Sage Instant Accounts

FOR

DUMMIES

A Wiley Brand

Sage Instant Accounts

FOR DUMMIES®

A Wiley Brand

by Jane Kelly

FOR DUMMIES®

A Wiley Brand

Sage Instant Accounts For Dummies®

Published by: **John Wiley & Sons, Ltd.,** The Atrium, Southern Gate, Chichester, www.wiley.com

This edition first published 2013

© 2014 John Wiley & Sons, Ltd, Chichester, West Sussex.

Registered office

John Wiley & Sons Ltd, The Atrium, Southern Gate, Chichester, West Sussex, PO19 8SQ, United Kingdom

For details of our global editorial offices, for customer services and for information about how to apply for permission to reuse the copyright material in this book please see our website at www.wiley.com.

The right of the author to be identified as the author of this work has been asserted in accordance with the Copyright, Designs and Patents Act 1988.

For general information on our other products and services, please contact our Customer Care Department within the U.S. at 877-762-2974, outside the U.S. at (001) 317-572-3993, or fax 317-572-4002.

For technical support, please visit www.wiley.com/techsupport.

A catalogue record for this book is available from the British Library.

ISBN 978-1-118-84805-0 (pbk), ISBN 978-1-118-84793-0 (ebk), ISBN 978-1-118-84800-5 (ebk)

Printed and bound in Great Britain by TJ International Ltd, Padstow, Cornwall

10 9 8 7 6 5 4 3 2 1

Contents at a Glance

Introduction *1*

Part I: Getting Started with Sage Instant Accounts *5*

Chapter 1: Introducing Sage Instant Accounts 7

Chapter 2: Creating Your Chart of Accounts and Assigning Nominal Codes..........35

Chapter 3: Setting Up Records 55

Chapter 4: Recording Your Opening Balances..75

Part II: Looking into Day-to-Day Functions *93*

Chapter 5: Processing Your Customer Paperwork..95

Chapter 6: Invoicing Your Customers.. 107

Chapter 7: Dealing with Paperwork from Your Suppliers 117

Chapter 8: Recording Your Bank Entries 127

Chapter 9: Maintaining and Correcting Entries 143

Chapter 10: Keeping Track of Your Products 153

*Part III: Running Monthly, Quarterly
and Annual Routines* *163*

Chapter 11: Reconciling Your Bank Accounts 165

Chapter 12: Running Your Monthly and Yearly Routines................................ 177

Chapter 13: Running Your VAT Return 191

Part IV: Using Reports *205*

Chapter 14: Running Monthly Reports... 207

Chapter 15: Tackling the Complicated Stuff 221

Chapter 16: Running Key Reports.. 235

Part V: The Part of Tens *251*

Chapter 17: Ten (Okay, Eleven) Funky Functions 253

Chapter 18: (Not Quite) Ten Wizards to Conjure 257

Appendix: Glossary *263*

Index *267*

Table of Contents

Introduction *1*

About This Book 1
Foolish Assumptions 2
Icons Used in This Book 2
Beyond The Book 3
Where to Go from Here 3

Part I: Getting Started with Sage Instant Accounts *5*

Chapter 1: Introducing Sage Instant Accounts **7**

Looking at Two Sage Instant Options 7
Installing the Software 8
    Getting what you need before you get started 9
    Moving to the installation itself 9
Setting Up with the Active Set-Up Wizard 14
Finding Out How Easy Sage Is to Use 22
    Burying the accounting jargon 22
    Looking at the screen layout 22
    Introducing process maps 23
Navigating Around Sage 26
    Exploring the Menu bar 26
    Navigating the Task pane, Links list and Module buttons 31
Using Wizards 33

**Chapter 2: Creating Your Chart of Accounts
and Assigning Nominal Codes** **35**

Understanding as Much as You Need to about Accounting 35
    Dabbling in double-entry bookkeeping 36
    Naming your nominals 36
    Preparing reports 37
Looking at the Structure of Your Chart of Accounts 38
    Checking out the default COA 38
    Identifying Balance Sheet codes 41
    Looking at Profit and Loss codes 43
    Leaving gaps and mirroring codes 45
    Accommodating floating nominals 46

Editing Your COA...46
    Amending your COA...47
    Creating a new COA...49
Checking Your COA...51
    Previewing errors 52
    Looking at some common errors.......................................53

Chapter 3: Setting Up Records 55

Choosing How to Create Your Records....................................55
    Getting a quick start using the Record icon....................55
    Switching off the process maps..56
    Following the wizards brick by brick 57
Creating Customer and Supplier Records................................57
    Setting customer and supplier defaults...........................60
    Deleting customer and supplier records 61
Creating Your Nominal Records..61
    Exploring your nominal records.......................................61
    Renaming existing nominal records 63
    Adding a new nominal record 63
    Looking for a nominal record 65
    Looking around a nominal record.....................................66
    Deleting a nominal code...67
Recording Your Bank Accounts...67
    Renaming an existing account 68
    Creating new accounts...68
    Deleting a bank record...70
Getting Your Product Records in Order....................................71
    Creating a product record...71
    Editing a product record..73
    Deleting a product record 73

Chapter 4: Recording Your Opening Balances 75

Timing Your Switch to Sage 75
Obtaining Your Opening Balances 76
Entering Opening Balances Using the Wizard 78
    Entering your default date...79
    Entering customer and supplier balances......................79
    Reversing the nominal balances in preparation for entering
        the Trial Balance 81
    Entering the Trial Balance from your accountant 82
    Entering the un-cleared transactions for your bank account 84
    Checking opening balances against the Trial Balance
        from your accountant 85
    Checking your data...85
    Backing up your data..86

Manually recording opening balances 86
Recording opening bank balances manually.........................87
Recording nominal opening balances manually 88
Putting in opening balances for products 89
Checking Your Opening Balances 90
Printing an opening Trial Balance 91
Dealing with errors 91

Part II: Looking into Day-to-Day Functions 93

Chapter 5: Processing Your Customer Paperwork 95

Posting Batch Entry Invoices 95
Creating Credit Notes...97
Registering Payments from Your Customers................................99
Matching payments to invoices 100
Giving credit where due – allocating credit notes.......................102
Recording payments on account 104
Deleting Invoices and Credit Notes 105
Managing Write offs, Refunds and Returns 105
Performing Customer Refunds..106

Chapter 6: Invoicing Your Customers 107

Deciding on an Invoice Type..107
Creating Invoices 108
Putting in the details 108
Getting to the main attraction.......................................109
Filling in the order details...112
Getting down to the footer details...................................112
Managing Your Invoice List..113
Printing..113
Using Quick Print 115
Updating..115
Deleting 116
Using defaults 116

Chapter 7: Dealing with Paperwork from Your Suppliers......... 117

Receiving and Posting Invoices 117
Setting up your receiving system 117
Posting invoices 118
Getting Credit..120
Allocating a Credit Note...122
Paying Your Suppliers..123
Managing Write offs, Refunds & Returns..................................124
Supplier refunds...125

Chapter 8: Recording Your Bank Entries. 127

Understanding the Different Types of Bank Accounts 127
Keeping up with the Current and
Deposit accounts (1200/1210) 128
Counting the Petty Cash account (1230) 129
Handling your Cash Register (1235) 129
Managing the company credit card (1240) and
credit card receipts (1250) 130
Tracking Bank Deposits and Payments 130
Transferring Funds between Accounts 132
Repeating Recurring Entries 133
Going for consistency with your bank entries 133
Repeating customer and supplier payments 135
Making regular journal entries – if you dare 136
Processing and posting recurring entries 137
Dealing with Petty Cash 138
Funding petty cash 138
Making payments from the tin 139
Reconciling the petty cash tin 139
Paying the Credit Card Bill 140
Making payments 140
Reconciling the credit card statement 140

Chapter 9: Maintaining and Correcting Entries 143

Checking and Maintaining Your Files 143
Checking data 144
Making corrections 145
Re-indexing data 147
Compressing data 147
Rebuilding data 147
Finding Ways to Find Transactions 148
Searching For Records 149
Backing Up Data 150
Restoring Data 152

Chapter 10: Keeping Track of Your Products 153

Taking Stock 153
Adjusting stock levels 156
Checking stock activity 157
Adjusting your Opening and Closing Stock 158
Stock Reports 160
Product Activity Report 160
Product List 161
Product Profitability 161
Stock Take report 161
Selling Stock 161

Part III: Running Monthly, Quarterly and Annual Routines 163

Chapter 11: Reconciling Your Bank Accounts 165
Recognising Reasons to Reconcile 165
Getting Ready to Reconcile 167
Doing the Actual Reconciliation 167
Troubleshooting when Your Account Doesn't Reconcile 173
Rounding Up Stragglers 173
    Listing un-presented cheques and outstanding lodgements 174
    Remembering recurring entries 175

Chapter 12: Running Your Monthly and Yearly Routines 177
Adding Up Accruals 178
Counting Out Prepayments 179
Depreciating Fixed Assets 180
    Writing down your assets 180
    Posting assets and depreciation 181
Entering Journals 182
Carrying Out Your Month-End Routine 184
    Ticking off your checklist 185
    Running the month-end 186
    Clearing stock transactions 187
    Clearing your Audit Trail 188
Doing a Year-End Routine 189

Chapter 13: Running Your VAT Return 191
Understanding Some VAT Basics 191
    Knowing your outputs from your inputs 192
    Cracking the codes 192
    Comparing Sage's VAT accounting methods 193
Running the VAT Return 194
    Calculating your VAT 195
Checking Your VAT Return 196
    Checking under the standard scheme 197
    Checking with cash accounting 198
Making Manual Adjustments to Your VAT Return 199
Reconciling Your VAT Transactions 200
    VAT Transfer 201
    Recording a VAT payment 202
    Submitting your return to HMRC 202
    Submitting your VAT return manually via HMRC 203

Part IV: Using Reports *205*

Chapter 14: Running Monthly Reports 207
    Making the Most of Standard Reports 207
    Checking the Chart of Accounts First 208
    Figuring Out the Financial Reports 209
        Trying for an initial Trial Balance 209
        Accounting for profit and loss 210
        Comparing profit and loss 212
        Weighing the Balance Sheet 214
    Viewing the Audit Trail 215
    Designing Reports to Suit Yourself 217

Chapter 15: Tackling the Complicated Stuff 221
    Exporting Data 221
        Sending spreadsheet stuff 221
        Transferring Microsoft Outlook contacts 222
        Exporting to Microsoft Word 223
    Linking to Your Accountant 224
        Sending accounts to your accountant 225
        Managing material changes 225
        Getting back adjustments and narratives 226
    Trying e-Banking 226
        Configuring your e-Banking 227
        Opting for e-payments 229
        Reconciling electronically 230

Chapter 16: Running Key Reports 235
    Checking Activity through the Nominal Codes 235
    Looking into Supplier Activity 238
    Tracking Customer Activity 239
    Checking Numbers with Supplier Daybook Reports 240
    Finding the Customers Who Owe You 242
    Paying Attention to Your Creditors 244
    Handling Unreconciled Bank Transactions 246
    Ranking Your Top Customers 249

Part V: The Part of Tens *251*

Chapter 17: Ten (Okay, Eleven) Funky Functions 253
    Browsing for Help with F1 253
    Calculating Stuff with F2 253
    Accessing an Edit Item Line for Invoicing with F3 254

Finding Multiple Functions at F4 254
Calculating Currency or Checking Spelling with F5 254
Copying with F6 254
Inserting a Line with F7 255
Deleting a Line with F8 255
Calculating Net Amounts with F9 256
Launching Windows with F11 256
Opening Report Designer with F12 256

Chapter 18: (Not Quite) Ten Wizards to Conjure **257**
Creating a New Customer Account 257
Setting up a New Supplier 258
Initiating a New Nominal Account 258
Creating a New Bank Account 259
Launching a New Product (For Sage Instant Accounts Plus Only) 259
Helping Out at Month-End: Opening/Closing Stock (For Sage
    Instant Accounts Plus Users Only) 259
Saving Time: Global Changes 260
Keeping Others in the Loop: Accountant Link 261

Appendix: Glossary *263*

Index *267*

Introduction

Sage is a well-known accounting system used in more than three-quarters of a million small- and medium-sized businesses in the UK. The range of business software continually evolves, and Sage's developers pride themselves on listening to their customers for feedback on how to improve the software. This evolution results in regular revisions and updates that add new features to Sage each time.

This book offers you a chance to understand how Sage Instant Accounts can help you run your business effectively.

About This Book

The aim of this book is for you to get the most from Sage. I use lots of screenshots to help you navigate your way around the system and offer tips to help you customise the programs and reports contained in Sage in language you can understand, even if you're not an accountant.

Wherever possible, I show you the quickest way to do something, because you can often do the same thing in more than one way. I understand that you want a quick start, so I show you the easiest methods of doing things. You can always add details later, when time permits.

This book presents information in a modular fashion so that you get all the information to accomplish a task in one place. I don't ask you to remember things from different parts of the book; if another chapter has information relevant to the discussion at hand, I tell you where to find it, so you don't have to read the chapters in order. You can read the chapters or sections that interest you when it suits you.

Foolish Assumptions

While writing *Sage Instant Accounts For Dummies,* I made some key assumptions about who you are and why you picked up this book. I assume that you fall into one of the following categories:

- You're a member of staff in a small business who's been asked to take over the bookkeeping function and will be using Sage.

- You're an existing bookkeeper who has never used Sage before or who needs to refresh your knowledge.

- You're a small-business owner who wants to understand how Sage can help in your business.

Icons Used in This Book

Every *For Dummies* book uses icons to highlight especially important, interesting or useful information. The icons used in this book are:

Look at this icon for practical information that you can use straightaway to help you use Sage in the most effective way.

This icon indicates any items you need to remember after reading the book – and sometimes throughout it.

This icon calls your attention to examples of specific tasks being carried out in Sage Instant Accounts. Read them through to see how Sage is used in a variety of accounting activities.

This icon indicates that a function is available only to users of Sage Instant Accounts Plus.

The paragraphs next to this icon contain information that is, er, slightly technical in nature. You don't *need* to know the information here to get by, but it helps.

This bombshell alerts you to potential problems you may create for yourself without realising it. Don't ignore this icon!

Beyond The Book

Find out more about Sage Instant Accounts by checking out the bonus content available to you at www.dummies.com.

You can locate the book's e-cheat sheet at www.dummies.com/cheatsheet/ sageinstantaccountsuk. Here you'll find handy Sage function key shortcuts, tips n backing up your data as well as a monthly management account checklist.

Be sure to visit the book's extras page at www.dummies.com/extras/ sageinstantaccountsuk for further Sage related information and articles.

Where to Go from Here

You're now ready to enter the world of Sage. If you're a complete beginner, starting at the beginning and gradually working through is probably best. If you're an existing user, but a little rusty in certain areas, you can pick the chapters that are most relevant to you, probably in Parts III and IV. This book is designed for you to dip in and out of. I hope that you find it a useful tool for developing and managing your business.

Part I

Getting Started with Sage Instant Accounts

getting started with

sage instant accounts

In this Part . . .

- ✔ Get yourself going! Install Sage Instant Accounts quickly and efficiently.

- ✔ Tailor Sage Instant Accounts to meet your business's book-keeping needs by creating your Chart of Accounts.

- ✔ Learn how to set up customer, supplier, nominal, bank and products records.

- ✔ Enter your opening balances and start using Sage Instant Accounts to improve your account keeping.

Chapter 1

Introducing Sage Instant Accounts

· ·

In This Chapter

▶ Introducing the Sage software range

▶ Considering SageCover

▶ Installing the software

▶ Getting help from the wizard

▶ Navigating around Sage

· ·

*I*n this chapter, I introduce you to Sage Instant Accounts. I show you how easily you can install the software and give you a guided tour, so that you can get up and running quickly – essential for busy people!

Sage works on the principle that the less time you spend doing your accounts, the more time you can spend on your business, so makes each process as simple as possible.

I also discuss SageCover, an optional technical support package, which is an addition worth considering. If you experience software problems, SageCover can help. For small businesses, this support is like having an IT department at the end of a phone.

Looking at Two Sage Instant Options

Sage offers two versions of Instant Accounts:

✔ **Sage Instant Accounts:** The entry-level program. Sage Instant Accounts provides all the features you require to successfully manage your accounts. You can professionally handle your customers and suppliers, manage your bank reconciliations and VAT returns and provide simple reports, including monthly and year-end requirements. This basic version is suitable for small businesses with a simple structure.

✔ **Sage Instant Accounts Plus:** Contains all the features of the entry model, but in addition includes a simple stock system and also the ability to have up to two users.

Deciding on SageCover

You can purchase SageCover at the same time as the software. SageCover provides you with technical support in case you have any problems using Sage. It may seem an additional cost burden to begin with, but is well worth the money if you've a software problem. Sage does currently offer 45 days of free telephone support, along with free online learning and access to guides and video tutorials.

Most people who use accounting packages know something about accounting, but don't necessarily know much about computer software. When the screen pops up with an error message that you simply don't understand, a quick phone call to your SageCover support line soon solves the problem.

For Sage Instant Accounts, you can choose between two different types of cover:

✔ **SageCover:** Provides telephone support during normal office hours, as well as email and online question and answer support. You also have access to a data repair service, where a member of the Sage in-house team will retrieve and repair your data if it becomes lost or corrupt. There's also a free subscription to Sage's business magazine *Solutions*.

✔ **SageCover Extra:** Includes all the benefits of SageCover, plus software upgrades, so you always have access to the latest version. You also gain the benefit of an Express data repair service rather than just the standard service. You're given priority telephone support with Sagecover Extra, including a call-back option and also have additional Remote Support, which means that, with your permission, Sage technicians can remotely access your PC to help you solve your queries.

Having someone on the end of a phone to talk you through a problem is a real bonus. Sometimes the Help button just doesn't answer your question. The technical support team can help you solve the most awkward problems that would otherwise have you throwing your laptop out of the window in pure frustration!

I recommend that you install Sage Instant on a Windows operating system. Windows 8 or 7, Windows Vista, Windows XP, Windows Server 2008, Small Business Server 2011 or Server 2003 are all recommended by Sage.

Installing the Software

In this section, I take you step by step through the installation process, showing you the screens as they appear on your computer and ensuring that you load up the software correctly. I also let you know about any problems that may crop up while loading, so that you can deal with them effectively.

Anyway, onwards and upwards!

Getting what you need before you get started

Your Sage software package contains a CD, a 'Getting Started with Sage Instant Accounts' guide and, more importantly, a serial number and activation key. Without these last two pieces of information, you can't successfully load the software. But don't worry, if you purchased a genuine copy of Sage software, you have the necessary activation information.

You also need a few details about your company:

- **When your company's financial year begins:** If you're not sure of the date, consult your accountant.

- **Whether and what type of VAT scheme you use:** Again, your accountant can tell you whether you operate the VAT cash accounting scheme or the standard VAT scheme. If you've a VAT registration number, keep it handy.

Moving to the installation itself

The following steps assume that you're loading Sage for the first time for a single company and single user. For those of you loading multiple-user programs, check the instructions provided with your software.

1. **Insert your CD into the disk drive.**

   If your CD doesn't immediately start, you may need to click Run.

2. **Follow the options on your screen to run the CD.**

   A Sage Instant Accounts opening screen appears. Click the Install button to continue as shown in Figure 1-1.

   For Vista users, the User Account Control window appears, asking you for permission to continue installing Sage; click Continue to proceed.

   The Sage system checker highlights any problems with loading your software, such as hardware speed and so on as shown in Figure 1-2. Click Install to continue.

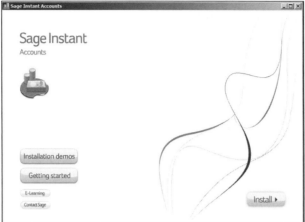

Figure 1-1:
The initial screen prior to installing the software.

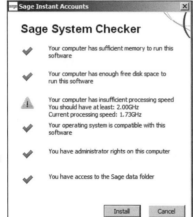

Figure 1-2:
System checker.

3. The Accounts Installshield wizard starts up when you click Install and this is followed by the Licence agreement as shown in Figure 1-3.

Be warned, the licence seems to go on forever, if you choose to read it! (Have a quick look through the software licence agreement though, just to see what you're signing up for!) Click Yes to accept the licence.

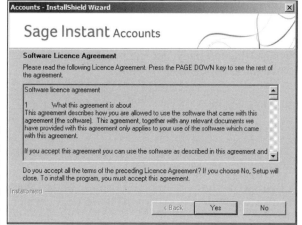

Figure 1-3:
Accepting
the software
licence
agreement.

4. **Select the installation type and destination folder and follow the prompts.**

   You've a choice between a Standard install and a Custom install, as shown in Figure 1-4. The choice you make is important.

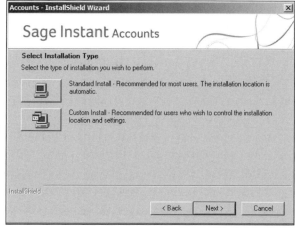

Figure 1-4:
Choosing
Standard
or Custom
install.

Standard install is recommended for most users; it copies the files to C:\Sage\Accounts.

Choose Custom install only if you want to control the destination of the programs being installed; for example, if you want to keep different versions of Sage separately on your computer.

Check with Sage (the company, not the program!) if you aren't sure whether to use the Custom install or not.

If you want to use Custom install and choose a different destination folder, follow these steps:

i. **Click the Custom install option.**

The destination folder at the bottom of the screen automatically defaults to C:\Sage\Accounts 2011.

ii. **Click Browse.** With the help of the Browse button you can change the destination folder, as shown in Figure 1-5. I have changed it to C:\Sage\Instant Accounts 2013. Click OK. The destination path has now changed to the new one that you've designated. Click Next to continue.

Select your Program folder – this window allows you to change the program folder to your preferred destination, as shown in Figure 1-6 you can now click Next to continue.

Sage now confirms the destination folders for the program as shown in Figure 1-7. Click Next to continue.

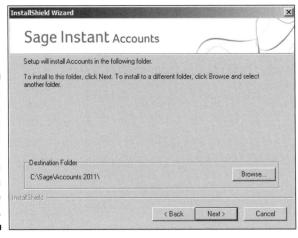

Figure 1-5: Click the browse button to find an alternative destination for the Sage program.

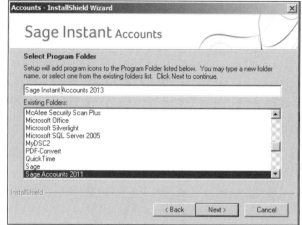

Figure 1-6:
Having
amended
to Sage
Instant 2013
directory.

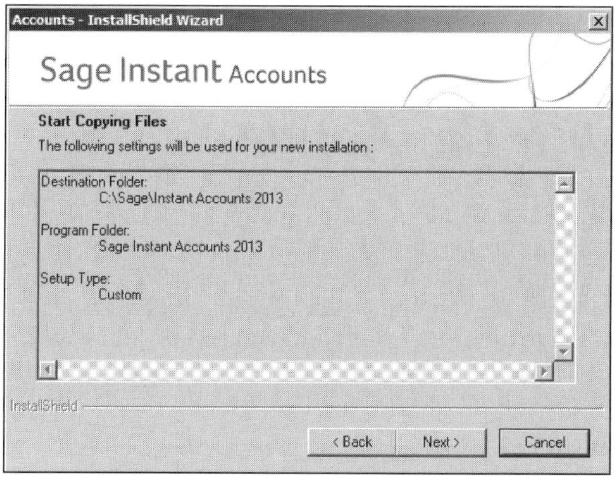

Figure 1-7:
Sage
confirms the
destination
folders for
Instant
Accounts.

The system then whirrs into action and starts the installation process.
It takes several minutes, so you probably have time to make a quick cup
of tea!

5. Click Finish when Sage tells you that the installation is complete.

That's it! You've successfully installed your Sage software. This is the message
you should see, shown in Figure 1-8. You should see a Sage Instant Accounts
icon on your desktop – now you're ready to rock and roll!

Figure 1-8:
Confirmation
of a
successful
installation!

Be sure to remove the CD and keep it in a safe place!

Setting Up with the Active Set-Up Wizard

Of course, you're champing at the bit and want to get going with Sage, so double-click the new Sage icon on your desktop to get started. You may get an RSS feeds message (see Figure 1-9) and you can decide whether you want to receive these or not by clicking on the tick box. Click OK to continue.

Figure 1-9:
Checking
your RSS
feeds.

The Activate Sage Software window opens as shown in Figure 1-10. You're asked to enter your activation key and serial number. You can find these on your delivery note or within your CD case. If you don't have this information, click the My Sage button and follow the online instructions.

Figure 1-10:
Activating
your Sage
Software.

When you've entered your activation key and serial number and clicked Continue, a confirmation message appears saying that your Sage Instant Accounts has now been registered. Click OK to continue, the Active Set-up wizard opens. The first screen, shown in Figure 1-11, gives you three options:

- ✔ **Set up a new company:** If you're new to Sage, choose this first option.

  You're then guided through the automatic steps of the Active Set-up wizard. The following numbered steps lead you through this process.

- ✔ **Use an existing company stored on your network:** If you already use Sage and are upgrading, choose this option, which lets you copy accounts data from your previous Sage installation.

- ✔ **Restore data from a backup file:** Choose this option if you're restoring data from an earlier version.

Choose whichever option is best for you and click Next.

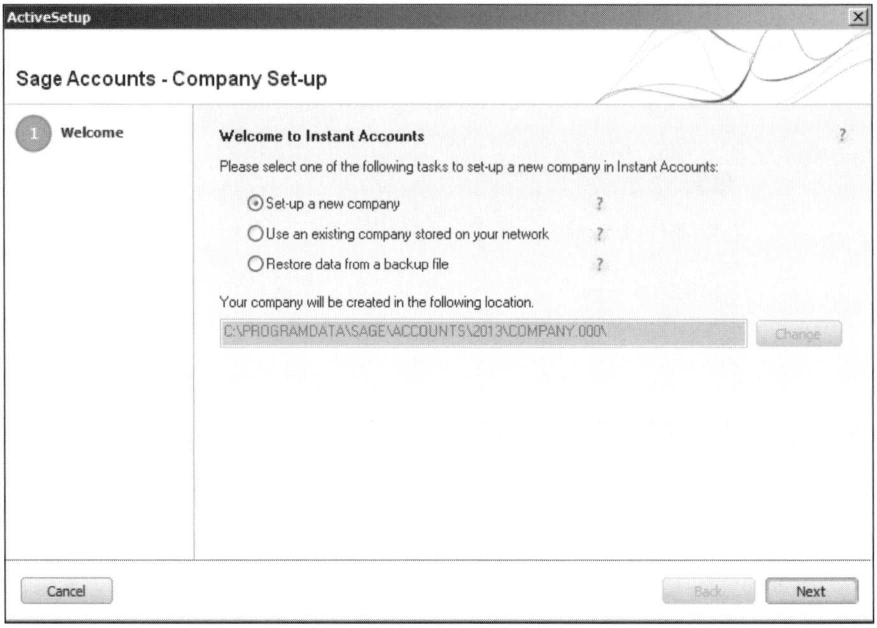

Figure 1-11:
Putting
the Active
Set-up
wizard to
work.

The following steps take you through the process of setting up Sage for the first time.

1. **Click Set Up a New Company, then click Next and then enter your company's details. Sage now takes you through a 7-step wizard.**

   You're prompted to enter your company information, such as name, address and contact details, as shown in Figure 1-12.

   Make the set-up speedier by putting in just the company name. You can complete the other information later by clicking Settings on the main toolbar and then selecting Company Preferences.

2. **Click Next. A screen appears that prompts you to Select Business Type, as shown in Figure 1-13.**

3. **Click the appropriate business type.** For example, I've chosen Limited Company, for Jingles. If you're in any doubt, contact your accountant, who'll be happy to assist. Whichever business structure you choose, Sage applies the appropriate nominal codes and Profit and Loss and Balance Sheet reports for your accounts.

   If you don't want to select any of the categories shown, you can click *I want to use a pre defined business type* and create your own business type. You can then use your existing nominal codes if you're transferring accounts from a different system.

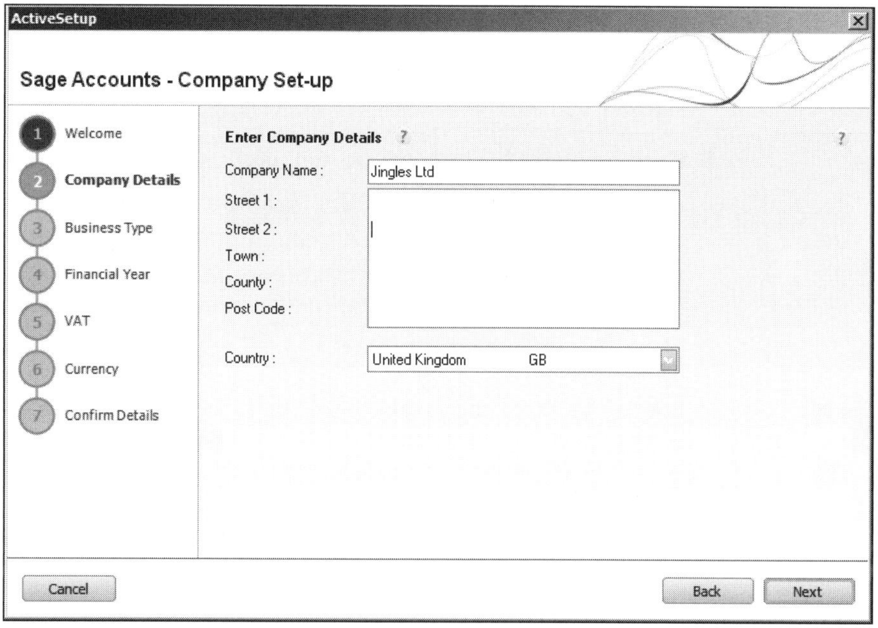

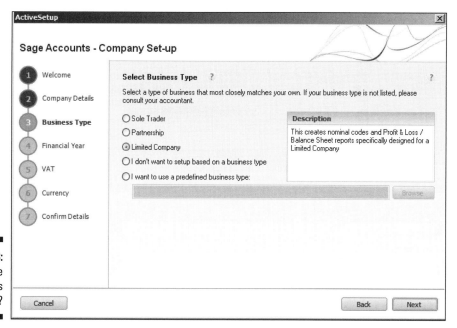

Figure 1-12:
Asking for the company contact information.

Figure 1-13:
What type of business are you?

4. **Click Next and select your financial year.**

   The fictional Jingles company I invented ends its financial year on
   31 March 2014, so the financial start date is April 2013, as shown in
   Figure 1-14.

5. **Click Next and fill in your VAT details.**

   If you're not VAT registered, click No and go to Step 6.

   If you're VAT registered, enter your registration number and, using
   the drop-down arrow, select the appropriate VAT rate, as shown in
   Figure 1-15. You must enter the current standard VAT rate if that's the
   rate you've selected. Jingles Ltd is VAT registered for the purposes of
   illustration.

   Don't enter any transactions until you're certain of which VAT scheme
   you operate. Failure to use the correct scheme means that your VAT
   is calculated incorrectly. Sorting out the wrong VAT scheme can be
   extremely messy!

6. **Click Next and choose the base currency that you use as shown in
   Figure 1-16.** Click Next again. Note: The currency option is only available
   if you've purchased the currency module.

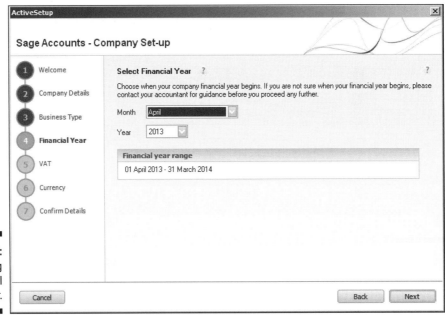

Figure 1-14:
Beginning
the financial
year.

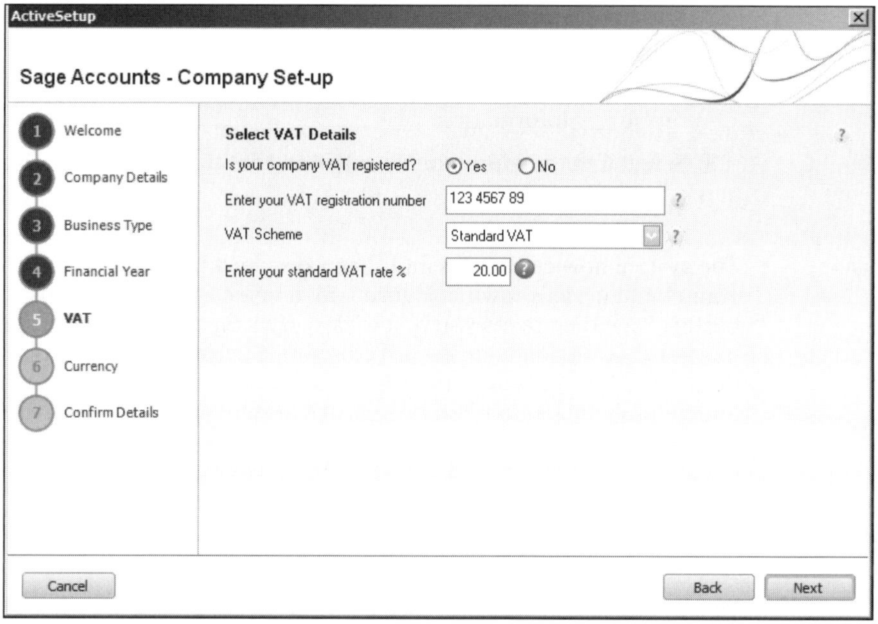

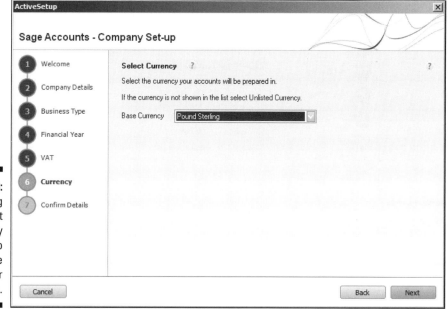

Figure 1-15:
Registering
your VAT
status.

Figure 1-16:
Telling
Sage what
currency
to use to
prepare
your
accounts.

7. **The final screen summarises the data you entered on your Active Set-up wizard, as shown in Figure 1-17.**

   If you need to make any changes to your data, you can click Back and revise any information.

8. **Select Create when you're satisfied that the information is correct.**

   You've finished!

The system now configures and then asks you whether you'd like to customise your company, as shown in Figure 1-18. If you click the Customise Company button, Sage then takes you to a wizard style menu, where you can choose to set up the defaults and records for your Customers, Suppliers, Banks, Products, Financials and the Administration areas of your software. You will find helpful videos that you can play to assist you in setting up the individual modules within Sage. Sage also has a tick box you can use when you've completed each section. If you click Setup Now, Sage automatically takes you to the default screen for whichever module you're setting up. See Figure 1-19 for an example of the Customer Default window.

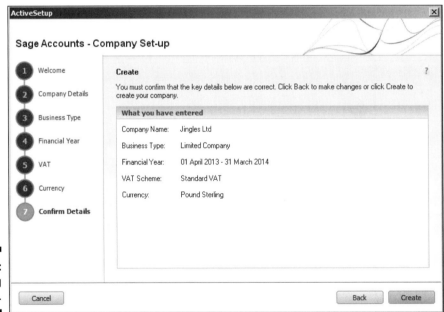

Figure 1-17:
Confirming
your details.

Figure 1-18:
Customising
your
company
details.

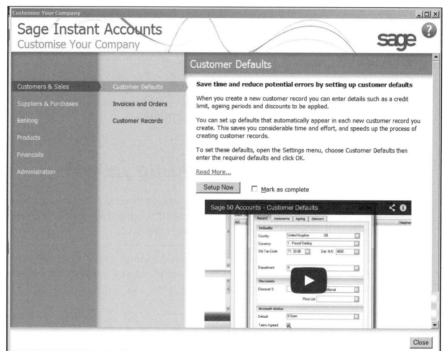

Figure 1-19:
Customising
your
customers!

When you start the customisation process, it can be time consuming to go through each section, and more than you can sensibly manage in one sitting. You can close the screen, which takes you to the Sage Welcome page. When you're ready to go back to the customisation wizard, click Help from the menu bar and then Customise your Company.

I would recommend setting up Sage manually, as you can take your time familiarising yourself with Sage. You're in danger of information overload if you try to set up all the modules in one go without taking time to navigate around Sage first.

I'm going to talk you through setting up the modules manually so that you can see where all the options are within the Sage software. The remainder of the chapter shows you how to do this.

Finding Out How Easy Sage Is to Use

Sage is a user-friendly system, using words and phrases that people easily understand rather than accounting jargon. Sage also has a lot of graphics to make the pages look more appealing and easier to navigate. For example, an icon appears next to the Bank module that looks like the entrance to a grand building – like the Bank of England, perhaps?

Burying the accounting jargon

Sage uses terms that users understand and steers clear of accounting jargon. So, instead of using *debtors* and *creditors*, Sage uses *customers* and *suppliers*; rather than *nominal ledger*, it uses *company*.

Accounting terminology isn't altogether done away with, for example you still have to print Aged Debtors reports and Aged Creditors reports, but most of the program uses simple language.

Looking at the screen layout

When you open Sage, the first screen you come across is the Sage Welcome screen, as shown in Figure 1-20. It provides useful links and various Help pages, including a Just Practice section, where if you're not sure how to do something, you can try it out in the practice company first.

Figure 1-20:
Welcoming
you to Sage.

If you look closely at the bottom of the screen, you find two tabs. The first is for the Welcome to Sage Instant Accounts screen, and the second is called Customer Process – the arrow points to it in Figure 1-20.

Introducing process maps

Process maps look like flow charts, they illustrate specific customer and supplier processes in a pictorial format. Click the Customer Process tab to see the process map, as shown in Figure 1-21.

Figure 1-21 shows the various stages of the customer paper trail in the Customer Process map, from the original quotation through to chasing the debt and receiving the money from the customer. You can click on any one of these boxes, and Sage takes you directly to the screen necessary to process that action. For example, if you click Customer Receipt you're taken to the Customer Receipt screen, so that you can process the payment received.

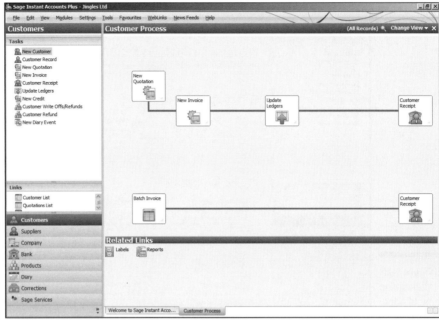

Figure 1-21:
Looking at
the inner
workings
of the
customer
process.

On the Customer Process screen, the words Change View appear in the top right corner. Clicking Change View produces a drop-down menu that gives you two more options to change the appearance of the screen:

✔ **Customers:** This view, shown in Figure 1-22, is the traditional Sage screen. The main body of the screen appears blank when you're starting out with Sage, but it eventually fills up with your customers' names, balances and contact details.

Across the top of the screen, below the Customers heading, the icons that form part of the customer pages appear – Customer Record, Activity, Batch Invoice and Batch Credit, to name just a few.

✔ **Customer Dashboard:** The dashboard offers a graphic representation of the customer information. It shows the Customer Cash Overview, Aged Debt and Today's Diary Events. This presentation appeals to people who want quick access to the key information in the accounts.

Before you input any data, the Customer Dashboard screen looks extremely boring. However, even just the Sage demonstration data illustrates the dramatic impact of presenting data in this way, as shown in Figure 1-23. To open Sage using demo data, click File from the top toolbar, then Open, then Open Demo data. At the screen login, choose Manager and no password, and then Sage opens with new company data called Stationery& Computer Mart UK.

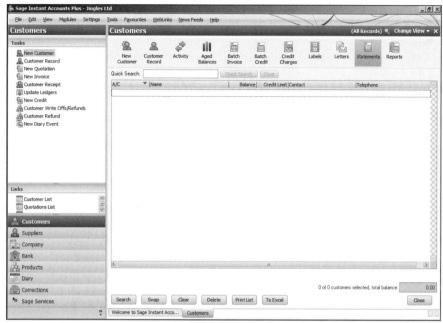

Figure 1-22:
Viewing the
traditional
Customers
screen.

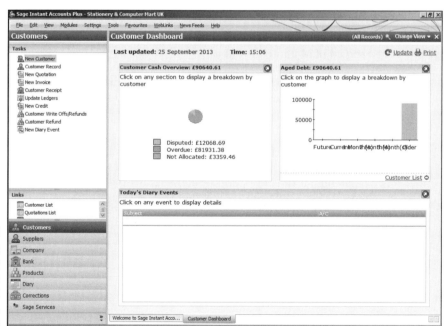

Figure 1-23:
Going
for the
graphical
view.

Alternatively you can use the Practice data to play around with Sage (you access the practice data in the same way as the Demo data).

Navigating Around Sage

At the very top of the Sage Welcome screen is the name of your version of Sage – Sage Instant Accounts Plus, for example – followed by the company name you entered when you set up Sage. (Refer to the 'Setting Up with the Active Set-Up Wizard' section, which walks you through getting Sage up and running.)

The Sage Instant desktop is divided into three key areas: The Menu Bar is found running horizontally across the top of the screen and is one method of navigating around Sage Instant. (See Exploring the Menu Bar later in this chapter)

The Navigation bar runs vertically down the left-hand side of the screen, (see the 'Navigating the Task pane, Links list and Module buttons' section later in this chapter for more detail). The navigation bar is further subdivided into three areas:

- ✔ The Tasks pane
- ✔ The Links pane
- ✔ List of Module buttons

The Work Area is the main central space of your screen and can be configured to your preferences by using Tools, and then Options from the Menu bar.

Exploring the Menu bar

The menu bar runs horizontally across the top of your screen and provides many navigational tools to help find your way around Sage. Refer to Figure 1-24 (later in this chapter) to see both the Menu bar and Navigation bar.

By clicking the different Menu bar options, you gain access to sub-menus and different parts of the system. The next sections talk about each option on the Menu bar in turn.

File

Nothing counter-intuitive here; clicking File gives you options for creating, accessing, saving and sharing data. The sub-menu options are:

- **New Report:** Takes you into Sage Report Designer, where you can use the Report wizard, which enables you to design new reports.

- **Open:** Enables you to access the demonstration data, practice data and open a report previously saved.

- **Close:** Closes the drop-down menu.

- **Backup:** Allows you to back up your data. You can also back up your data when you exit the program.

  Back up your data each time you use Sage, or at least at the end of each day. Back up more often during the day if you're processing significant amounts of data.

  Sage automatically gives the backup a filename, which is usually SageAccts then your company name, followed by the date and some numbers, then 001. (Sage backup files always have the file extension .001.) If you do more than one backup on the same day, differentiate the file name by adding a different number, otherwise Sage may overwrite the previous backup.

- **Maintenance:** Enables you, among other things, to correct data, delete records, check data or even, as a last resort, rebuild the data. I talk about maintenance in more detail in Chapter 9.

- **Restore:** Allows you to retrieve data from a previous backup, if necessary. You may need to utilise this function if you have problems with the current data – perhaps the data has been corrupted and you want to return it to a known point in time when it was free of problems.

- **Import:** Allows you to import records, such as customer, supplier, stock, assets, nominal accounts and project records, from other sources, like Microsoft Excel, as long as they're in a pre-determined CSV (comma separated values) format. This option is useful when you're setting up Sage and have other information or records that you wish to import. You can speed up the data-entry process if you import information instead of keying in each individual record. I cover importing and CSV formatting in more detail in Chapter 15.

- **Microsoft Integration:** Using this option, you can export data to Microsoft Excel, Word or Outlook (if you've a compatible version of Microsoft Outlook).

- **Send:** Enables you to send a message by using your default email program.

- **Exit:** Lets you exit the program altogether. You can also exit the program by clicking the black cross in the top right corner of the screen.

Edit

You can use Edit to cut, copy, paste, insert/delete rows and duplicate cells.

View

The *status bar* is the narrow strip across the bottom of your screen, showing the name of your Sage product, today's date, the start of the financial year and the current transaction number. You can switch it on and off. You can also view the user list, which shows who is currently logged onto Sage.

Modules

The *modules* are essentially the different components that form the whole of the Sage accounting system. The modules include the usual accounting ledgers, such as Customers, Suppliers, Bank, Nominal Ledger and reporting functions, but they also include the Invoicing function, wizards and a diary.

Access modules by clicking Modules on the *M*enu bar and selecting the module of your choice, or by clicking the much larger buttons on the *N*avigation bar at the bottom left of the screen. I prefer the buttons at the bottom – they're easier to use and more visible.

Settings

The settings include the Configuration Editor and Company Preferences, which hold some of the basic information about your company and the way that Sage was set up upon installation. Settings also include many of the default screens for the ledgers, which save you time when setting up records at a later date.

If you used the Customisation Wizard when you installed Sage, then you may have already seen these default screens.

If you need to change the system date or check the financial year, you can do it within settings. You also have access to the security settings for accessing the software and can set up passwords to protect your accounts data. The settings include:

- ✔ **Configuration Editor:** Holds the basic information you enter when you complete the Active Set-up wizard. Have a look at the numerous tabs within this option and familiarise yourself with them. Examples of things you can do include: editing your customer and supplier trading terms; amending your VAT codes; grouping your product categories, editing your custom fields and applying a status such as 'on hold' to your customer/ supplier records.

- ✔ **Company Preferences:** Allows you to enter extra information if you didn't add it all when using the Active Set-up wizard. You may want to update your address information, for example, or perhaps check your VAT details. Company Preferences provides many more tabs to look at, too many to comment on here, so have a flick through at your leisure.

✔ **Customer/Supplier/Bank/Product/Invoice and Email Defaults:** Gives you the opportunity to amend parts of the default data you set up on installation.

✔ **Financial Year:** Identifies the start of the company's financial year, as input during the Active Set-up wizard. This date is fixed when you start to enter data.

✔ **Change Program Date:** Allows you to change dates when running a month-end or a year-end report. The date is normally set to the current day's date, but there may be times, such as period ends, when you wish to change the date, albeit only temporarily.

✔ **Lock Date:** You have the ability to enter a lock date into the system, which means that you can prevent postings before a specific date that you enter. This feature is useful when you're processing year ends. Only users with access rights to Lock Dates can post.

✔ **Currencies:** Enables you to edit your currency requirements if you're using multiple currencies.

✔ **Countries:** Lists all the countries in the world in the Countries table, together with country codes, and identifies those countries that are currently members of the EU.

You can amend the Countries table as and when countries enter or leave the EU.

✔ **Control Accounts:** Gives you an at-a-glance list of all the control accounts within Sage. A *control account* is a summary of all entries contained within a specific ledger. For example, the Sales Ledger control account includes all transactions for all sales ledger accounts and the balance on the control account tallies with the sum of the sales ledger accounts. Control accounts are used as a check on the numerical accuracy of the ledger accounts and form part of the double-entry system that Sage performs when you enter transactions.

If you're going to change the control accounts, do so before you enter any transactions; otherwise, leave them alone.

You can reconcile a control account. Just click Help and follow the instructions for reconciling debtors or creditors.

✔ **Change Password:** Allows you to change your password periodically as part of your data protection and security routine.

Tools

The tools option is a hotchpotch of items. You can run the Global Changes wizard, run period ends, open up Report Designer and convert reports, to name but a few. The options are outlined below:

✔ **Global Changes:** Allows you to globally change customer or supplier credit limits, turnover values and product sales or purchase prices.

✔ **Activation:** Allows you to upgrade your program and enable third-party integration.

Third-party integration enables you to use add-on software, developed by a third party, which is tailored to your specific industry.

You can use the Upgrade Program option to register after your initial 30-day Sage trial period runs out.

✔ **Opening Balances:** Presents you with a series of actions that need to be completed to enter your opening balances. Chapter 4 guides you through the Opening Balances wizard.

✔ **Period End:** Enables you to run the month-end and the year end, as well as clearing the audit trail and clearing stock. (See Chapter 12 for further information on clearing stock and audit trails.) When you run your year-end, Sage sets your Profit and Loss nominal accounts to zero for the new financial year.

✔ **Transaction Email:** The Transaction Email Control Panel opens, but it can only be configured if you have Microsoft Office set up.

✔ **Report Designer:** Allows you to edit or create new reports, customised for your business.

✔ **Options:** Gives you options to change the settings and appearance of Sage. For example, you can change the default view of the Customers and Suppliers screens from the process map to customer or supplier lists, using the View tab.

✔ **Convert Reports:** This option opens the Batch Report Converter. Click F1 Sage Help for more details.

✔ **Internet Options:** Here you can vary the Sage update criteria, enter Sage Cover login details, change network settings and view SData settings, which provide remote access to business information held in your Sage software.

Favourites

You can store your favourite reports under this heading. To find out how to set up favourite reports, use the Help menu supplied with Report Designer (which can be accessed via Tools on the browser toolbar – Chapter 15 goes into more detail about the Report Designer).

Weblinks

Weblinks gives you a number of links to useful websites, such as Sage shop and HM Revenue and Customs, Sage Stationery, Sage e-banking and Sage Pay, provided that you're hooked up to the Internet.

News Feeds

Sage provides news feeds data that you can access, to provide information on relevant Sage updates and topics.

Help

Help is the last entry on the menu bar, but probably one of the most useful. If you want to understand more about the system and want to know how to do something, click the Help option. The program has several help options you can choose from, all of which take you to a web help page, where you can enter your keyword and click search to find the answers to your problems. A list of relevant options are presented and you can select the one you require. In addition you can find the 'Customise your Company' wizard which you may have discovered when you first installed Sage. You can access these screens at any time and amend your module defaults and other administrative functions.

The About page now contains a raft of information about your computer, including system details, licence information, contact details for Sage and much more. Sage support staff find this page useful when trying to identify any problems that you may be experiencing with your software. If you choose Help from the main toolbar and click About, the Sage support page opens up and shows you the mass of information held about your computer.

Navigating the Task pane, Links list and Module buttons

An alternative method of navigation, and probably the easiest, is to use the navigation bar, which is down the left side of the screen. It includes a Task pane and Links list, as well as buttons at the bottom of the bar for opening up your modules.

Sage offers a variety of ways to navigate to the same point. For example, if you want to open a new customer record, you can click New Customer in the Task pane or use the menu bar and click Modules, Customers and then the New Customer icon (assuming you changed the view to Customers not the process map – refer to the 'Looking at the screen layout' section earlier in this chapter).

As you get used to using Sage, you'll see that the first navigation bar to open is the Customers bar. Figure 1-24 shows the navigation bar in the Customer module, where you can see these features:

- ✔ **Task pane:** The topmost menu is the Task pane, which is different for each module.

- ✔ **Links list:** The Links list offers different links for each module within Sage. The Customer Links list takes you to customer-orientated pages, such as Customer Invoices, Aged Balances or simply a list of customers.

✔ **Module buttons:** These buttons sit at the bottom left side of the screen and enable you to switch between modules. They're wide buttons that start with a little icon and then a description. The first button is Customers, followed by Suppliers, Company, Bank, Products, Diary, Corrections and Sage Services.

Just below the Diary button is a tiny chevron with a small arrow directly beneath it. Clicking on the chevron gives you the option of showing fewer buttons or adding or removing buttons. You can play about with the buttons and decide which display you prefer. The Diary button assists with credit control and also allows you to create diary tasks or events to help meet deadlines.

Sage Services is a relatively new feature that provides access to an online service (see the 'Introducing the Sage Services button' sidebar for more information).

Clicking the various Tasks, Links or Module buttons automatically moves you to the relevant part of the system.

Menu
bar

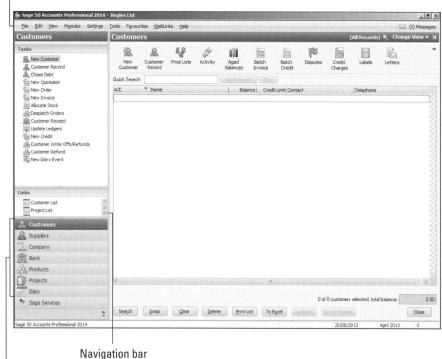

Figure 1-24:
Identifying
the
Navigation
bar, the Task
pane, the
Links list,
the Modules
buttons and
the Modules
toolbar as
viewed
from the
Customers
module.

Navigation bar

Module buttons

Introducing the Sage Services button

The Sage Services button gives you the ability to access a number of online Sage services, such as SageCover and Sage software updates. Prior to this service being available, SageCover was only available via the phone, and software updates came by CD or more recently online from the main Sage website, which involved opening up another browser session on your computer. You can now quickly access useful websites directly from your Sage software without having to open a separate Internet browser, but you need to create an account on the www. sage.co.uk website and obtain a Sage login and password first. You can record the details in your Sage software. (To do this, select the Tools menu, and then Internet Options and finally select the Sage Account tab, where you can enter your login details.)

I prefer the Module buttons, as I find it easier to navigate with them as they're more visible and easier to click than the Task pane or Links list.

Using Wizards

A number of wizards wield their technological magic through Sage. You can access these helpful creatures, whose job is to help you through a wide variety of setups and tasks, by clicking Modules on the browser toolbar and then Wizards.

A wizard's job is to make your work easy; all you have to do is follow the prompts and enter the information the wizard requests.

Wizards can help you in both setting up Sage and day-to-day processing. They can assist you in setting up new records for customers, suppliers, nominal accounts, bank accounts and products. But you can also use them to do the otherwise tricky double-entry bookkeeping for items such as opening and closing stock. In addition, whenever you click the New icon on the Modules toolbar, you go straight into the Record Set-up wizard; if you click the Customer module and click the New Customer icon, for example. See Chapter 18 for more details about wizards.

Chapter 2

Creating Your Chart of Accounts and Assigning Nominal Codes

In This Chapter

▶ Getting familiar with some accounting concepts

▶ Charting your accounts

▶ Adding nominal codes in your Chart of Accounts

▶ Changing your Chart of Accounts

*I*n this chapter, I get down to the nitty-gritty of the accounting system – the Chart of Accounts (COA), which is made up of nominal codes. Think of the Chart of Accounts as the engine of the accounting system. From the information in your COA, you produce your Profit and Loss report and your Balance Sheet. Set it up properly, and the Chart of Accounts grows with your business, but set it up wrongly and you'll have problems forever more!

Luckily, Sage gives you a lot of help and does the hard work for you, but you still need to understand why Sage is structured in the way that it is and how you can customise it to suit your business.

Understanding as Much as You Need to about Accounting

To use Sage, it helps if you have an appreciation of accounts and understand what you're trying to achieve. But you certainly don't need to understand all the rules of double-entry bookkeeping. The next sections give you the basics of accounting principles so that you can use Sage more comfortably.

Dabbling in double-entry bookkeeping

Accounting systems and accounting programs such as Sage use the principle of *double-entry bookkeeping,* so called because each transaction is recorded twice. For every debit entry, you record a corresponding credit entry. Doing the two entries helps balance the books.

For example, if you make a cash sale for £100, your sales account receives a £100 credit and your cash account gets a £100 debit.

Some knowledge of double-entry rules helps. That way, you can interpret information a little more easily. The following is a short summary of the rules of double-entry bookkeeping:

- ✔ **Asset and expense accounts:** Debit the account for an increase in value; credit it for a decrease in value.

- ✔ **Liability and income and sales accounts:** Debit the account for a decrease in value; credit it for an increase in value.

Fortunately, you don't need to book yourself into a bookkeeping evening class, as Sage does the double-entry for you . . . phew! (If you're intrigued by the double-entry system, though, pick up a copy of *Bookkeeping For Dummies* by Jane Kelly, Paul Barrow and Lita Epstein (Wiley), which explains double-entry and more.)

Having said that, understanding the double-entry method does help, particularly if you intend to do your own nominal journals. This knowledge also comes in handy if you intend to produce monthly management accounts. Sometimes, you need to post nominal journals to correct mistakes, and understanding the principles of double-entry bookkeeping lets you confidently process journals. Some familiarity with the double-entry method is important, but thorough knowledge isn't essential. If you struggle with journals, leave them to your accountant or at least seek advice if you aren't sure.

Naming your nominals

In accounting and in Sage, you bump into the term *nominal* quite a bit. And for good reason, as several key concepts use the word:

- ✔ **Nominal account:** Every item of income, expense, asset and liability is posted to a nominal ledger account. The nominal ledger accounts categorise all your transactions. The individual nominal accounts are grouped into ranges and can be viewed in your Chart of Accounts.

✔ **Nominal code:** A four-digit number given to each account that appears in the nominal ledger. For example, 7502 is the nominal code for office stationery, which is an account in the nominal ledger.

Sage categorises each nominal code into nine different ranges, and these categories form the basis of your Chart of Accounts.

✔ **Nominal ledger:** The nominal ledger is an accumulation of all the nominal accounts – this ledger is the main body of the accounting system. Each nominal account shows all the transactions posted to that specific code, so it follows that the nominal ledger represents all the transactions of the business in one place. Deep joy, I hear you say!

Sage tries to complicate things by referring to the nominal ledger as Company.

✔ **Nominal record:** An individual record for each nominal code. So, to create a new nominal code, open up a new nominal record and give it the new nominal code as its reference. See Chapter 3 for more details about nominal records.

Sage categorises the nominal codes in a specific way, so don't change them without careful consideration. Using common sense and planning at the early stages of implementing Sage can pay huge dividends in the future. You need to correctly categorise your nominal codes in order to create meaningful reports.

Preparing reports

One of the reasons you're investing in Sage is probably so that you can run reports to see how your business is doing. And your money is well spent, for Sage has many reports that you can run at the click of a button. The important thing to remember is that reports are only as good as the information contained within them. The old saying, 'Rubbish in, rubbish out' is never truer.

The two key financial reports every business and every accounting system use are:

✔ **Balance Sheet:** This report shows a snapshot of the business. It identifies assets and liabilities and shows how the business is funded via the capital accounts.

✔ **Profit and Loss report:** This report shows the revenue and costs associated with the business for a given period and identifies (as the name suggests!) whether the business is making a profit or incurring a loss.

The Profit and Loss and Balance Sheet reports are created from the information in the COA, so you must make sure that you get the COA right!

I discuss the Profit and Loss report and the Balance Sheet more fully in Chapter 14, where I also cover producing monthly accounts and the types of reports you're likely to need.

Looking at the Structure of Your Chart of Accounts

The Chart of Accounts (COA) is a list of nominal codes, divided up into the nine categories below:

- ✔ Fixed Assets
- ✔ Current Assets
- ✔ Current Liabilities
- ✔ Long-term Liabilities
- ✔ Capital and Reserves
- ✔ Sales
- ✔ Purchases
- ✔ Direct Expenses
- ✔ Overhead

The first five categories form the Balance Sheet; the remaining categories create your Profit and Loss report. So the COA is a pretty important part of the system!

A look at the nominal list on the Nominal Ledger screen shows that the list runs in numerical order, with the Balance Sheet codes first. If you click the Chart of Accounts icon within the Nominal Ledger, and look at the default layout of accounts, you'll notice a tab for Profit and Loss and another for Balance Sheet. You can click on either of these two tabs and a preview of the report appears on the right side of the screen.

Checking out the default COA

Being a caring, sharing software developer, Sage provides a default COA for you to use, with a ready-made list of nominal codes. (You select the type of COA you want using the Active Set-up wizard, which I go through in Chapter 1.) Your COA is determined by the type of business you operate. You're asked what business type when you install Sage. I use the Limited Company business type to demonstrate Sage in this book.

While Sage can spot whether a new nominal code is outside the range of the usual COA, it can't really help with the structure of the coding system that you choose to use, so plan ahead to avoid costly mistakes.

You can also customise the default COA to suit your business. (I tell you how in the 'Editing Your Chart of Accounts' section a little later in this chapter.)

The COA is in the Company module. To display it, click Modules on the main (browser) toolbar and then select Company, or you can simply click the Company button from the Navigation bar down the left side of the screen. (Make sure that you click Show More Buttons at the bottom of the Navigation bar so that all the buttons are visible.)

The Navigation bar is in full view all the time you're using Sage.

The opening screen for the Company module is shown in Figure 2-1. On the navigation bar, Sage uses the word Company as a title for the Nominal Ledger module, and you access the COA from there.

Check out the name of the opening screen of the Company module – Nominal Ledger, the name Sage uses within the Company module. Sage has slipped seamlessly into accounting mode – are you visualising the grey suits? The Nominal Ledger screen shows a series of icons, one of which is COA. You can also create and amend nominal codes from this screen, and create journals, as well as run a series of Nominal Ledger reports.

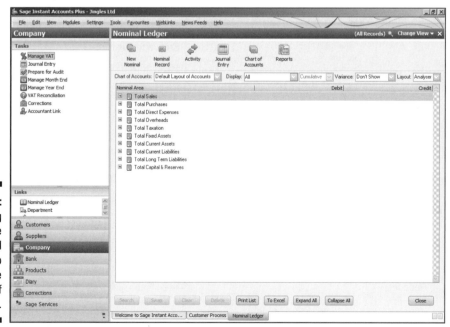

Figure 2-1:
Going through the Nominal Ledger to get to the Chart of Accounts.

For a better look at the COA screen, follow these steps:

1. **Click the COA icon on the Nominal Ledger toolbar.**

   The COA icon is second from the end of the icons across the top of the screen. The Chart of Accounts window opens, which gives you a list of all the Charts of Accounts you created. At first, only the Default Layout of Accounts shows, but any subsequent Charts of Accounts you create also show here.

2. **Highlight the Chart of Accounts you want to view and click the Edit button at the bottom of the next screen.**

   Initially, the Chart Of Accounts you want is the Default Layout of Accounts.

   The Edit Chart of Accounts window for the Default Layout of Accounts screen opens as shown in Figure 2-2. This screen shows the category types and a description in the top left of the screen, and the Category Accounts list showing the nominal codes associated with those categories outlined below. To the right of the screen, you see a preview of the Profit and Loss report layout.

   As you click each category type in the first box, you can see that the nominal codes shown in the Category Account List below change to match the category type. Have a go and see for yourself.

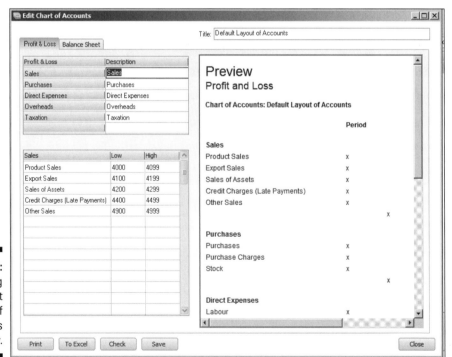

Figure 2-2:
Looking
at the Edit
Chart of
Accounts
window.

The first category shown is Sales, as displayed in Figure 2-2. Because Sales is highlighted in the first box, you'll notice that the Category Account list below shows the High and Low ranges of nominal codes within each Sales category. I explain the nominal code ranges in the next two sections.

If you're not sure which nominal codes fall into the range described, you can print a complete list of nominal codes. Alternatively, you can click the number in the Low or High column and use the drop-down arrow next to the field to see which account the nominal code is referring to. You can then scroll down the list of accounts that appear and view the range of codes.

To print a hard copy of the nominal list, use the following steps. The list usually consists of two or three pages, but the length depends on the number of codes you create. The more codes, the longer the list!

1. **From the navigation bar, click the Company button.**

2. **Click the Print List button at the bottom of the screen.**

   A command is sent to your printer to run off a hard copy of the existing codes.

The list of nominal codes may look rather daunting at first, but I talk you through the basics in the next sections.

Identifying Balance Sheet codes

The *Balance Sheet* is a snapshot of the business at a fixed point in time. It identifies the company's assets and liabilities and shows how the business has been funded via the capital accounts. To achieve this snapshot, the Balance Sheet looks at the assets the business holds and its liabilities, so it draws on the numbers in a range of nominal codes:

✔ **Fixed assets (0010–0051):** A *fixed asset* is an item likely to be held in the business for a long period of time – more than 12 months. The range of fixed-asset codes is used for transactions relating to freehold and leasehold property, and other items the company plans to hold for a while. You can add other capital items, such as computer equipment, to this list.

✔ **Current assets (1001–1250):** A *current asset* is an item that has a lifespan of 12 months or less. You should be able to *liquidate* (turn into cash) current assets reasonably quickly. Common current assets include stock, debts owed to the business, and bank and cash items. Current assets are normally ordered in the least liquid order first, meaning that items that take the longest to convert into cash appear at the top of the list. Therefore you expect to see cash, which is so liquid it runs through some people's hands like water, at the bottom of the current assets list.

✔ **Current liabilities (2100–2230):** *Current liabilities* are amounts that the business owes, normally outstanding for less than 12 months. At the top of the list is the Creditors control account, which is basically the total owed to all suppliers. But it also includes amounts owed to HM Revenue and Customs, which include VAT and PAYE, if applicable.

✔ **Long-term liabilities (2300–2330):** These liabilities are amounts owed by the business for a period of more than 12 months. They include long-term loans, hire-purchase agreements and mortgages.

✔ **Capital (3000–3200):** Capital accounts show how the business is funded. These codes include those for share issues, reserves and the current Profit and Loss balance.

Reserves is another word for earnings retained within the business – they're officially called *retained earnings*. Annual profits swell this account and any distributions of dividends to owners of the business reduce the balance.

In order for the Balance Sheet to balance, the capital account includes the current-year profit, as shown in the Profit and Loss report.

Table 2-1 shows the range of nominal codes that form the Balance Sheet.

Table 2-1	Balance Sheet Nominal Codes	
Category	*Low*	*High*
Fixed Assets		
Property	0010	0019
Plant & Machinery	0020	0029
Office Equipment	0030	0039
Furniture & Fixtures	0040	0049
Motor Vehicles	0050	0059
Current Assets		
Stock	1000	1099
Debtors	1100	1199
Bank Account	1200	1209
Deposits & Cash	1210	1239
Credit Card (Debtors)	1250	1250
VAT Liability	2200	2209

Category	Low	High
Current Liabilities		
Creditors: Short Term	2100	2199
Taxation	2210	2219
Wages	2220	2299
Credit Card (Creditors)	1240	1240
Bank Account	1200	1209
VAT Liability	2200	2209
Long-term Liabilities		
Creditors: Long Term	2300	2399
Capital & Reserves		
Share Capital	3000	3099
Reserves	3100	3299

Looking at Profit and Loss codes

In the default set of nominal codes, all codes from 4000 onwards are Profit and Loss codes, which, appropriately enough, include the numbers that show how much money the business brings in and how much it spends. The Profit and Loss codes include the following:

- **Sales (4000–4999):** Sales codes apply to goods or services that your business offers; they indicate how you earn your money. The 4000–4999 range also includes income other than sales, for example royalty commissions.

  The default descriptions against the sales codes are nonsense. Sales Type A, B, C, D and so on are not meaningful to anyone; they're just a starting point. You need to change the sales types to make them applicable for your business. If you own a card shop, for example, instead of Sales type A, you may have nominal code (N/C) 4000 for birthday cards, sales type B may become N/C 4005 for get-well cards, and so on. I look at editing nominal codes in Chapter 3.

- **Purchases (5000–5299):** These codes identify material purchases and purchasing costs such as carriage, packaging and transport insurance. *Material purchases* is a general term for the purchase of the raw materials used to make the products that the business sells. For example, flour is a material purchase for a bakery.

✔ **Direct expenses (6000–6999):** A *direct expense* is a cost directly associated with the product being manufactured or created by the business. Labour costs, including sub-contractors, come under these codes, which also include expenses such as sales commissions, samples and public relations costs that can be associated directly with the products.

✔ **Overheads (7000–9999):** By far the largest range of codes is *overheads,* which covers all other expenses not directly associated with making and providing the products or service. Table 2-2 shows the smaller sections into which overheads can be broken.

Table 2-2 lists the nominal codes that form the Profit and Loss report.

Table 2-2	Profit and Loss Nominal Codes	
Category	*Low*	*High*
Sales Revenue		
Product Sales	4000	4099
Export Sales	4100	4199
Sales of Assets	4200	4299
Credit Charges	4400	4499
Other Sales	4900	4999
Purchases		
Purchases	5000	5099
Purchase Charges	5100	5199
Stock	5200	5299
Direct Expenses		
Labour	6000	6099
Commissions	6100	6199
Sales Promotion	6200	6299
Miscellaneous Expenses	6900	6999
Overheads		
Gross Wages	7000	7099
Rent & Rates	7100	7199
Heat, Light & Power	7200	7299
Motor Expenses	7300	7399
Travelling & Entertainment	7400	7499
Printing & Stationery	7500	7599
Professional Fees	7600	7699

Category	Low	High
Overheads		
Equipment Hire & Rental	7700	7799
Maintenance	7800	7899
Bank Charges & Interest	7900	7999
Depreciation	8000	8099
Bad Debts	8100	8199
General Expenses	8200	8299
Suspense & Mispostings	9998	9999

Use Suspense and Mispostings nominal accounts when you can't find a suitable nominal code to put something to. They serve as holding pens – somewhere to post an item while you're trying to find a better code to post it to. At the end of each month, you need to review the Suspense and Mispostings accounts and put the items in their correct locations. Unfortunately, the suspense account in particular can become a dumping ground. Avoid the use of these accounts as far as possible and only use them when absolutely necessary.

Leaving gaps and mirroring codes

Notice that the ranges of codes in the preceding sections leave plenty of gaps between the categories. For example, Sales codes start at 4000 and the next range of Purchase codes doesn't begin until 5000. You can fill the large gap between 4000 and 4999 with Sales codes, which provides a great deal of flexibility for a growing business.

I suggest leaving gaps of ten between each code to allow for growth, but you need to decide for yourself the best fit for your business.

You may consider mirroring corresponding Sales and Purchase codes, so that the last two digits are the same for the sale and purchase of each item, as in Table 2-3, which shows a few of Jingles' nominal codes. (Jingles is the fictional card shop and party-planning company I created to serve as an example throughout this book.)

Table 2-3	Mirroring Nominal Codes		
Nominal Code	**Description**	**Nominal Code**	**Description**
4000	Sale of greetings cards	5000	Purchase of greetings cards
4020	Sale of party balloons	5020	Purchase of party balloons
4030	Sale of party gifts	5030	Purchase of party gifts

Accommodating floating nominals

A *floating nominal* is a code that can be placed as a Current Asset or Current Liability, depending on whether the balance is a debit or a credit. For example, if your bank account is in the black, the account is a Current Asset, but if the account is overdrawn, it should show as a Current Liability. Another example is the VAT Liability account, as you can sometimes get a refund from HM Revenue and Customs.

The Sage program automatically places the code to the correct side of the Balance Sheet, but only if you've identified those specific codes that can be treated as an asset or as a liability in the Floating Nominal Accounts section on the Edit Chart of Accounts screen. Sage normally designates accounts as floating nominal codes, so you don't have to do anything.

Editing Your COA

One of the first things to consider when setting up Sage is how well the COA suits your business. Have a look at the categories and nominal codes to make sure that they contain suitable descriptions for your products or services. For example, the Product Sales category doesn't suit a business that primarily provides a service. You may want to change a few categories, or you may decide to make wholesale changes, in which case it may be simpler to create an entirely new COA. The next sections tell you how to change and create COAs.

If you place a nominal code in the wrong category, it can cause inaccuracies in the reports you produce; miscodings are every accountant's nightmare! When creating new codes, be sure that you know whether the code should be a Balance Sheet or a Profit and Loss item. You can usually rely on your common sense, but if you're unsure, give your accountant a quick call. Accountants don't mind answering a quick question like this, but they do mind if you mix up Balance Sheet and Profit and Loss codes and they then have the task of unpicking your mistakes!

Amending your COA

You can edit the default COA to suit your business.

In Figure 2-2 (in the earlier 'Checking out the default COA' section), the category types showed Profit and Loss items on the first tab and Balance Sheet items on the second tab. If you move your cursor down the list of categories in the first box, you notice the details in the Category Account list below change to reflect the heading names and nominal codes contained within the highlighted category types. To view the nominal code ranges in more detail, click the nominal code and then use the drop-down arrow to identify the name of the nominal code.

You can change the description of each of the categories in the first box on the COA screen. You can also change the description of the ranges of nominal codes shown in the Category Account list. One of the first things to change is the Product Sales headings. These headings are general descriptions and won't suit all businesses. For example, if you're a baker using Sage, you may want to change the sales types to bread sales, cake sales and so on.

The headings in the COA show up in your Profit and Loss report and Balance Sheet (which you can see previewed on the right-hand side of the COA screen), so you need to give careful consideration to which headings you want to see on your financial reports. If you don't want an extensive list of different types of sales categories on your Profit and Loss account, consider grouping together several nominal codes under more general headings.

After you decide on the level of detail you want to show on your reports, you're now ready to amend your COA by following these steps:

1. **From the navigation bar, click Company and then click Chart Of Accounts.**

2. **Make sure that you highlight Default Layout of Accounts and then click Edit.**

3. **Make any changes to headings within the category account.**

   Changes available are:

   - **Rename a heading:** Simply click the title and overtype with the new name.

     For example, Jeanette, the owner of Jingles, would change Product Sales to Shop Sales.

     When you rename a heading, make sure that all the nominal codes included within the renamed heading relate to the new heading. (Check Chapter 3 section 'Creating Your Nominal Records' for more help with this.)

• **Insert a new heading:** To insert a line in the Category Account list, click the line below where you want to insert a line and press the F7 function key. A message comes up to say that inserting a line moves all categories down by one. Click Yes and don't panic when the codes above disappear from view! They're still there – they've just moved up. Scroll up the category accounts to see where your line has been inserted. Type the name of the new heading and then enter the range of nominal codes to which it relates.

Figure 2-3 shows the newly created Party Fees heading for Jingles. At the moment, the new heading has only one relevant nominal code (4350 Party Organising), so this code is both the Low and High range. If Jeanette wants to add more nominal codes at a later date, she can include them in the High range. So if the new code was 4370, the range of nominal codes for Party Fees would be 4350–4370.

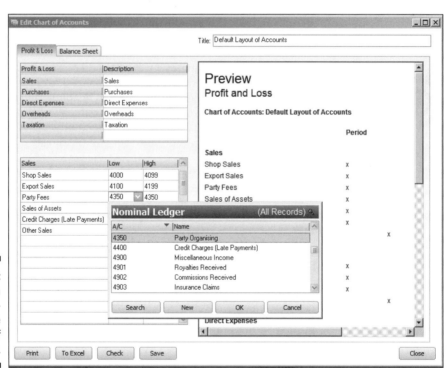

Figure 2-3:
Inserting a new heading in the Chart of Accounts.

- **Delete a heading:** You can use F8 to delete a heading line, but you must ensure that you're not likely to want to use those nominal codes.

4. **Click Save when you're happy with the changes you've made.**

   You need to go through your COA for errors, so take a look at the 'Checking Your COA' section later in this chapter.

Creating a new COA

If the existing COA doesn't suit your business at all, you may find that creating your own COA is less work than adapting the one that Sage provides. You may decide to use your existing nominal codes from your old accounting system, in which case you can customise the COA with these existing codes.

Alternatively, you may find that your business has particular geographical locations or segments that you wish to report on. You can create a new COA for each segment or location, but make it specific for your business. For example, you may have an office in London and one in Edinburgh. With the creation of suitable nominal codes, you can produce a Profit and Loss report to the gross profit line for each office. So you group together all the Sales codes associated with the London office and deduct from them all London office Purchases and Direct Costs. This calculation results in a London office gross profit. You can do the same exercise for the Edinburgh office with a separate COA, and then you can compare the two, to see which office was the most profitable.

Being able to analyse any further than gross profit requires an extremely complex set of nominal codes. Speak to your friendly accountant, who can assist with complicated nominal code structures.

When adding a new COA with the purpose of producing a Profit and Loss report to gross profit level, be aware that you can only select the nominal codes specific to that geographical location or segment of the business. As a result, the word *partial* appears after the COA name because you haven't selected all the nominal codes. In addition to the Gross Profit reports, you must always have a fully complete COA for the whole business, which must be checked for errors prior to running reports. See the 'Checking Your COA' section later in this chapter. Don't try to check a COA that has *partial* in the title, as Sage always brings up a list of codes that are missing; always check your complete COA for accuracy.

To add a COA, follow these steps:

1. **From the navigation bar, select the Company module and click Chart Of Accounts.**

2. **Click Add from the Chart Of Accounts window.**

   The New Chart of Accounts window appears.

3. **Enter the name of your new COA and click Add. A new Edit Chart of Accounts window opens, with the title of your new COA in the top right corner.**

4. **Select each category type by clicking the Description field in the first box and then enter a description in the Category Account List box below. Enter new headings and assign a range of codes for each heading for both the Profit and Loss tab and the Balance Sheet tab.**

Figure 2-4 shows a new COA called Jingles Card Shop. The Jingles business consists of two definite parts. One is the card shop, which sells cards, balloons and so on, and the other is party planning. To see the gross profit made on each part of the business, I created a separate COA for each segment. I selected only the nominal codes specific to the card shop and ignored any party-planning codes. Because I didn't include all the nominal codes in this COA, Sage includes the word *partial* in the title.

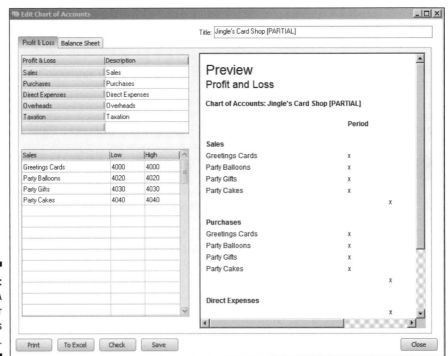

Figure 2-4:
A new COA created for the Jingles Card Shop.

Deleting a COA

You may find that while you've been playing around designing new COAs, you created too many variations and want to delete some of them.

Follow these steps:

1. **Click Company and then Chart of Accounts.**

   The Chart of Accounts window opens.

2. **Highlight the COA that you want to delete and click Delete.**

3. **Click Yes to confirm that you want to delete it.**

   If you decide that you don't want to delete, click No and return to the main Chart of Accounts window.

However, to get accurate reports for the whole of the business, I need to use the default COA, as this COA includes all nominal codes.

After you add a new COA, you can run your Profit and Loss report to see what information pulls through. Pay attention to the descriptions that you use in your COA, as they transfer through to your Profit and Loss and Balance Sheet reports. At this point, you can see the gross profit for each part of the business and determine what is making money or not, as the case may be.

When editing your COA, you can use the F7 function key to insert a line and the F8 key to delete a line.

Also, if you want just one code within the range, then the code is the same in both the High and Low columns.

Checking Your COA

After you make any changes to your COA, you need to ensure that your COA doesn't contain any errors. If an error is present, the Profit and Loss or Balance Sheet reports may be incorrect, and a warning message flashes up every time you run these reports.

To check your COA, follow these steps:

1. **Go to the Company module and click Chart of Accounts.**

2. **Click Edit.**

3. **Click Check.**

If no problems are present, Sage tells you that no errors were found in the COA, and you can breathe a sigh of relief. However, if a little window entitled Chart of Accounts Errors appears, be prepared to take corrective action.

Previewing errors

The Chart of Accounts Errors window gives you four output options for displaying the error report:

- ✔ **Printer:** Sends the report directly to your printer.
- ✔ **Preview:** Lets you look at the errors on the screen before deciding to print or exit.
- ✔ **File:** Saves the report to a new location.
- ✔ **Email:** Offers the facility to email the document to another person.

Usually, the best method is to preview the report first, to make sure that it's providing you with the information you expected, and then you can print a hard copy if you like what you see.

Make sure that the option you want has a filled-in circle next to it and then click the Run button at the bottom of the pop-up screen. Figure 2-5 is a sample Error report, showing that two account ranges are overlapping one another. Shop Sales shows nominal codes 4000–4100 and then Export Sales shows from 4100–4199. We can see that 4100 is incorrectly included in both ranges. We need to correct the ranges to stop the Error report coming up.

Figure 2-5:
An error shows up in a COA Error report.

Looking at some common errors

Whenever you add new nominal codes, the chance exists that they may not fit within the nominal code structure currently in place. This common oversight leads to errors within the COA.

Check the steps in the 'Amending your COA' section earlier in this chapter for advice on how to fix the errors I list here.

Other common errors include:

- **Overlapping ranges:** The same nominal code occurs in two different ranges and is therefore counted twice (as described in the example under heading 'Previewing errors'.)

- **Enclosing one range within another range:** Assigning a range of codes that's within another range is a big no-no.

  For example, Jeanette assigned the Sale of Balloons category a range from 4020 to 4029, and then assigned the Sale of Party Gifts codes from 4025 to 4028, which is within the Sale of Balloons range. She needs to fix it so that she knows whether she's selling mostly balloons or party favours.

- **Using a floating code in one category but not in its complementary category:** You may require a floating code so that an item such as the Bank Account can be both a Current Asset or a Current Liability, depending on whether the account is overdrawn or not. If you set up a floating code in Current Assets but not in Current Liabilities or vice versa, you get an error message.

Chapter 3

Setting Up Records

. . . .

In This Chapter

▶ Choosing a quick start or step by step

▶ Setting up records for customers and suppliers

▶ Registering your bank accounts

▶ Accounting for your products

. . . .

*A*fter you install your Sage software, you quickly realise that the hard work is only just beginning! You now have to create the records necessary to operate your accounting system, including those for your customers and suppliers and your existing bank accounts. Depending on your business, you may also need to set up stock records. This chapter tells you how.

Choosing How to Create Your Records

Setting up records may seem a daunting task, but Sage provides at least two ways of doing things: a quick way, using the Record icon within the relevant module and the step-by-step way, which involves using the wizards. If you like the belt and braces approach, choose the wizards, as they help you complete each section of the record thoroughly. However, if you're a bit of a speed freak and want to get on with things as quickly as possible, and don't mind leaving a few less important data fields blank (you can always update them later), choose the quick start option outlined in the next section. I always use this method, as time is invariably of the essence.

Getting a quick start using the Record icon

If you're looking for a quick start, the first thing you need to do is locate the Record icon. To set up records for customers, suppliers, nominal accounts, bank accounts and products, click the relevant module button from the navigation bar, and you're presented with the associated icons for each module, including the Record icon. You can also click the relevant edit option on the Task pane for each module. A record opens for you to start entering data.

For customer and supplier records, after you click the module button from the navigation bar, you're presented with a process map, which is currently the default screen. If you prefer not to have the process maps as a default and want to see a list of customers and suppliers with icons across the top of the screen, you can switch the process maps off. (See the 'Switching off the process maps' section later in this chapter.)

If you want to keep the Process screen as your default screen, you can simply use the Task pane to open up the Customer or Supplier Record screen. To do this, click the relevant module and then Customer/Supplier Record in the Task pane to bring up the Record screen.

You can then start entering your customer/supplier details; I tell you how in the later 'Creating Customer and Supplier Records' section.

As soon as you close the Process screen, the default screen reverts to opening with the process map.

Switching off the process maps

You can choose not to display the process maps as your default screen for customers and suppliers. I personally don't like the process maps, as I prefer to use the icons shown on the Toolbar screen. Incidentally, for those of you who have used Sage before, the Toolbar screen is more like the screens used to be before all the fancy graphics. (Now I'm showing my age!)

If you want to switch off the process maps and see the Customers or Suppliers screen instead, follow these steps:

1. **From the Menu bar, click Tools.**

2. **Select Options.**

3. **Click Yes to the confirmation screen, if you've other windows open.**

4. **In the Options menu, select the View tab. Click the small drop-down arrow next to Customers Process Maps and select Customers List. Do the same for Suppliers.**

   Figure 3-1 shows the Options screen.

5. **Click OK.**

Now, as soon as you enter the customer or the supplier ledger, the default screen shows the icons. You can click the Customer/Supplier Record icon to create as many records as you require. See the 'Creating Customer and Supplier Records' section later in this chapter.

Following the wizards brick by brick

Like Dorothy and friends finding their way to the Emerald City, going brick by brick or step by step can take some time, but it most assuredly gets you where you need to be. This method is slower than using the Customer/Supplier Record icon, as it guides you through the completion of every box in each record. For example, if you're keen on keeping customers within their credit limit and offer discounts for early settlement, you may want to use the Customer wizard to guide you through setting up the intricacies of your credit control.

To awaken a wizard, click the module you want to create a new record within and then click New Customer/Supplier. The program takes you through a step-by-step wizard, which prompts you to dot every 'i' and cross every 't'. The wizard is thorough, but using it can be time-consuming. (For more information about wizards, check out Chapter 18.)

Creating Customer and Supplier Records

Because setting up customer and supplier records is essentially the same process, I cover both of them in this section. Wizards can walk you through creating both types of records (just click New Customer/Supplier in the relevant module), but for the quick start method, read on.

Click the Customer Record icon using one of the methods outlined in the preceding 'Getting a quick start using the Record icon' section. A blank customer record appears, as shown in Figure 3-2.

Notice that several tabs appear across the top of the record:

✔ **Details:** Type the usual contact details in these fields.

Decide how you want to set up the account reference prior to beginning your data entry. Think carefully about this first data-entry field and the eight-digit short name you give each account. Sage recommends that you use an *alphanumeric* reference, meaning that you use letters and numbers. Sage suggests this method because you may have a number of clients with the same surname, for example Smith, so you need to give them unique references, such as Smith01, Smith02 and so on. Alternatively, ignore any numbers and continue with just words. For example, Julian Smith is SmithJ, Sarah Smith becomes SmithS and so on.

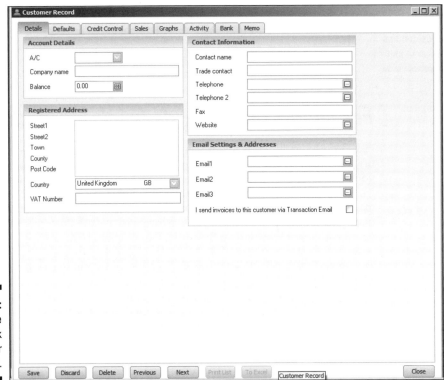

Figure 3-2:
An example of a blank customer record.

After typing in the account reference, you can tab through the other fields and enter the relevant information.

If you're transferring from a different computer package, you may be able to import the customer records from your old system to Sage. See Chapter 15 for details about how to do this.

✔ **Defaults:** The basic defaults are shown in each record, and you can override the details for each individual record if desired. You can specifically tailor the defaults for your customers as well.

For example, the default nominal code is currently set at 4000, but if you have a customer for whom this code never applies, you can easily change the code to something more suitable. For example, Jingles may sell one customer only balloons, therefore it makes sense to set the default nominal code to Sale of Balloons for that customer.

✔ **Credit Control:** You can enter your credit control details here for both customers and suppliers. For example, you can set credit limits so that, if a customer exceeds those limits, Sage warns you and you can take steps to get that customer account back under control. You can note details such as credit reviews and settlement discounts to assist you in your credit control.

To avoid a nervous breakdown, tick the Terms Agreed box in the bottom left corner of the Credit Control screen. If you don't, every time you open that record, you get an audio and visual prompt saying that terms haven't been agreed with this account. This prompt will drive you crazy after a very short space of time! So if you do nothing else with this page, make sure that you tick the Terms Agreed box.

✔ **Sales (customer record):** You can view a history of all invoices, credit notes, balances, receipts and payments against this account. Doing so identifies trends in your customer's monthly transactions.

✔ **Purchases (supplier record):** You can view a history of all invoices, credit notes, balances, payments and receipts applied to this supplier account. Again, you can see trends developing in your transactions with this particular supplier.

✔ **Graphs:** Prepare to be wowed with a graphical representation of the history of the transactions month by month.

✔ **Activity:** I use this screen a lot. It shows a list of every transaction ever made on the selected account. You can see all the invoices and credit notes, payments and receipts. It also shows a balance, amounts paid or received and turnover for that account.

Each line on the Activity list represents a single invoice, credit note, receipt/payment or a payment on account. You can drill down into additional detail, where it exists, by clicking the plus sign (+) on the left side of the transaction line. You can also view the aged detail of your customer or supplier accounts, shown at the bottom of the Activity tab. Future, Current, 30 days, 60 days, 90 days and Older buttons show values according to the age of the outstanding amounts.

✔ **Bank:** You can enter bank details on each record. This option is useful if you do a lot of online banking, particularly payment of suppliers.

You can also make notes about your customers and suppliers.

Setting customer and supplier defaults

Whenever you create a customer or supplier record, you enter details such as the credit limit, discounts and terms of payment. If all the same terms apply to all your customers or suppliers, you can set up this information once only, and it then applies to all customer or supplier records that you create. This option can save you time, particularly at the start when you're creating lots of records. If terms are different for a few individual customers or suppliers, or if the terms change for some reason, you can over-ride the defaults for each individual customer or supplier record at any time. If all your customers and suppliers are different, then don't set up defaults.

The following steps apply to setting up the Customer defaults, but you can use the same process for Supplier defaults:

1. **Click Settings from the Menu bar, and then Customer or Supplier Defaults.**

   The Customer Defaults screen opens on the Record tab. Here you can enter the country, edit the VAT code, nominal code and any discounts, as applicable. You can also edit the account status of the customer/ supplier.

2. **Click the Statement tab to amend the wording that you want to appear on your statements. For example, the default for invoices is Goods/ Services; you can change this to Shop Sales.**

3. **Click the Ageing tab if you want to switch from Period Ageing to Calendar Monthly Ageing.**

   Period Ageing sets periods of less than 30, 60 and 90 days, and 120 days or more. So if an invoice is dated 15 January 2013, it falls into the current period between 15 January to 13 February (within 30 days) and the 30-days-plus period between 14 February and 14 March, and so on.

   Calendar Monthly Ageing means that all the month's transactions are classed as outstanding on the first day of the month. For example, if the invoice is dated 15 January 2013, the invoice falls into the current period if an aged report is run between 1 January and 31 January. If the aged report is run between 1 February and 29 February, the invoice falls into Period 1, and so on.

If you've set Sage up using the Customise Your Company option, you'll have already looked at the Customer and Supplier defaults, so you can ignore this section of the chapter. However, if you want to revisit the Customisation pages, you can access them from the Menu bar by clicking Help, then Customise Your Company. You can then choose the appropriate modules that you wish to amend.

Deleting customer and supplier records

You can delete a record only if no transactions exist on the account and the account balance is zero. If neither condition is met and you try to delete an account, Sage lets you know in no uncertain terms that you can't do it! But if you can, and if you must, find out how here.

You may want to delete a record if you set up duplicate accounts in error. For example, you set up a new account before checking to see whether one was in existence already.

If no transactions exist on the second account, you can delete it following the steps here. If you've unwittingly added transactions to the duplicate account, you can change them by using the File Maintenance option, which I tell you how to use in Chapter 9. You then need to rename the second account with the words *Do Not Use!* in the title.

To delete a record, follow these steps:

1. **Open the customer or supplier ledger as appropriate and select the account you want to delete.**

2. **Click Delete, and when the confirmation message appears, click Yes.**

Creating Your Nominal Records

Nominal records are the main body of an accounting system. They're categorised into a Chart of Accounts structure, which I explain in Chapter 2.

Exploring your nominal records

To explore your nominal records, click Company to open up the Nominal Ledger screen. You can change the way the information is presented on the Nominal Ledger screen by using the drop-down arrow next to the Layout field. Figure 3-3 shows the Analyser layout.

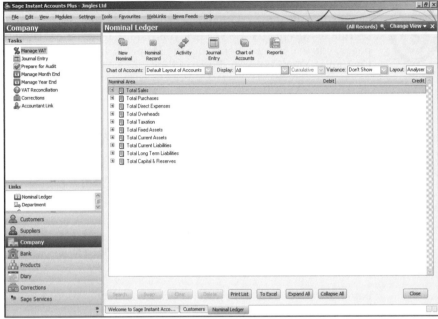

Figure 3-3:
Looking at
the nomi-
nal ledger
through the
Analyser
layout.

The main body of the screen shows the categories of the nominal codes. To
see which codes lie within the categories, click the plus sign (+) next to each
category. Doing so drills down to the next level and shows the sub-categories.
You can click the plus sign next to a sub-category to see the actual codes that
form part of that sub-category.

Alternatively, you can view all the nominal codes at a glance. To do so, follow
these steps:

1. **Click the Layout drop-down menu at the top right corner of the screen.**

2. **Select List.**

   The screen changes its appearance and shows a list of all your nominal codes along with a description/name. After you have transactions
   entered, you also see Debit and Credit columns with figures in, next to
   each nominal code.

3. **Scroll up and down this page to see the numerous codes.**

   They start at 0010 and finish at 9999! You may think that this range
   includes an awful lot of numbers, but the numbering system has gaps. I've
   never felt inclined to count them all, but suffice it to say, Sage has a lot!

You can choose the Graph layout, which shows a pie chart layout of the nine
categories of accounts within the nominal ledger. This option is colourful, but
not particularly useful. My preferred option is the List layout, which shows
the nominal codes in their clearest format.

Renaming existing nominal records

You may want to rename some of your nominal records. For example, Sage helpfully gives you several Sales Type codes from A to E – meaningless descriptions that you need to change to suit your business.

For example, Jeanette, the owner of Jingles, wants to change nominal code 4000, currently designated as Sales Type A, to Sale of Greeting Cards.

Follow these steps to rename the nominal records:

1. **Click Company.**

2. **On the Nominal Ledger toolbar, click the Nominal Record icon.**

3. **Type the number of the nominal code you want to change in the N/C (nominal code) box and press Enter.**

   In the Jingles example, Jeanette types in 4000.

4. **Place your cursor in the Name box and delete the current name. Replace it with the name of your new sales type.**

   For Jingles, Jeanette replaces Sales Type A with Sale of Greeting Cards.

5. **Click Save and then Close.**

Adding a new nominal record

When you're adding a new nominal record, you need to make sure that the nominal code you use fits into the correct part of the Chart of Accounts. Refer to Chapter 2 to see the nine different ranges of nominal codes that make up the Chart of Accounts.

If you're adding new codes into your range, you need to decide where you can slot them into your existing structure. For example, if you want to add a nominal record (which requires a new nominal code) for mobile phones, look at the Profit and Loss account, because mobile phones is an expense item. Mobile phones is not a direct product cost, so place it in the Overhead section, close to the telephone costs for the business, around the 7500 range of nominal codes.

In the Jingles example, Jeanette wants to add a new Sales nominal record, Sale of Birthday Cakes, with a new nominal code, 4040.

Here's how to add a new nominal record:

1. **Click Company.**

2. **On the Nominal Ledger toolbar, click the Nominal Record icon.**

3. **In the N/C box, type the new nominal code number and then tab to the Name field.**

   The new nominal code for Jingles is 4040.

   The words *new account* pop up next to the nominal code because Sage doesn't recognise this nominal code; it isn't part of the default list of nominal codes.

4. **In the Name field, type the name of your new record.**

   For Jingles, Jeanette enters Sale of Birthday Cakes.

5. **Click Save and close the box.**

Figure 3-4 shows Jingles' new nominal record.

You need to check that your Chart of Accounts is free of errors; refer to Chapter 2 for instructions on how to do this.

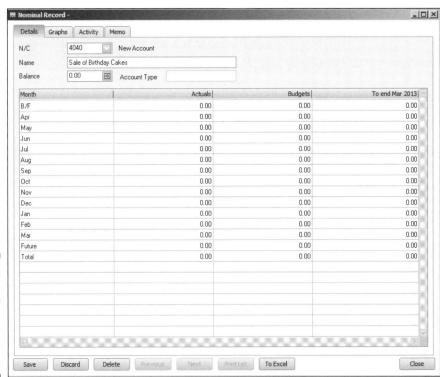

Figure 3-4: Adding Sale of Birthday Cakes to Jingles' nominal ledger.

Looking for a nominal record

Each nominal record has its own nominal code, but not every nominal code is immediately easy to find. Not that Sage tries to make things difficult, but an awful lot of codes need slotting into categories. Some codes slot into categories better than others.

Because I know a lot of the nominal codes by heart, I know where to start looking, but as a beginner you need to have a few tricks up your sleeve to find those elusive codes!

Searching for a record alphabetically

If you know the name of the record you're trying to find, but not the number (nominal code), follow these steps:

1. **Click Company and then Nominal Record.**

2. **From the N/C (nominal code) field, click the right drop-down arrow.**

   A list of all your nominal codes appears, in numbered order.

3. **Click the grey heading Name to reorganise the nominal codes into alphabetical order. Press the appropriate letter and locate the code you're interested in.**

   If you're looking for the nominal record for Telephone, press **T** on the keyboard, and Sage takes you to the first record beginning with the letter 'T', which just so happens to be Taxation . . . . Yuck! Scrolling down the codes, you find that Telephones and Fax is the next option. The nominal code is 7550.

To see where a record sits in the overall range, sort the nominal records back into number order by clicking the grey A/C (account code) heading and scrolling down to the appropriate codes.

After you sort the records back into number order, if you want to get to a specific number range again, type the first digit of the nominal code. Sage takes you to the first code that starts with that number, so you save time.

Finding a record numerically

If you know the approximate nominal code range, 7500 for example, but you don't know the specific code to use, follow Steps 1 and 2 from the preceding section and then click the grey A/C heading, which then sorts the nominal codes into numerical order. Enter 7 to find the 7000 codes and then scroll down the screen until you find the code that you need.

Looking around a nominal record

Sage provides a number of different ways to view the information contained within a nominal record. It also provides you with demonstration data, and I sometimes find it helpful to explore parts of the system with dummy data already entered.

To view the demonstration data, use the following steps:

1. **From the menu bar, click File⇨Open⇨Open Demo Data. Click Yes to the confirmation window that appears.**

2. **Type** manager **into the Logon field. No password exists, so click OK.**

3. **Click Company and then Nominal Record.**

4. **Type a code in the Nominal Code field and press Enter.**

   To follow this example, type **4000** to bring up the Sales North nominal record, which is shown in Figure 3-5.

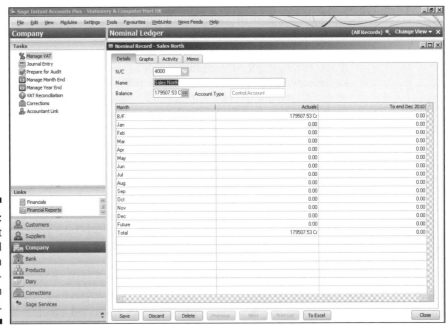

Figure 3-5: Looking at a nominal record with Sage's demonstration data.

Notice the four tabs at the top of the nominal record:

- ✔ **Details:** You're already in the Details screen. This screen shows you actual amounts posted to this account on a month-by-month basis, your budget figures and prior-year figures if they're available. You can edit the Budget field and enter figures directly into each month for each nominal record as part of your budget-setting process. These figures then appear on the Budget report, which I tell you about in Chapter 16.

- ✔ **Graphs:** You can view a graphic format of the account information with lots of pretty colours!

- ✔ **Activity:** One of the most well-used screens! You can scroll up and down the screen to see exactly what transactions have been posted using this nominal code. Any credit notes or journals also show here.

  As 4000 is a sales code, you can see exactly which invoices have been posted.

- ✔ **Memo:** You can make notes that relate to this account.

Deleting a nominal code

You can delete nominal codes that you never use, to tidy the list. For example, if you sell just one product, you may want to delete the codes associated with Sales Types B, C, D and E. Just follow these steps:

1. **Click Company.**

2. **On the Nominal Ledger toolbar, click the Nominal Record icon.**

3. **In the N/C box, type the number of the code you want to delete and press Enter.**

4. **Click Delete. Click Yes when the confirmation box appears.**

You can only delete a nominal record if no transactions are associated with that code.

Recording Your Bank Accounts

Sage automatically gives you seven bank accounts, as shown in Figure 3-6. The accounts range from an Ordinary Bank Current Account to a Credit Card Receipt account. You need to review the list of bank accounts and rename some, add new ones or delete those that don't apply to your business. The next sections tell you how to do these tasks.

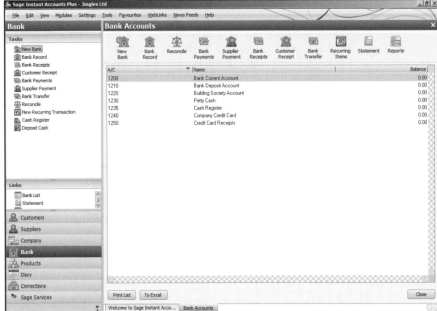

Figure 3-6:
The default
list of bank
accounts
that Sage
provides.

Renaming an existing account

You may find that the number of bank accounts that Sage gives you is sufficient, but you probably need to rename them to suit your business. For
example, you may want to specify the name of the bank or type of account,
such as number one account, number two account and so on.

Don't create a new account if you can simply rename an existing one. You
then don't need to amend your Chart of Accounts for new nominal codes.

To rename an account, follow these steps:

1. **Click Bank and then Bank Record.**

2. **Use the drop-down arrow to select the account you want to rename
   and then overtype the new name in the Nominal Name field.**

3. **Click Save.**

Creating new accounts

If you've a lot of bank accounts, you may need to create additional bank
account records to accommodate your business needs. You can choose from
three ways of creating a new account. You can:

✔ Set up a new account by using the wizard. Simply click New Bank on the Task pane while in the Bank module, or the New Bank icon from the Bank Account Module toolbar.

✔ Duplicate an existing account. From the Bank module, highlight the account you want to duplicate and click the Duplicate button at the bottom of the screen. Give the account an appropriate nominal code and name, click Save and off you go.

✔ Use a blank record and follow the steps I give here.

I demonstrate how to create a bank record with the same method used for creating customer, supplier and nominal records so far. The steps are:

1. **From the Bank module, click Bank Record.**

   The default bank account record opens.

   The screen shows the account reference as 1200, which is the default nominal code for the Bank Current account.

2. **Click the drop-down arrow in the Account Reference box.**

   All the existing bank accounts and their nominal codes are listed.

3. **Decide on a new nominal code reference for your new bank account and enter it in the Account Reference field.**

   Try to keep all the current accounts and deposit accounts between 1200 and 1229 and credit card accounts between 1240 and 1249. The Chart of Accounts is more presentable that way. I've used nominal code 1205 to create a new bank account for Jingles, as shown in Figure 3-7.

4. **Tab down to the Nominal Name field and give your new account a name.**

5. **From the Account Type box, use the drop-down arrow to select cash, cheque or credit card account.**

6. **Skip the Balance box – don't enter anything.**

   Have a look at Chapter 4 for information on opening balances.

7. **Tick** No bank reconciliation **if you're not intending to reconcile this bank account.**

   You probably only need this option for the Petty Cash account. You need to reconcile all accounts, including credit card accounts, to a bank or credit card statement to get a good picture of how your business is doing.

8. **Click Save.**

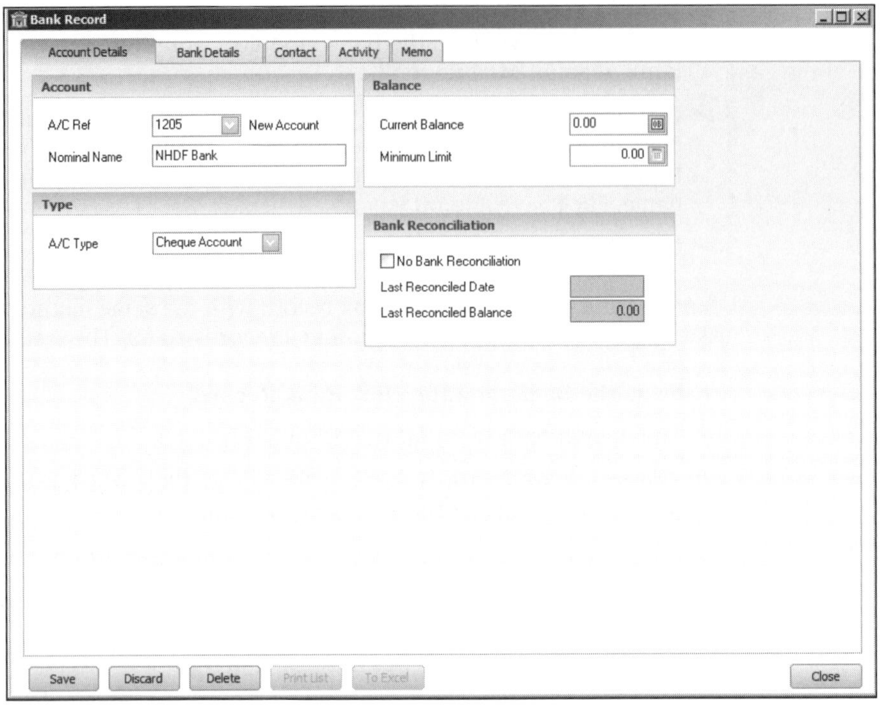

Figure 3-7:
Creating a
new bank
record.

Deleting a bank record

You may find that you want to delete a bank record. For example, Sage
provides you with a Building Society account, which you may not want.
Although you may decide to rename this account, you can choose to delete
the account completely and tidy up your bank account list. However, you can
only delete the account if the following conditions apply:

- The bank account has no transactions associated with it.
- The balance is zero.
- The account is not a control account.

If the account meets these conditions, highlight the bank account concerned
and click Delete. You receive an affirmation message. Click Yes to continue or
No to return to your original record.

Getting a handle on control accounts

Sage uses control accounts to make double-entry postings. The Debtors and Creditors control accounts enable you to see total figures for all your debtors and creditors without having to add up all the individual invoices and credit notes.

To see a list of all the control accounts, click Settings and then Control Accounts on the main toolbar. You don't need to alter these accounts because they're default accounts. In fact, if the Debtors, Creditors and Sales Tax or Purchase Tax control accounts have balances on them, you can't make any changes to these codes. Only journal to them if you're confident with your double-entry bookkeeping. Otherwise, leave them to your accountant!

Getting Your Product Records in Order

Planning your nominal codes is important, but planning your product records is just as crucial. The product records that you create eventually become your product list – a list of all your stock items. As the business grows, the number of stock items also grows, so you need to design a stock-coding system that's easy to use and can easily identify products. You need to be able to identify a product type quickly and easily from a stock list or stock report.

Creating a product record

Three methods exist for creating a product record:

- ✔ Using the wizard: Click Products and then New Product (from the Task Pane or by clicking the New Product icon).
- ✔ Duplicating an existing record: Click the product and then Duplicate.
- ✔ Typing your details directly into a blank product record, as detailed here.

Follow these steps to use the blank record method:

1. **From the Products module, click Product Record.**

   The Details screen, shown in Figure 3-8, appears.

2. **Enter your chosen product code, using 30 digits or fewer.**

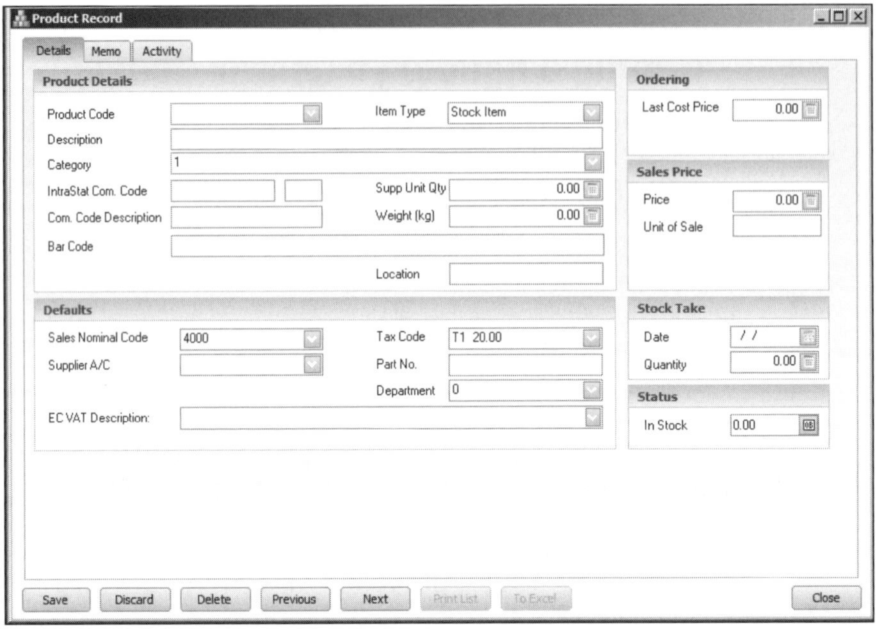

Figure 3-8:
Viewing a blank product record.

3. **Type in a description of the product and fill in as many of the product details as you can. (Note: the product field allows you to enter the bar code for your product, alphanumerically and up to 60 characters in length.)**

   In the default section, you may need to change the default sales nominal code. For example, a stock record for birthday cards requires a nominal code for birthday cards. You need to check the nominal codes and change if necessary.

   When entering your product details, you can choose an Item Type:

   • **Stock Item:** A regular item of stock, which has a product code and description.

   • **Non-Stock Item:** An item that isn't a usual item of stock, perhaps purchased for use within the business instead of to sell.

4. **When you've finished entering your product details, click Save.**

   Your first record is saved, and the screen goes blank again, waiting for your next record.

   The other tabs that belong to the product record are outlined next.

   • **Memo:** You can enter additional notes about the product.

   • **Activity:** Shows the individual transactions created for each product, for example goods in, out or transferred, or stock adjustments. You can also view the quantity of the item in stock.

Editing a product record

You can edit a product record at any time by double-clicking the chosen product. The Product Record screen appears. You can then make the necessary change, click Save and close the screen.

Deleting a product record

As with the other records, you can only delete a product record if the following criteria are met:

- ✔ The product record has no transactions on the product activity. Any history needs to be removed, using the Clear Stock option; see Chapter 12 for information on how to do this.
- ✔ The In Stock is zero.

If all these conditions are met, you can delete the product with a couple of steps:

1. **From Products, highlight the product you want to delete.**
2. **Click Delete. An affirmation message appears. Click Yes.**

Chapter 4

Recording Your Opening Balances

In This Chapter

▶ Choosing the right time to switch to Sage

▶ Getting your opening balances

▶ Recording your opening balances

▶ Checking for accuracy

*I*n this chapter I explain how to transfer the individual account balances from your previous accounting system, whether manual or computerised, into Sage Instant Accounts. Effectively, you're taking the values that make up what your business is worth on the day you swap from your old system and start using Sage. You need to set up your nominal records before recording balances, so check out Chapter 3 if you haven't done that yet.

Opening balances give you a true picture of your business's assets and liabilities to use as a starting point. If you don't enter your opening balances, you don't have accurate information about who owes you money, how much money you owe or how much money you have in the bank. You won't even be able to reconcile your bank balance. In short, without opening balances, the information in your Sage program isn't worth the paper it's printed on!

Entering your opening balances can be a bit tricky, so make sure that you're not going to be disturbed too much! After you've entered your opening balances, you can print an opening balance sheet, which is an important tool to check that your balances have been entered correctly.

Timing Your Switch to Sage

The best time to start with a new system is at the beginning of a financial year. You roll the closing balances from the previous year-end forward so that they become your opening balances for your new year. Take advice from your accountant if you have one, as everyone's circumstances are different.

If you can't wait until the new financial year to switch to Sage and you're VAT registered, at least wait until the start of a new VAT quarter. This way, you avoid having a mixture of transactions in your old and new system that makes reconciling your data extremely difficult.

Enter your opening balances before you start entering transactions. You can then check your accuracy by proving that your opening Trial Balance matches your Closing Trial Balance from your previous system. Without the clutter of day-to-day transactions, you can check much more easily!

Obtaining Your Opening Balances

Whether you're transferring from a manual bookkeeping system or a computerised one, the process is still the same. Essentially, you transfer into Sage the balance sheet information that shows the net worth of your business.

An opening *Trial Balance* is a list of all account balances carried forward from the previous year-end. Your previous accounting system is your source for your Trial Balance. As you zero-down your Profit and Loss items at the end of the financial year, any retained Profit and Loss items from the previous year now sit in your balance sheet, so an opening Trial Balance contains only balance sheet codes. An opening Trial Balance report looks quite short and shows debit and credit entries for all your balance sheet items, with grand totals at the bottom of both your Debit and Credit columns.

If you're starting to use Sage at the beginning of a new financial year, your accountant can provide you with your opening balances.

If you're transferring from a manual bookkeeping system, you need to ensure that you've balanced off all your individual accounts for the previous period. You may find it easier to print off a list of your newly created nominal accounts in Sage and create two columns: one for debit balances, and the other for credit balances. (To print a nominal list, click Company, which takes you to the Nominal Ledger screen, and then click Print List.) You can then total each column to create an opening Trial Balance.

The figures contained within a Trial Balance are simply the accumulated value of items. For example, the Debtors control account is simply the combined value of all monies owed by customers at that point in time. To establish your opening balances, you need to know the specifics of exactly which customers owe you money and what invoices are outstanding. The same applies to your suppliers: you need to see a full breakdown of who you owe money to. You obtain this information from a variety of sources. Table 4-1 shows the types of reports you need from a computerised system or a manual one.

Table 4-1   Information Sources for Entering Opening Balances

Category	Computerised System	Manual System
Customers		
For a standard VAT system, record the transaction including VAT. For a VAT cash accounting scheme, record both the net and VAT amount. If this figure isn't the same as your opening Debtors Balance, you need to investigate why.	An Aged Debtors report, showing a breakdown of who owed you money at the start of the year/period.	A list of customers who haven't paid at the year-end, including the amount outstanding.
Suppliers		
For a standard VAT scheme, include the VAT amount. For a VAT cash accounting scheme, show both the net and VAT amount. If this figure isn't the same as your opening Creditors Balance, you need to investigate why.	An Aged Creditors report, showing a breakdown of who you owed money to at the start of the year/period.	A list of suppliers who you haven't paid at the year-end, along with the monies owed.
Bank		
When you start reconciling the first month's bank account, you may see cheques from the prior year clearing through the bank account. You don't need to worry about these un-presented cheques and lodgements as they've already been taken into account in the previous year and are included in the opening balance for your bank account. Simply mark the items on your bank statement as being prior-year entries. Don't post the items through again.	A copy of the bank statements showing the balance at the year-end. A copy of the bank reconciliation showing a list of any un-presented cheques or outstanding deposits. (Your accountant can help with this task.)	A copy of the bank statements showing the balance at the year-end. A copy of the bank reconciliation showing a list of any un-presented cheques or outstanding deposits. (Your accountant can help with this task.)

(continued)

Table 4-1 (continued)

Category	Computerised System	Manual System
Products		
	A stocktake list showing the number of items in stock at the start of the year/period.	A stocktake list showing the number of items in stock at the start of the year/period.

Entering Opening Balances Using the Wizard

Sage has developed a wizard that can help you magically enter your opening balances with ease. To access, click Tools and then Opening Balances from the Menu bar. The Opening Balances window opens as shown in Figure 4-1.

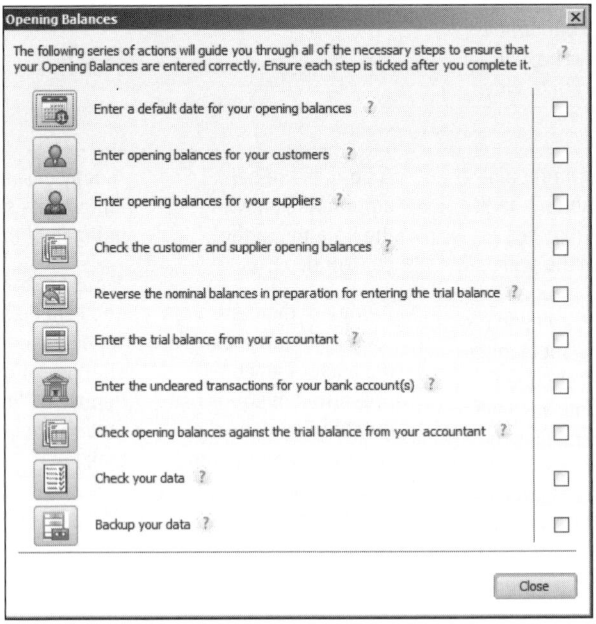

Opening Balances

The following series of actions will guide you through all of the necessary steps to ensure that your Opening Balances are entered correctly. Ensure each step is ticked after you complete it.

- Enter a default date for your opening balances ?
- Enter opening balances for your customers ?
- Enter opening balances for your suppliers ?
- Check the customer and supplier opening balances ?
- Reverse the nominal balances in preparation for entering the trial balance ?
- Enter the trial balance from your accountant ?
- Enter the uncleared transactions for your bank account(s) ?
- Check opening balances against the trial balance from your accountant ?
- Check your data ?
- Backup your data ?

Close

Figure 4-1: Entering your opening balances using the wizard.

The opening balances represent the financial position of your business on the day you start entering transactions into Sage. Even a new business has opening balances as the funds used to start it up need to be accounted for – the owner's money or grant funding, for example.

In the following section, I take you through the steps necessary to enter your opening balances using the wizard as your mystical guide. Click the first button on the list of icons shown in Figure 4-1 and you can begin to enter your default date.

After you've performed each task, Sage puts a tick in the box next to that task. Go through the list in the given order to ensure maximum accuracy.

Entering your default date

Don't panic – the default date is usually the last day of the previous month, normally the day before the start of your financial year. So, if your financial year starts on the 1 April 2013, your default date is 31 March 2013.

When you click the first button a new window opens, as shown in Figure 4-2, and you're asked to enter your default date. If you're not sure of the default date, check with your accountant. Click Save when you're happy that the date is correct.

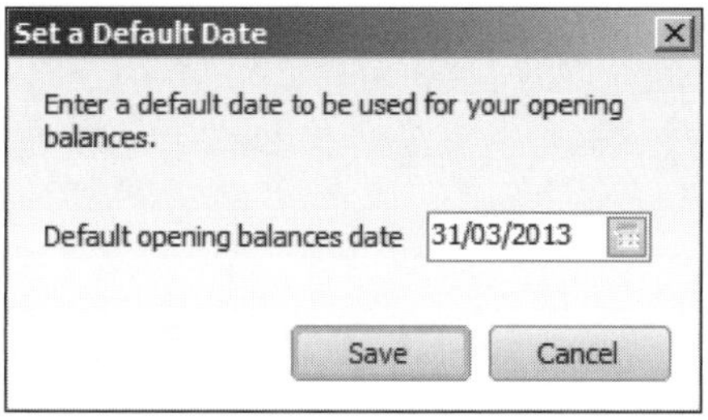

Figure 4-2: Entering your default date.

> **Set a Default Date**
>
> Enter a default date to be used for your opening balances.
>
> Default opening balances date `31/03/2013`
>
> [Save]   [Cancel]

Entering customer and supplier balances

Despite the fact that customers owe you money and you owe money to suppliers, the process for entering opening balances for both is pretty much the same, so I talk about them together in this section.

Using your Aged Debtors report or debtor list for customers and your Aged Creditors report or creditor/supplier list for suppliers, access each individual account and enter each opening balance, recording each invoice individually.

Enter your opening balances as separate invoices, as doing so helps with ageing the debts and affects any future reports that you may run. It also depends on which VAT scheme you use, as you definitely need to enter transactions separately if you choose to use VAT cash accounting or the UK flat VAT rate (cash-based).

When you click the customer or the supplier icon, you're presented with a similar screen. Figure 4-3 shows the entry screen for entering Customer Opening Balances.

Using the drop-down arrow, simply select the customer for whom you have an opening balance to record and click OK. The screen displays the full account name and the default date is automatically entered. The ref O/Bal is used to identify the transaction, but you may wish to enter a further reference in the Ex.Ref column to identify your invoice number. You also have the opportunity to enter a department reference.

Notice that the word 'Invoice' has already been entered in the Type column. If you've credit notes to enter, use the drop-down arrow at the side of the Type column and select Credit Note instead.

Finally, you need to enter the gross value of the invoice.

When you're happy with the details on the screen, click Save.

You now see a tick against the Customer and Supplier line.

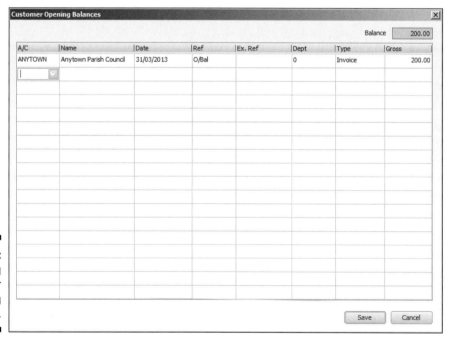

Figure 4-3:
Entering
Customer
Opening
Balances.

You only need to record customer balances if you keep customer records. So if you run a shop that collects all receipts at the till and doesn't send out invoices, you don't need to keep customer records.

If you send invoices to your customers, keep records for each customer and record how much each one owes you at the start of your new accounting period with Sage.

If you used wizards to create your customer and supplier records, you've already entered your opening balances because the wizard asks for them.

Reversing the nominal balances in preparation for entering the Trial Balance

Wow, what a mouthful! If you're struggling to understand what this heading means, don't worry, the process is automatic and Sage does all the hard work for you. In a nutshell, when you've entered the balances for your customers and suppliers, Sage enters values into the nominal account for both Debtors and Creditors. When you start entering the information from the Opening Trial Balance in the next step, you're duplicating entries for Debtors and Creditors, but thankfully Sage intercepts at this point and reverses out the duplicated entries. Phew!

All you need to do is click the icon next to Reverse the Opening Balances. Sage asks if you want to make a backup before proceeding (you should always make a backup!). After you've done so, a new screen opens called Opening Balances Reversals, as shown in Figure 4-4.

Sage has already completed the journals for you, but you can check them prior to clicking Reverse in the bottom right corner. If you're not happy, you can click Cancel, and Sage returns to the Opening Balances wizard.

When you click Reverse, Sage brings up a warning message saying that the date is prior year. Click Yes as you're entering a prior year date. The screen then returns to the Wizard list.

It may look as if Sage hasn't actually done anything, but in reality it has. You can check on the financials page to see evidence of reversing journals having been posted.

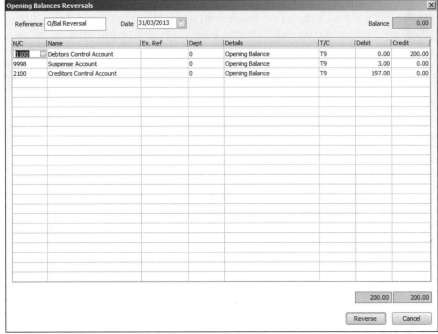

Figure 4-4:
Reversing the nominal balances in preparation for Opening Trial Balance.

Entering the Trial Balance from your accountant

You may be in the lucky position of already having an Opening Trial Balance from your accountant; if not, asking for one is a good idea. You only need an Opening Trial Balance if you've already been trading the previous year and you're simply moving your accounts from your old system to Sage.

(If you're a business start-up, and have no previous accounts records, you may simply want to enter the odd invoice or transaction as an opening balance. You can do so manually, as explained in the 'Manually recording opening balances' section, later in this chapter.)

Click the icon next to *Enter the trial balanace from your accountant* and the Trial Balance Entry window opens, as shown in Figure 4-5.

Using your Opening Trial Balance, enter each item systematically into the Trial Balance Entry window.

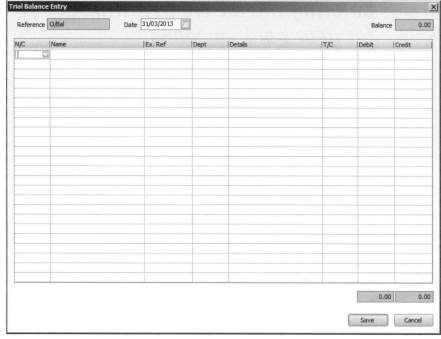

Figure 4-5:
Entering
your
Opening
Trial
Balance
from your
accountant.

If you're using the Sage default set of nominal codes, use common sense and match the items from your Opening Trial Balance to those of Sage. For example, Accruals in Sage has the nominal code 2109. Take the balance for Accruals from your opening Trial Balance and use nominal code 2109.

If you're using your own existing nominal codes, enter them here. (If you're using your own codes, you need to have elected to use a customised Chart of Accounts when you set up Sage – refer to Chapter 1 for company set-up information.)

After you've entered your opening Trial Balance, check that the debits and credits columns on both your Sage Trial Balance and your Opening Trial Balance match. Check each individual entry and ensure that each account is correctly entered. When you're satisfied, click Save.

You return to the Opening Balance Wizard list. A tick should now show in each step you've completed.

Entering the un-cleared transactions for your bank account

This is where you need to enter the items that haven't yet cleared your bank account. These items are your un-presented cheques that may have been written out prior to the previous year-end but haven't yet cleared the bank account, so they won't be included in the bank balances that you entered in your Opening Trial Balance from your accountant.

You should be able to easily identify these transactions by checking your cheque stubs against your bank statements and seeing which items are considered to be un-presented cheques.

In addition, you may have bank receipts that you paid into the bank close to the year-end, but which may not have cleared into your bank account. You need to enter these items so that they show up on the bank reconciliation screen and are available for you to select when reconciling each bank account.

Click the icon next to `Enter the uncleared transactions for your bank accounts` and the screen shown in Figure 4-6 opens.

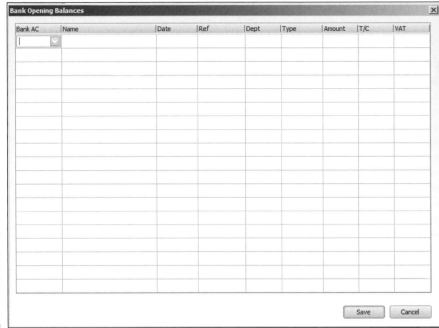

Figure 4-6: Entering un-cleared bank transactions.

Using the drop-down arrow, select the appropriate bank account. Sage prefills some of the columns, but you must select the type of transaction, such as Receipt or Payment. You then need to enter the amount and the appropriate VAT code.

Note: The amount is the Net amount if you're selecting VAT code T1.

Once you're happy with the details, click Save.

As an additional prompt, I enter the cheque number or paying-in slip reference in the reference field (next to where it says O/Bal) – this extra detail makes reconciling the bank account a lot easier.

Checking opening balances against the Trial Balance from your accountant

When you click on the icon next to the line Enter the trial balance from your accountant, Sage simply opens up Criteria Box for the Trial Balance report. If you use the drop-down arrows, select the brought forward date for your Trial Balance Report, as shown in Figure 4-7.

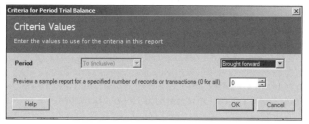

Figure 4-7: Selecting the opening Trial Balance Report.

Click OK and your Opening Trial Balance appears on the screen. You can print it out and double-check it against your accountant's opening trial balance.

Checking your data

Sage gives you an option to check your data to ensure that everything is okay. I do so just for peace of mind.

Click the icon next to `Check your data`. Sage automatically runs the File Maintenance process and informs you of any errors or warnings associated with your data.

Backing up your data

Finally, Sage asks you to back up your data. When you click on the icon, Sage asks whether you want to check your data (which you already did in the previous step). Click No, and Sage takes you straight through to the backup window. Choose an appropriate filename, perhaps something referring to the backup after posting Opening Balances, and click OK.

That's it! You've now completed all the steps necessary to enter your opening balances.

Manually recording opening balances

As with most things in life, you can always do things in more than one way. I'm not a great fan of using wizards to enter records and data, as I find them rather cumbersome and slow to use. However, many other people find them incredibly useful. That said, the Opening Balances wizard is much more useful than most, and I believe it guides you correctly and smoothly through the whole process, allowing you to check details as you go along. It also provides you with a visual aid of your progress, as you can see at a glance which items have already been ticked off the list.

But perhaps you want to enter the Opening Balances the old-fashioned way and prefer to manually enter information. Here's how you do so.

Depending on whether you're entering balances for customers or suppliers, you start from different places:

✔ **Customers:** From the Customer module, click Customer Record.

✔ **Suppliers:** From the Supplier module, click Supplier Record.

Then follow this process:

1. **Select the account using the drop-down arrow and then click the OB (Opening Balance) button located to the right of the Balance box.**

   The Opening Balance Setup window appears. Figure 4-8 shows the location of the OB button.

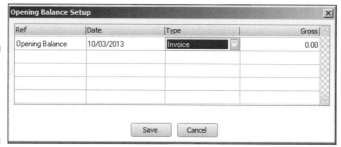

2. **Click the Reference field, and type** opening balance.

3. **Tab to the Date field and enter the original date of the invoice/credit note.**

   Entering the original invoice date ensures that the invoices are allocated to the correct period when printing Aged Debtors or Creditors reports.

4. **Tab to the Type field and select Invoice or Credit.**

5. **Enter the invoice or credit amount in the Gross field.**

   Record the gross amount including VAT for standard VAT accounting users; record the net amount and VAT separately if using the VAT cash accounting scheme.

6. **Press Enter to move down to the next line if you've more transactions to enter for that customer/supplier and repeat Steps 2 to 6.**

7. **Click Save to accept the details you've entered. Click Cancel if you aren't happy with the accuracy of your entries and want to return to the main customer record without saving.**

8. **Check that your customer balance agrees with your Aged Debtors or customer list for customers, and your Aged Creditors or supplier list for suppliers.**

Recording opening bank balances manually

You need to record the opening balance for each bank account associated with your business.

Use the following steps to enter opening balances for each bank account:

1. **From the Bank module, highlight the bank account you wish to enter an opening balance for and click Record.**

2. **Click the OB button next to the Current Balance box.**

   The Opening Balance Setup window opens. The Reference automatically defaults to O/Bal (Opening Balance), which is fine; leave it as it is.

3. **Enter the date.**

   You want to enter the prior year's end date. For example, if you're starting with Sage on 1 April 2013, the date should be 31 March 2013 to ensure that Sage posts you're opening balance into the correct period.

   The closing balance as at 31 March is the same as the opening balance as at 1 April.

4. **Enter the account balance.**

   If the account is in the black, enter the account balance in the Receipt box. If the account is overdrawn, put the amount in the Payment box.

5. **Click Save when you're happy that the opening balance figure is correct.**

You may have un-cleared payments or receipts already included in your bank balance shown on the opening Trial Balance. The best way to deal with un-cleared payments is to obtain a copy of your bank reconciliation statement at the year-end and identify those items shown as un-presented cheques or outstanding paid-in items. After your bank statement arrives, mark these items on your statement as being pre-year-end transactions. When you come to reconcile your bank account in Sage, you can ignore these items as they're already included in your opening balances.

Recording nominal opening balances manually

If you're manually entering your opening balances and you've been following the order of this chapter, you've already entered the Debtors control account, the Creditors control account and the opening bank balances, so you don't want to enter them again.

When you enter the individual opening balances on to each customer record, Sage does some double-entry in the background, crediting the Sales account and debiting the Debtors control account; therefore when you come to enter the remaining nominal account balances from your Trial Balance, don't post the Debtors control account total, otherwise you're double-counting. If you do post the Debtors control account balance in error, you need to reverse the posting by using a nominal journal. Turn to Chapter 12 for information on journals.

If you choose the Opening Balance Wizard, Sage does the reversing journals automatically for you, so you don't need to worry about double-counting anything.

Working in a methodical manner (using your opening Trial Balance), enter all the remaining balances, such as fixed assets, stock, loans and so on, using the following steps:

1. **From Company, click Company Record.**

2. **Enter the nominal code.**

   If you're using the Sage default set of nominal codes, use common sense and match the items from your opening Trial Balance to those of Sage. For example, Accruals in Sage has the nominal code 2109. Take the balance for Accruals from your opening Trial Balance and use nominal code 2109.

   If you're using your own existing nominal codes, enter them here. (If you're using your own codes, you should have elected to use a custom- ised Chart of Accounts when you set up Sage – refer to Chapter 1 for company set-up information.)

3. **Click the OB button next to the Balance box.**

   The Opening Balance Setup window appears.

4. **Keep the reference (Ref) as O/Bal (opening balance) and tab along to the Date field and enter the closing date of the prior period.**

5. **Tab to the Debit or Credit column and enter a debit or credit figure from the opening Trial Balance.**

6. **Click Save.**

You must use the prior year-end date as your opening balance date so that the Trial Balance you bring forward is correct. If you inadvertently enter 1 April as your date, the figure you enter drops into the current year and not into the brought-forward category. To rectify this problem, enter a nominal journal to reverse the previous journal that Sage automatically posted for you. (See Chapter 12 for help.) If you want to view the automatic journal that Sage has posted, click Company from the navigation bar and then click Financials from the Links list.

Putting in opening balances for products

You only need to put in opening balances for products if you want to track stock items.

Make sure that you create product records for all the items of stock that you wish to put an opening balance to before you try to enter opening product balances. (Refer to Chapter 3 for information on creating records.)

Jingles, the fictional card company, is serving as the example in the following steps. Jeanette, the owner, created a record with the product code Card-HB for birthday cards. Her stocktake at the year-end showed 1,000 cards in stock.

1. **From the navigation bar, click Products. Highlight the product you want to enter an opening balance for and click Product Record.**

   For Jingles, Jeanette highlights Card-HB.

2. **Click the OB button, which is located in the Status box in the bottom right corner of the Product Record.**

3. **Keep the reference as O/Bal and enter the date as the prior year-end.**

4. **Enter a quantity and cost price for the item.**

   In the Jingles example, Jeanette enters 1,000 as the quantity and 50p as a cost price, as shown in Figure 4-9.

Figure 4-9: Entering product opening balances.

Opening Product Setup				
Ref	Date	Quantity	Cost Price	
O/BAL	31/03/2013	1000.00	0.50	
	Save	Cancel		

5. **If you're happy with the details entered, click Save.**

   If you're not happy, click Cancel to return to the product record and start again from Step 2.

After you click Save, Sage posts an Adjustment In (AI) transaction to the product record, which you can see in the Activity tab. To view activity on an item, from the main screen, click the stock item you want to view and double-click the product to take you into the record. Click the Activity tab to see the adjustment posting.

The product opening figures don't automatically update a stock value into your nominal ledger. Opening stock is one of the figures you enter as part of your nominal ledger opening balances – see the 'Recording nominal opening balances' section earlier in this chapter.

Checking Your Opening Balances

If you've entered your opening balances manually, you need to make sure that the figures you entered are correct and agree with the opening Trial Balance you used to enter those figures. The best way to make sure is to print your own opening Trial Balance from Sage and compare it to the document you've been working with. If you find discrepancies, you can go back and fix them.

Printing an opening Trial Balance

Follow these instructions to run an opening Trial Balance:

1. **From the navigation bar, click Company and then click Financials in the Links list.**
2. **From Financials, click the Trial Balance icon at the top of the page.**
3. **Select Preview and Run in the Print Output box.**
4. **Change the date in the Criteria Values box to Brought Forward, using the drop-down arrow.**
5. **Click OK.**

   This previews the opening Trial Balance.

6. **Click the Print icon to print the Trial Balance and check your report.**

Look for the following information on the report:

✔ Check that the *suspense account* (the temporary account where you put problematic transactions until you determine where they properly belong) shows a zero balance.

✔ Check that the totals on your new Trial Balance are the same as the totals on the Trial Balance from your previous system.

If you've problems with either of these balances, see the next section.

Dealing with errors

If the suspense account doesn't have a zero balance, first check that you haven't entered the Debtors or Creditors control account twice. If you've entered something twice, turn to Chapter 16, which tells you how to reverse the duplicated item using a nominal journal.

If you find that your total balance doesn't match the total of your opening Trial Balance, make sure that you've entered an opening balance for each nominal code and that you haven't missed anything out by mistake.

After you enter all of your opening balances and your opening Trial Balance matches that of your previous system, you're ready to begin entering your transactions. Chapter 5 covers processing your customer-related paperwork.

Part II
Looking into Day-to-Day Functions

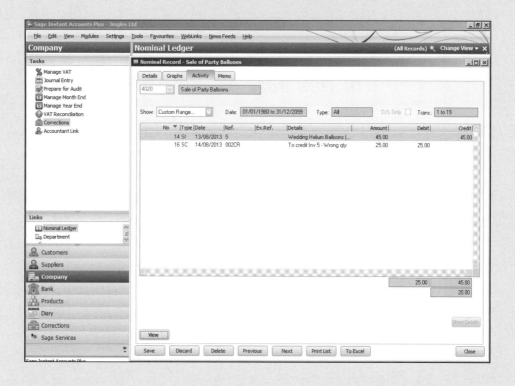

Go to www.dummies.com/extras/sageinstantaccountsuk for free online bonus content.

In this part . . .

✔ Get a handle on your business's finances and brush up on the day to day record keeping duties within Sage Instant Accounts.

✔ Be in-the-know with invoices: create sales invoices and enter supplier invoices and credit notes.

✔ Cover every corner: clue yourself up on credit cards and petty cash.

✔ Protect yourself and your business by learning how to make corrections to your data.

✔ Get to know the Products module – carry out stock takes and amend your stock on the system.

Chapter 5

Processing Your Customer Paperwork

In This Chapter

▶ Entering sales invoices manually

▶ Posting credit notes

▶ Allocating customer receipts

▶ Dealing with invoices and credit notes

▶ Managing write offs, refunds and returns

*I*n this chapter I tell you how to process the sales invoices for your company. If you want to process invoices created manually or from another system, such as Microsoft Word, this chapter is the one for you! Alternatively, if you prefer to produce your sales invoices directly from Sage, check out Chapter 6.

Posting Batch Entry Invoices

Don't you just groan when you see a huge pile of invoices that need entering? Well, Sage can help you speed your way through them by allowing you to post batches of invoices. In other words, you can enter several invoices on the same screen and post them all at the same time as a batch onto the system. (*Post* is a way of saying *enter information into an account.*)

Use this method to record sales invoices raised from a system other than Sage. For example, you can issue invoices with Microsoft Word and then enter the invoices onto Sage by using batch entry.

 You can enter any number of invoices in one sitting. For example, if you've 20 invoices to process for the day, you can enter them all onto one screen and then check the total of that batch to ensure accuracy. Larger companies often process large quantities of invoices in a number of smaller batches, which makes processing a more manageable task.

You can enter one invoice per line on your Batch Entry screen, but remember that if you've an invoice where the value needs to be split into two different nominal codes, you need to use two lines for that one invoice.

When you've a batch of invoices in front of you, follow these steps:

1. **Click Customer and then click the Batch Invoice icon.**

   The Batch Customer Invoices screen appears.

2. **Click the A/C (Account) field and use the drop-down arrow to select the correct customer account for the invoice.**

3. **Enter the invoice date.**

   Sage automatically enters the system date, which is usually the current day's date. Make sure that you change this date to the one on the invoice.

4. **Enter the invoice number in the Ref (Reference) field.**

   Every invoice needs a unique number derived from a sequential system.

5. **Add any additional references in the Ex.Ref field.**

   You can choose to leave this field blank or enter order numbers or other references.

6. **Change the nominal code, if necessary, in the N/C (Nominal Code) field.**

   This field automatically defaults to 4000, unless you changed the nominal default code on the Default tab of your customer record.

7. **Click the department (Dept) applicable for your invoice.**

   You can leave this field blank if you don't have any departments set up. If, on the other hand, you want to be able to analyse information from different offices or divisions within the company, setting up departments is the way to go:

   • From the navigation bar, click Company.

   • Click Department from the Links list.

   You can then enter departments as you wish, by clicking the actual department number from the Department main screen and then the Department Record icon.

8. **Describe what the invoice is for in the Details field.**

9. **Enter the amount net of VAT in the Net field.**

10. **Choose the tax code applicable for this invoice in the T/C (Tax Code) field.**

Some common VAT codes:

- T0: Zero-rated transactions.

- T1: Standard rate 20 per cent.

- T2: Exempt transactions.

- T4: Sales to VAT-registered customers in the European Community (EC).

- T5: Lower VAT rate at 5 per cent.

- T7: Zero-rated purchases from suppliers in the EC.

- T8: Standard-rated purchases from suppliers in the EC.

- T9: Transactions not involving VAT, for example journal entries.

The system updates the VAT field according to the tax code you choose.

Make sure that the VAT that Sage calculates is the same as the amount on the invoice. Sometimes Sage rounds up the VAT, and you may find that you have a penny difference. If that happens, overwrite the VAT amount in Sage so that the amounts match.

11. **Perform a quick check of the total value of the invoices you're about to post.**

To do this:

- Add up the gross value of the pile of invoices you've just entered.

- Check this total against the total on your Batch Entry screen (in the top right corner of your Sage screen).

If the totals are different, check each line on your Batch Entry screen against the invoices.

12. **Click Save when the totals in Step 11 are the same.**

To speed up the entry of invoices, you can use the function keys. To see how the F6, F7 and F8 keys can help you, have a quick look at Chapter 17.

Creating Credit Notes

A *credit note* is the opposite of an invoice. Instead of charging the customer, as you do with an invoice, you refund money to a customer through a credit note. Posting a credit note reverses or cancels an invoice that you entered previously.

You use credit notes for a number of different reasons. Invoices may need to be cancelled because the product sent was wrong, the goods have been returned and so on.

To ensure that you raise the credit note correctly, you must identify which invoice you're trying to correct. You need to know the invoice number, the date it was raised and the nominal code it was posted to. Make sure that you use the same nominal code on your credit note as you used on your invoice. This way, the double-entry bookkeeping posts the entries in the correct nominal codes, so you don't find odd balances showing in the accounts!

You can produce credit notes from the Invoicing module described in Chapter 6, but if you're not invoicing directly from Sage, you must use the batch-entry method for processing them, which is what I describe here.

To enter a credit note, follow these steps:

1. **Click Customer and then the Batch Credit Note icon.**

   Note that the font colour changes from black to red. This feature is useful, as the Credit Note screen looks identical to the Invoice screen. You wouldn't be the first person to merrily continue entering credit notes rather than invoices!

2. **Select the account (A/C) you wish to enter the credit note against.**

3. **Change the date in the Date field if necessary.**

   Unless today's date is acceptable, remember to change it to your desired date for raising the credit note.

4. **Put the credit number in the Credit No field.**

   Use a unique sequential numbering system for your credit notes and file them separately to your sales invoices.

5. **Enter any additional references in the Ex.Ref field.**

   This step isn't necessary if you don't have any further references.

6. **Make sure that the nominal code (N/C) is the same as the invoice that you're trying to reverse.**

7. **Select the department (Dept) that the original invoice was posted to.**

8. **Use the Details field to record the specifics of the credit note.**

   Put something like 'Credit note against Invoice No. 123', and if possible add a description as to why the credit is necessary – the goods were faulty, for example.

9. **Enter the Net, Tax Code and VAT.**

   If you're completely refunding the invoice, these three values are the same as on the original invoice. Otherwise, you need to apportion the net amount and allow the VAT to recalculate.

10. **Click Save when you're happy with the information you've entered.**

    Sage posts the credit note: it debits the Sales account and credits the Debtors control account.

You can check to see whether the credit has been posted properly by viewing the Activity screen for the nominal code you used. (See Figure 5-1 for an example.) You can see the original invoice being posted to the sales nominal code as a credit and then the credit note showing the debit in the nominal code at a later date. If you've written a description in the Detail field linking the credit note to the invoice, it comes in useful here.

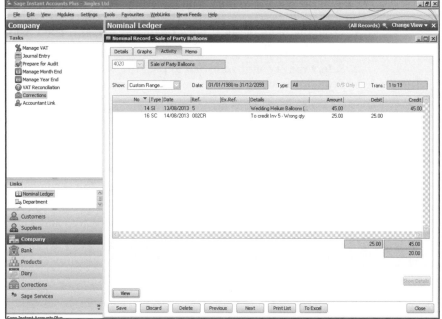

Figure 5-1:
A credit note and invoice on the Activity screen for nominal code 4020.

Registering Payments from Your Customers

Whenever you're dealing with money, whether a payment to a supplier, a cheque from a customer or any other kind of money transaction, use the Bank module. Don't forget this advice as you process your transactions!

The Bank module has several icons across the top. Use the Customer Receipt icon to post a customer receipt.

Don't go directly to the Receipt icon as the information under it helps you process things like bank interest received, grants received and so on – it doesn't record the money you receive from customers.

Matching payments to invoices

Ideally, when a customer sends you a cheque you also receive a *remittance advice slip*. This slip identifies which invoices the customer is paying with the cheque sent in. You then pay the cheque into the bank, using a *paying-in slip*, which is kept for your accounting records.

To match the cheque to the correct invoices, follow this procedure:

1. **From the Bank module, click Customer Receipt. The Customer receipt window opens.**

2. **Select the account you wish to post the receipt against by using the drop-down arrow.**

   As soon as you open an account, Sage displays all outstanding items for that customer on the main body of the screen. The first column shows the transaction number and the second column displays the transaction type: *SI* marks a sales invoice; *SC* indicates a sales credit.

   The top part of the Customer Receipt screen is split into three sections: the first column identifies the bank account; the second shows the customer details and the third shows the receipt details.

   Figure 5-2 shows a list of two outstanding invoices and a credit note on the Village Shop account – a Jingles Card Shop customer.

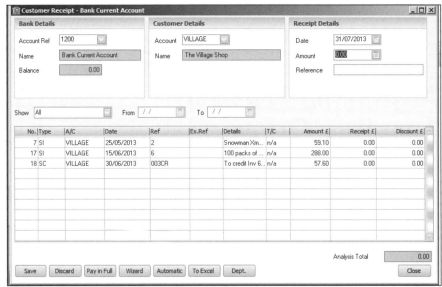

Figure 5-2:
Outstanding items on a customer's account.

3. **Enter the date that the money was received in the Receipt Details column.**

   If you're recording a cheque paid into the bank, type the date from the paying-in slip.

4. **Tab past the Amount field without entering an amount.**

5. **Type** BACS **(for Bankers' Automated Clearing Services) in the Reference field if the invoice is being paid automatically. Alternatively, put a paying-in slip reference if paid by cheque.**

6. **To allocate a receipt against a specific invoice, click the receipt column on the line of the invoice that you want to allocate the receipt against.**

7. **Click the Pay in Full button at the bottom of the screen.**

   The top-right box (the Amount field you ignored in Step 4) now shows the amount of the invoice paid. In the Jingles example in Figure 5-3, the amount shows £59.10, which is the total of the first invoice.

8. **Click Save at the lower left of the screen if you're happy that the receipt amount is correct.**

   If things aren't right, click Discard. A confirmation button appears: click Yes to continue discarding and your data is cleared ready to start again.

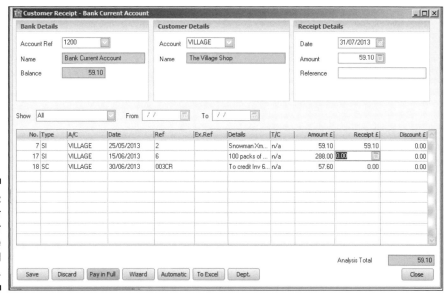

Figure 5-3:
A customer receipt after clicking the Pay in Full button.

After you click Save, the screen returns to the original Customer Receipt screen ready for your next customer receipt.

9. Click Close to finish after you've finished entering all your receipts.

You need to enter and save each receipt individually.

If you want to see what's happened in your Customer account, click the Activity tab. Figure 5-4 shows the Activity tab for Jingles' customer, the Village Shop. The sales receipt is showing on the account. However, two unallocated items still remain on this account. In the next section, I show you how to allocate credit notes to invoices, rather than payments to invoices.

Giving credit where due – allocating credit notes

Allocating means matching a specific invoice to a specific payment or credit note. As well as knowing how to allocate a payment specifically to an invoice, you also need to know how to allocate a credit note against an invoice. Because a credit note is usually raised to cancel the whole or part of an invoice, it stands to reason that the two are matched off against one another.

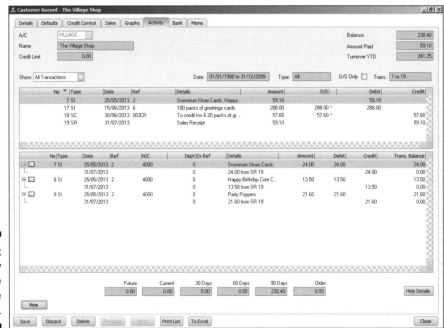

Figure 5-4:
The Activity tab for the Village Shop.

Referring back to Figure 5-4, you can see that two of the entries each have an asterisk against them. The asterisk means that the item is unallocated or unmatched. The two unallocated items are sales invoice number 6 and the credit note 00003Cr. You can tell that they should be allocated against each other because the description on the credit note refers to invoice 0006. However, the value of the credit note doesn't exactly equal the invoice, so you need to be careful, as you can't match the two items by using the Pay in Full button.

The steps to allocating a credit note are almost identical to allocating a customer receipt:

1. **From the Bank module, click Customer Receipt.**

2. **Select the customer account that you need to allocate the credit note to.**

3. **Put the date of the credit note in the Date field.**

   In the example, the date is 30.06.13.

4. **Tab past the Amount field and the Reference field, down to the Credit Note line. With the cursor sitting in the Receipt column on the Credit Note line, click Pay in Full.**

   Figure 5-5 shows the Village Shop account with a –£57.60 balance in the Analysis Total field in the bottom-right corner. This indicates that the credit note value is ready to allocate against the invoice.

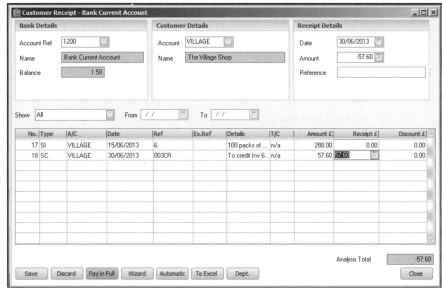

Figure 5-5:
Allocating a credit note to a customer invoice.

5. **Click the Receipt column on the line that has the invoice you wish to allocate against and manually enter the value of the credit note you're allocating.**

   The Analysis Total now reduces to zero.

6. **Click Save if you're happy that you've allocated the correct amount against the invoice.**

The Customer Activity tab for the Village Shop now shows an outstanding balance of £230.40 – the remaining part of invoice 6. The small letter 'p' against the balance indicates that that balance has been part paid or part allocated.

Recording payments on account

You may receive payment from a customer that you can't match to a specific invoice. For example, a customer may have inadvertently paid an invoice twice (it does happen) or have forgotten to include the remittance advice slip, so you're not sure which invoice to allocate the payment to.

You can still enter the receipt onto your customer account, but you may not be able to allocate it against a specific invoice.

To enter the receipt, follow these steps:

1. **From the Bank module, click Customer Receipt and then select the customer account.**

2. **Enter the date of the receipt in the Date field.**

3. **Enter the amount received in the Amount field.**

4. **Note in the Reference field why the payment isn't allocated against an invoice.**

   For example, if you believe that the customer has duplicated a payment, enter 'duplication'.

5. **Click Save.**

6. **Click Yes after you see the message saying that you've an unallocated balance and asking if you want to post this payment on account.**

The Customer Activity screen shows a payment on account as transaction type SA. In the event of a customer overpaying, you may find that the account now has a negative balance. To rectify this, you can send the customer a cheque or leave the balance on account and wait until you start raising more invoices to net this balance off against.

Deleting Invoices and Credit Notes

The traditional accounting method for reversing an invoice is to create a credit note for the same amount. However, Sage has made it even easier to sort out such problems: you can simply delete the invoice. That way, you don't have to raise the credit note or allocate it to the invoice. You maintain an audit trail, as any deleted items still show and are highlighted in red, so your accountant can always see what you've been up to!

You can use the Maintenance option to cancel unwanted transactions. See Chapter 9 for details on how to delete a transaction.

Managing Write offs, Refunds and Returns

Life can throw the occasional oddity at you, and accounting is no different. You may be confronted with an awkward refund, for example. But fear not, help is at hand in the shape of Sage wizard – created to help with those difficult adjustments that make your brain hurt when trying to work out how to deal with them in your books.

You can find this wizard by clicking on Customers and then looking at the Task pane. Here you find Customer/Write Offs/Refunds as shown in Figure 5-6. When you click on the link, you're presented with a four-step wizard, which helps you deal with Customer Invoice Refunds, Customer Cheque Returns, Refund Credit Notes and Payment on Account Refunds. In addition you can Write Off Customer Accounts, Customer Transactions and Small Overpayments.

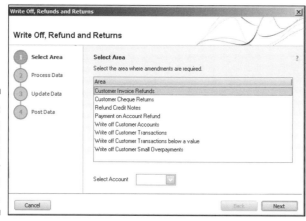

Figure 5-6: Sorting out those awkward Customer refunds and returns.

Once you've selected the type of transaction you'd like to undertake, simply follow the on-screen instructions and Sage guides you through the process.

Performing Customer Refunds

You can often find yourself in blind panic when you discover that you need to refund a customer and you're not sure how to deal with it. Sage has made it easy for you to process Customer Refunds, should they occur by allowing you to post a sales payment against a customer account in one easy step. All you need to do is:

- Click on Customers.
- From the Task pane, click Customer Refund.
- Select the customer you wish to complete a refund for.
- Click Save when you've entered the details, and *voila,* the refund has been made!

Chapter 6

Invoicing Your Customers

. . . .

In This Chapter

▶ Choosing an invoice type

▶ Setting up product and service invoices

▶ Printing, updating and deleting invoices

▶ Amending your defaults

. . . .

*Y*ou can generate invoices directly from your Sage accounting software, which means that you can streamline your paperwork process by printing invoices quickly. This feature means that you've more time to make more money for your business – or more time to take a break from making money for your business.

Sage is an integrated system, which means that when you produce a sales invoice, the system automatically updates the nominal ledger and the customer account, along with your stock system (if you're using one).

Deciding on an Invoice Type

Depending on the type of business you run, you issue mainly one of two types of invoices:

  ✔ **Product invoices:** Used for businesses that sell physical items – cards, widgets and what-have-yous. A manufacturing company issues product invoices, using product codes.

  ✔ **Service invoices:** Used for businesses that don't sell tangible products, but provide a service to their clients.

A business that sells physical products may need to generate a service invoice occasionally. For example, manufacturers of widgets may service some of the products they manufacture, and the engineer's time is charged using a service invoice. However, a business that provides services rarely needs to send a product invoice. For example, a consultant charges for the time spent providing a service, but usually doesn't need to issue product invoices.

Creating Invoices

You can create both product and service invoices in much the same way, so I combine the two methods in this section and simply highlight the differences between the two as I go along.

Before you start your product invoices, make sure that you've set up your product records, which I explain how to do in Chapter 3.

To begin creating your invoices, from the Customers Task pane, click New Invoice. The Product Invoice screen comes up, as shown in Figure 6-1. The next sections cover the four tabs on the Product Invoice screen.

Putting in the details

The Invoice screen opens with the Details tab, where the default invoice type is for a product invoice, as indicated in the upper-right corner of the screen.

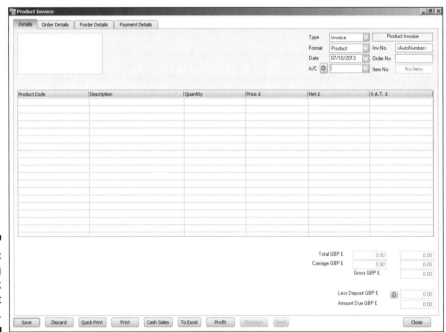

Figure 6-1:
Creating
a blank
product
invoice.

Starting in that corner, you can set options for your invoice, including:

- ✔ **Type:** Use the drop-down arrow if you want to change from an invoice to a credit note.

- ✔ **Format:** You can choose a product or service invoice.

- ✔ **Date:** This option automatically defaults to today's date, so change it if necessary.

- ✔ **Account:** Select your customer account, using the drop-down arrow.

- ✔ **Invoice Number:** The Autonumber notation here unsurprisingly indicates that Sage automatically numbers your invoices. It starts with number 1 and then automatically increases by one for each subsequent invoice. If you want to start with a different number, click Settings from the Menu bar and then Invoice Defaults and select the Options tab.

- ✔ **Order Number:** You can enter your own order number here or leave it blank.

- ✔ **Item Number:** This option shows the item line of the invoice that the cursor is currently sitting on.

Getting to the main attraction

The main body of the invoice has the most differences between product invoices and services invoices. As you would expect from a product invoice, you must select the product code, which in turn comes up with the product description and a Quantity field. A service invoice doesn't require these items; instead it has a Details field.

Producing product invoices

Enter the following fields when creating a product invoice:

- ✔ **Product Code:** Normally you set up product codes within product records. You can type in the relevant product code directly or use the drop-down arrow.

  You may encounter instances where a regular, everyday product code isn't suitable and you need a special product code, such as:

  - **M Message Line:** Use this code to add extra lines of description or to make comments about the products.

  - **S1 Special Product Item Tax Chargeable:** Use this code for product items that are standard VAT rated and don't have their own product code.

  - **S2 Special Product Item Zero Rated:** Use this code for zero-rated items that don't have their own product code.

✔ **Description:** The product description displays automatically from the product record, but you can overwrite it if necessary. You can also click F3 to edit the item line and add any one-off product details or comments.

✔ **Quantity:** Enter the number of items that you're invoicing. Sage automatically shows a '1' if a quantity is in stock or '0' if no items are in stock. If you don't have enough stock for the quantity you enter, Sage issues a warning – you can't (not to mention illegal!) charge people without delivering the product, so pay attention to the warning.

✔ **Price:** The unit price for the product record appears here, but you can change this price if you need to.

Selecting service invoices

A service invoice has fewer columns in the main body than a product invoice.

After you enter the header details for your invoice (customer details, date and so on), you then need to add the details of the service provided.

✔ **Details:** You can expand the information entered in the Details field by using the F3 key. This function allows you to add additional information to the invoice detail. You can only use F3 after you've entered information into the Details field.

✔ **Amount:** You can enter the amount using the Edit Item Line window – this window appears if you used the F3 key in the Details field. Alternatively, if you didn't need to use the F3 key for additional details, add only one line of detail on the main screen and then tab across to the Amount column and enter the amount there.

Figure 6-2 shows what happens after the insertion of the detail Hire of Clown for Party into the Details field. As soon as you type in the description, press F3 and the edit box appears. Sage duplicates the words typed into both the Description and the Details field.

You can now apply the number of hours the clown worked and enter the unit price. You can also check that the nominal code is one that you want to use or adjust it where necessary. In this case, you may choose to change the nominal code shown in the Jingles illustration from 4000 for Sale of Cards (the default nominal code) to a more suitable code, such as Party Organising. Because Party Organising isn't an existing code, you then need to create a new nominal code. Refer to Chapter 3 to see how to do this.

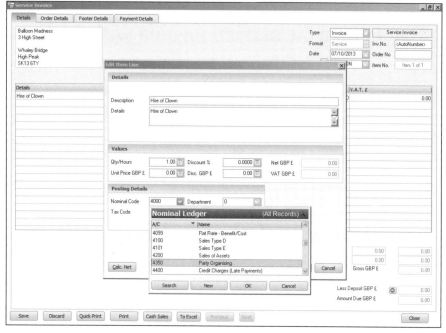

Figure 6-2:
Using the
F3 function
key to
expand the
details of
the service
invoice.

After you're happy with the details on the main body of the invoice, the following steps are the same for both product and service invoices:

✔ **Net:** This calculation is automatic, and also applies any discount attached to this customer account. Change the discount by using the F3 key if you need to.

An additional Discount and Discount Percentage column shows if you selected this option within Invoice defaults. Click the Discount tab and tick the Show Discount on Main Invoice/Order box.

✔ **VAT:** Sage automatically calculates this column. You can only edit it if you selected the Item VAT Amendable box on the VAT tab of Company Preferences on the main toolbar.

Then you get to the bottom of the Invoice screen, where Sage does much of the work for you:

✔ **Total:** Sage totals the invoice, showing net, VAT and any carriage charges applied.

✔ **Deposit:** This feature has a smart link – a little grey arrow that takes you to the Payment tab of the invoice if you click it, so you can record any deposits you've received against the invoice.

Editing the service invoice with the F3 key

When you press F3 from the Description line of an invoice, an edit box appears where you can amend some of the detail of your invoice. The nominal code, tax code and department all appear in the posting details in this edit box. The details shown are those chosen as defaults. You can amend both the tax and nominal codes for each item line on the invoice by using the drop-down list. Alternatively, if you want to use the same nominal code and tax code for all lines of the invoice, you can click the Footer Details tab of the invoice and enter the appropriate codes in the Global section. The new codes then overwrite any code used on an individual line of the invoice.

Filling in the order details

You can use the Order Details tab to fill in details of where the goods are being delivered and who took the order. You can also add up to three lines of text. If the order can be left outside by the chicken shed, this tab is the place to share that information!

Getting down to the footer details

You can enter carriage terms, settlement terms and global details in the Footer Details tab:

- ✔ **Carriage terms:** You may want to assign carriage costs to the invoice. You may have postal or courier costs. You can set up specific nominal codes to charge carriage costs. If you set up departments, use the drop-down list to select the appropriate one.

  To set up a courier on your Footer Details tab, click Help from the main toolbar. Using the Contents and Index option, type in **couriers** to see how to add a new courier.

- ✔ **Settlement terms:** Some information may already be present in these boxes if you entered the details on the customer record. You can enter the number of days during which an early settlement discount applies, if any. You can see what discount percentage is applied, if any. It also shows you the total value of the invoice.

- ✔ **Global:** This section enables you to apply global terms to the whole of the invoice or credit note. If you choose to do this, only one line is added to the audit trail, although carriage is always shown as a separate line.

You can apply one nominal code to the whole invoice. If you do, you can also enter details to accompany the posting to the nominal ledger. Up to 60 characters are available for additional details, which appear on your reports.

The same global effect can be applied to your tax code and also your departments (if required).

 Credit notes are prepared in a similar way to product and service invoices. The screens look exactly the same; however, after you type in the details of the credit note, the font becomes red.

Follow the same process as that for creating an invoice, but make sure that you change the Type box on the Details tab to credit note. Refer back to previous sections of this chapter for assistance.

You need to remember to update your credit notes in the same way as you do invoices. If you don't, the credit notes aren't updated to the nominal ledger.

Managing Your Invoice List

After you safely save an invoice, it appears on your Invoice List, and you can do all sorts of business-like things with it. The next sections tell you how.

Printing

As soon as you save your invoice, you can print it. If you still have the invoice open in front of you, simply click Print. The Layouts window opens, as shown in Figure 6-3. Select Layouts and the right-hand side of the window displays the different report options. When you scroll down the screen and highlight your chosen report, floating icons appear giving you the options to preview, print, export, export to Microsoft Excel or email the document. If you haven't got the invoice open in front of you, click Customers from the Navigation bar and select Invoice List from the Links list. Highlight the invoice you want to print from the list and click the Print icon to open the Layout window, then select Layouts as before and choose the appropriate report required, then click the floating print icon window.

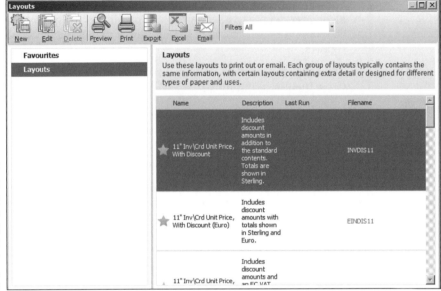

Figure 6-3:
Choosing
your invoice
layout
prior to
printing your
invoice.

The layout choices are pretty self-explanatory; you choose one based on paper size and whether the customer is offered a discount.

You can preview the invoice prior to printing to make sure that the details are correct. Click the floating preview icon and the system then loads the invoice onto the screen for you to view. If you're happy with what you see, you can print the invoice directly from this screen, or choose to email it directly to the customer.

You can print the invoice without previewing it, but I always check to ensure that I'm happy with the details. You can edit or change an invoice at any point prior to sending it to the customer and updating the ledger.

You can print off a number of invoices at the same time by highlighting all the invoices you want to print and clicking Print. Then follow the instructions as shown earlier in this chapter for selecting the desired invoice layout.

You can choose an invoice layout as a favourite, by clicking the star at the side of the report when you select an invoice layout. This action copies the invoice to the favourite screen, which is the first screen to open when you click the print icon. This feature saves you time from scrolling through all the layouts to select the one you want.

When you've printed an invoice, you'll notice that the column titled Printed on the Invoice List has the word 'Yes' in it. You can still reprint at any time, but this feature helps you to easily identify which invoices have already been printed.

Using Quick Print

Sage has a feature called Quick Print, which allows you to select a default print layout and then print items with a single click. The Quick Print icon sits alongside the Print icon (see previous section).

This is an extremely quick way of printing off invoices, particularly if you want to select more than one. Be aware, though, that you won't be able to see a preview of the invoice before it prints, so you need to be sure that you've selected the correct layout.

If you try to use the Quick Print icon without having set up the default layout, a warning message appears, and Sage asks you whether you want to set up the default now. If you know which report layout you wish to use, click Yes. You're then directed to the Layout window, where you can click the appropriate layout. Highlight the invoice layout you require and click OK. The report now prints. Be aware that you won't get the opportunity to preview this invoice.

Another way of setting up your default Quick Print invoice layout is to click Settings, followed by Invoice defaults and then click the Quick Print tab. Here, you can select the default print layouts for invoices and quotations.

Updating

After you're 100 per cent happy with your invoices, you're ready to *update ledgers,* a process that posts the invoice to both the nominal ledger and the customer ledger.

You can update invoices individually or in batches. First, check to see which invoices have been updated and printed already. To find out the status of each invoice:

1. **From Customers, click Invoice List.**

2. **Look at the last two columns – the Posted and Printed columns.**

   The word 'Yes' indicates whether an invoice has already been printed and/or posted.

To update the invoices:

1. **Highlight the invoices you want to update.**

2. **Click Update Ledgers.** The Update Ledger box opens and you have the opportunity to print, preview or send to file. I usually leave Preview highlighted, so that when you click OK, you can view all the invoices you've updated. Notice that the main screen now has a 'Yes' against that invoice in the Posted column.

You can print this report if you want to, but you don't really need to.

Deleting

Deleting invoices and credit notes is easy, but be aware that if you've already posted the invoice to the nominal ledger, deleting the invoice or credit note doesn't reverse the posting in the ledger.

To delete an invoice or credit note:

1. **From Customers, click Invoice List. Select the required invoice or credit note from the Invoice list.**

2. **Click Delete. An affirmation message appears. Click Yes to continue or No to exit.**

That's it; your invoice is deleted from the Invoice list.

Using defaults

You may have invoices and credit notes with similar items or characteristics, and as such you can enter defaults for them. For example, you may want to assign carriage costs to your customers.

To access the defaults, from the Menu bar, click Settings and then Invoice Defaults. To adjust carriage defaults, click Footer Details.

For help with other invoice defaults, select Help from the main toolbar and then click Contents and Index and select Invoices, followed by Defaults.

Alternatively, you can click Help and then Customise Your Company. Here you've access to both the Customer defaults and also the Invoice defaults. You can amend at your leisure!

Chapter 7

Dealing with Paperwork from Your Suppliers

. . . .

In This Chapter

▶ Getting and posting bills

▶ Entering credit notes

▶ Recording supplier payments

▶ Sending remittance advice notes

▶ Managing write offs, refunds and returns

. . . .

*Y*ou receive lots of invoices from your suppliers, so you need to put systems in place to enable you to easily locate them if you need them. Sometimes Sage contains enough detail to answer a query about an invoice, but on some occasions you need to pull the actual invoice out of the file.

As you process each invoice, Sage allocates it a sequential transaction number. Use this transaction number as a reference, so you can always track down an invoice quickly and easily.

Receiving and Posting Invoices

You need a good system for capturing all the purchase invoices that come into your business, so that bills get paid, and you can continue doing business. You need two steps to make sure that bills get paid efficiently: receiving the invoices properly and then posting them.

Setting up your receiving system

Send all invoices to one person or department (a choice that depends on the size of your business). You don't want lots of different people receiving the invoices, as more people means more chance of invoices getting misplaced or entered incorrectly.

Enter invoices onto the accounting system as soon as possible after receiving them so that the liability is recorded in the business accounts. Depending on the size of your business, you may want to make a copy of the invoice so that you can keep one copy within the Accounts department and send the other copy to the person who requested the goods, so that they can check the details for accuracy and also get the invoice authorised for payment.

Posting invoices

The term *posting* doesn't mean posting the invoice into a letter box! In accounting terms, *posting* means processing an invoice to the nominal ledger. (Chapter 2 talks about the nominal ledger.)

You can post a number of invoices in one sitting. If you've large quantities of invoices to process, separate them into smaller batches and total the values of each batch so that you can check those same values against Sage to ensure that you haven't made any mistakes.

Sort the invoices into date order before separating them into batches. By doing so, you ensure that you enter them in chronological order, which helps when you're viewing them on screen.

To enter a batch, follow these steps:

1. **From Suppliers, click the Batch Invoice icon.**

   Doing so brings up the Batch Suppliers Invoice box.

2. **Select the correct supplier account for the invoice.**

   When you have several items on an invoice, enter each item from the invoice separately on the Batch screen as you may need to give each item a different nominal code. However, you can use the same supplier account, date and reference, so that Sage can group those items together.

   After you post the invoice, you can view it on the Supplier Activity screen, which is split into two parts. The top part has one line entry for each transaction (in other words, all the individual lines of each invoice are grouped together), and the bottom part has the detail of each transaction. Clicking an invoice highlights it in blue, and the bottom part of the screen shows each line entry of that invoice.

3. **Put the invoice date in the Date field.**

   Be careful as Sage automatically defaults to today's date, so you need to overtype the invoice date here. If you don't, Sage won't age the invoice correctly, and you end up with a distorted view of the transaction on the Aged Creditors reports.

4. **Enter your sequential number in the Ref (Reference) field.**

   Your *invoice reference number* is the number order in which you file your invoices.

   I tend to give each invoice a sequential number and mark this number in pen at the top right-hand corner of the invoice. I then use the Ref field to enter this number into Sage.

5. **Add details in the Ex.Ref field, if desired.**

   You can add more references here or leave this field blank. I always enter the suppliers own invoice number here, as it acts as a secondary means of identification. This additional reference is helpful when you wish to retrieve an invoice from your filing system, particularly if you have invoices from a supplier with the same value.

6. **Select the nominal code in the N/C field, using the drop-down arrow, otherwise Sage uses the default code 5000.**

7. **Click the department applicable for your invoice in the Dept field.**

   You can leave this field blank if you don't have any departments set up.

8. **Enter information describing what the invoice is for in the Details field.**

   Put as much detail as you can here. In addition to entering the suppliers invoice number in the Ex Ref field, I also enter the supplier's invoice number in the details column, followed by the description. You can then identify the invoice quickly using the supplier's number. If you need to contact the supplier about an invoice, it helps to use their reference numbers, so it makes sense to record these numbers here.

   Note: I use both the Ex.Ref field and the Details columns for the suppliers invoice number, because different reports sometimes include one but not the other. While this method is a bit 'belt and braces', experience has taught me that this system works!

9. **Enter the amount net of VAT in the Net field.**

10. **Choose the tax code applicable for this invoice in the T/C (Tax Code) field.**

    Depending on the tax code, Sage updates the VAT field.

    Make sure that the VAT Sage calculates is the same as the amount on the invoice. Sometimes Sage rounds up the VAT, and you need to overwrite the amount in Sage to match the VAT on the invoice.

11. **Repeat Steps 2 to 12 for each invoice in your batch.**

12. **Check that the total of your batch of invoices matches the total in the right corner of the Batch Entry screen (see Figure 7-1), and if it does, click Save.**

    Doing the check ensures that the data you entered is accurate. When you click Save, Sage posts the invoices to the nominal ledger, posting a debit to the Cost account and a credit to the Creditors control account.

| A/C | Brilliant Balloons | | | | | | | Tax Rate | | 20.00 |
| N/C | Purchase of Party Balloons | | | | | | | Total | | 606.00 |

A/C	Date	Ref	Ex.Ref	N/C	Dept	Details	Net	T/C	VAT
PAPER	01/05/2013	1	5467	5030	0	500 Sheets of ...	286.00	T1	57.20
DERBY	13/05/2013	2	4536A	5000	0	10 birthday car...	64.00	T1	12.80
DERBY	13/05/2013	2	4536A	5000	0	10 Get well so...	28.00	T1	5.60
DERBY	13/05/2013	2	4536A	5000	0	10 Cute cards	25.00	T1	5.00
BRILLIAN	23/07/2013	3	113	5020	0	Helium Balloon...	50.00	T1	10.00
BRILLIAN	23/07/2013	3	113	5020	0	Helium Balloon...	40.00	T1	8.00
BRILLIAN	23/07/2013	3	113	5020	0	10 assorted pa...	12.00	T1	2.40

505.00   101.00

Save | Discard | Calc. Net | To Excel | Close

Figure 7-1:
A batch of
purchase
invoices
entered
onto Sage
prior to
posting.

Check out Chapter 17 to see how the function keys can help speed up the
batch-entry process.

Getting Credit

Credit notes can be raised for a variety of reasons. The goods delivered may
have been faulty or the wrong colour, for example. The supplier assumes that
you've already posted the original invoice supplied with these goods and sends a
credit note to reduce the amount you owe them. The credit note may completely
reverse the value of the original invoice or partially credit the invoice.

You process a credit note in much the same way as you process an invoice,
so follow the steps in the previous section, 'Posting invoices', paying special
attention to the following points:

- ✔ **From Suppliers, click the Batch Credit icon instead of the Invoice icon
  and select the account to enter the credit note against.** The screen
  looks similar to that of the Invoice screen, but the font colour is red
  rather than black to alert you to the fact that you're processing a credit
  note. You wouldn't be the first person to merrily continue entering
  credit notes, when they should be invoices!

- ✔ **Remember to change the date, unless today's date is acceptable.**

- ✔ **Enter a credit number instead of a reference number.** Use a unique
  sequential numbering system for your credit notes. Some people prefer
  to have a separate numbering system for credit notes, others just use
  the next available invoice number. It really doesn't matter, as long as
  you're consistent.

✔ **Make sure that the nominal code (N/C) is the same as the invoice you're reversing.** This check ensures that the correct cost code is reduced in value.

✔ **Put a notation in the Details field.** Something like 'Credit note against Invoice No 123' plus a description of why the credit note necessary, if possible, is fine.

✔ **If the credit note is reversing just part of an invoice, apportion the Net and VAT amounts.**

When you click Save, Sage posts the credit note, crediting the Purchase account and debiting the Creditors control account.

You can check to see whether everything is posted by viewing the Activity screen for the nominal code you used. The Jingles example in Figure 7-2 shows the Activity screen for nominal code 5000. You can see transaction number 22, the purchase of get-well-soon cards (debiting code 5000) and transaction 28, the credit note (crediting the nominal record). The Activity screen shows the original invoice posted to the purchase nominal code as a debit and then the credit note shows at a later date, crediting the nominal code. Here's where having a description in the Details field linking the credit note to the invoice comes in handy.

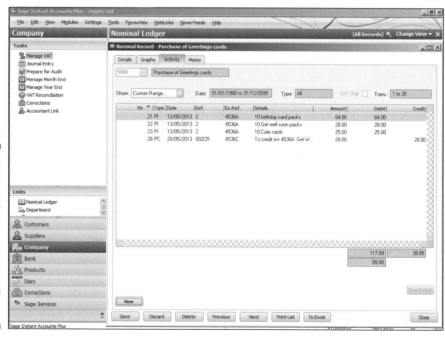

Figure 7-2:
The nominal code Activity screen showing a credit note posted for the purchase of cards.

Allocating a Credit Note

You allocate credit notes in the same way as you make payments, though you need to allocate a credit note specifically against an invoice.

You can tell if something hasn't been allocated if a transaction in the Supplier Activity screen has an asterisk against it.

To allocate a credit note, follow these steps:

1. **From Bank, click Supplier Payment.**

2. **Select the account you require.**

   All outstanding transactions are shown.

3. **Enter the date, usually the date of the credit note.**

4. **In the Payment column, click Pay in Full Against the Credit Note.**

   Doing so puts a negative value in the Analysis total at the bottom right side of the screen.

5. **Move up to the invoice that you wish to allocate the credit note to, and type in the value of the credit note.**

   The Analysis total becomes zero.

6. **Click Save.**

   By doing so, you post the allocation, as shown in Figure 7-3.

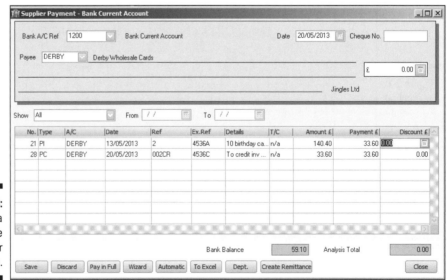

Figure 7-3:
Allocating a credit note to a supplier invoice.

Paying Your Suppliers

When you come to process the payments for your supplier, you need to use the Bank module.

1. **From Bank, select Supplier Payment.**

   A screen that looks a bit like a cheque book opens up.

2. **Check that the Bank A/C Ref field shows the correct account.**

   This field automatically defaults to account 1200, which is usually the Bank Current account. If this account isn't the one you wish to use, select the appropriate account.

3. **Enter the supplier name or use the drop-down arrow to select the payee.**

   As soon as you select an account, Sage brings up a list of outstanding transactions for that account.

4. **Enter the payment date in the Date field.**

   Usually you use the date on your cheque stub or the date of the direct debit or other form of payment.

5. **Record the cheque number or method of payment in the Cheque No. field.**

   Type **DD** for direct debit, **BP** for bank payment or any other short description that helps you identify the transaction when you reconcile your bank account.

6. **Click the Payment column.**

   You've several options here:

   - **To pay in full,** click the Pay in Full button at the bottom of the screen. Doing so puts an amount in the £ box at the top of the screen, as Figure 7-4 shows.

     Note: If you're taking a discount for early payment, enter the discount amount in the Discount column, and Sage calculates the amount you owe and shows this value in the £ box and in the Payment column.

   - **To pay part of an invoice,** enter the amount you wish to pay against that invoice. That amount shows up in the £ box at the top of the screen.

   - **To make a payment on account,** enter the amount you wish to pay in the £ box.

     You may find that you need to make a payment against a supplier account, but can't specify an invoice to allocate the payment to. You can make a payment into the supplier account without matching it to a specific invoice.

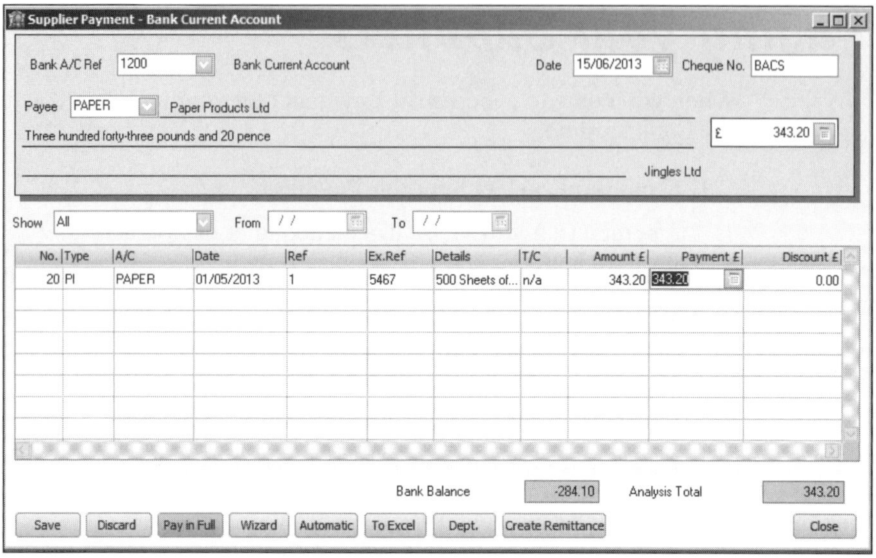

Figure 7-4:
A happy
supplier,
paid in full.

7. **Click Save.**

   If you make full or partial payments to an invoice, the payment posts to that invoice in the supplier account.

   If you make a payment on account, Sage gives you a confirmation message, asking 'There is an unallocated cheque balance of £x. Do you want to post this as a payment on account?' Click Yes to accept or No to cancel.

Managing Write offs, Refunds & Returns

As we all know, life can throw the occasional oddities at us, and accounting is no different. For example, sometimes we have to figure out what to do with an awkward refund. Help is at end in the shape of this useful wizard that Sage has created to help us with those difficult adjustments that can begin to make your brain hurt when trying to work out how to deal with them in your books.

You can find this wizard by clicking on Suppliers and then looking at the Task pane. Here you find Supplier/Write offs/refunds as shown in Figure 7-5. When you click on the link, you are presented with a four-step wizard, which helps you deal with supplier invoice refunds, supplier cheque returns, refund credit notes and payment on account refunds. In addition you can write off supplier accounts, supplier transactions and small overpayments.

Once you've selected the type of transaction you wish to undertake, simply follow the on-screen instructions and Sage guides you through the process.

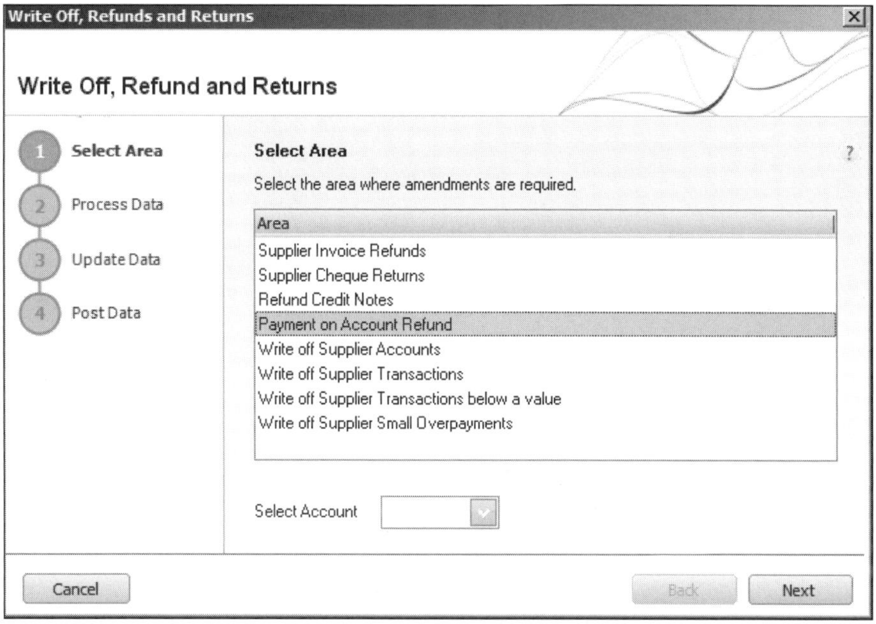

Write Off, Refunds and Returns

Write Off, Refund and Returns

1. **Select Area**

2. Process Data

3. Update Data

4. Post Data

Select Area   ?

Select the area where amendments are required.

Area
Supplier Invoice Refunds
Supplier Cheque Returns
Refund Credit Notes
Payment on Account Refund
Write off Supplier Accounts
Write off Supplier Transactions
Write off Supplier Transactions below a value
Write off Supplier Small Overpayments

Select Account

Cancel   Back   Next

Figure 7-5:
Sorting
out those
awkward
supplier
refunds and
returns.

Supplier refunds

Sage has made it easy for you to process supplier refunds, should they occur.
You may find it an occasion for blind panic when you see a refund come into
your account and you're not sure how to deal with it. Sage has given this
problem an easy solution by allowing you to post a purchase receipt against
a supplier account in one easy step. All you need to do is click on Suppliers
and then from the Task pane, simply click Supplier Refund and then select
the supplier you wish to complete a refund for. Click Save when you've
entered the details, and *voila,* the refund has been made!

Chapter 8

Recording Your Bank Entries

. . . .

In This Chapter

▶ Looking at the different types of bank accounts

▶ Processing bank receipts and payments

▶ Dealing with bank transfers

▶ Setting up recurring transactions

▶ Keeping track of petty cash

▶ Balancing credit card transactions

. . . .

*I*f you're the sort of person who likes checking your bank accounts and keeping track of what's been spent on the company credit card, then this chapter is for you! Here I tell you how to process bank payments and receipts that aren't related to sales invoices or purchase invoices. I look at how to process credit card transactions and deal with petty cash (one of the bookkeeping jobs that can be a real pain in the backside if not dealt with properly!).

I also show you how you can transfer money between bank accounts – perhaps to take advantage of earning extra interest (every little helps!). And, as many businesses often have a lot of banking transactions, I show you ways to speed up the processing by using recurring entries.

Understanding the Different Types of Bank Accounts

Clicking Bank shows you the default bank accounts that Sage provides, which include:

✔ **Bank accounts:** Current, Deposit and Building Society accounts, for example.

✔ **Cash accounts:** For example, the Petty Cash account.

✔ **Credit card accounts:** These accounts include a Credit Card Receipts account for those of you who receive customer payments via credit card.

You can, of course, add new bank accounts, rename existing accounts or delete accounts that you don't think you need – refer to Chapter 3 to find out how.

In the following sections, I show the account number or range of account numbers that Sage assigns to each account. These account numbers are the same as the nominal code for that bank account.

Keeping up with the Current and Deposit accounts (1200/1210)

The Bank Current account is the default bank account in Sage, the one that automatically pops up when you enter a bank transaction. Of course, you can choose another bank account if the Bank Current account isn't the right one for your transaction.

Most people use the Bank Current account for the majority of their transactions, although you may have additional bank accounts for different areas of your business. If you've surplus cash that you want to earn a bit of interest on, you may have a deposit account and transfer surplus cash between the current account and the deposit account to take advantage of higher rates of interest. (I talk about transferring money between accounts in the 'Transferring Funds between Accounts' section later in this chapter.)

I know of a number of companies that regularly transfer funds to a separate deposit account from their current account to accumulate enough money to pay their VAT bills or PAYE.

 Change the name of the Bank Current account to that of your own business current account and, if you've more than one, include the account number within the bank account name – for example, Barclays Current Account 24672376. You can add or amend bank accounts – for more information, refer to Chapter 3.

Sage's Deposit account functions in the same way as the Bank Current account. You can make transfers between Deposit and Bank Current accounts in Sage.

Sage also includes a Building Society account, although I don't know of many businesses that actually have one of those. You can rename or delete it as appropriate.

Counting the Petty Cash account (1230)

Use the Petty Cash account for cash stored somewhere other than a bank or building society – a strong box or safe in the office, perhaps (*not* under your mattress!).

You can operate this account in the same way as a normal bank account, although most people don't choose to reconcile it as you don't have bank statements to reconcile to.

You can transfer funds into this account from any of the other Sage bank accounts and make payments accordingly. I give further details in the later section 'Dealing with Petty Cash'.

Handling your Cash Register (1235)

You also have a separate bank account to handle your Cash Register transactions. Your business may wish to use this Cash Register function to record receipts of cash and card payments. This type of transaction allows for the sale, supply and payment to happen at the same time. A Cash Register sale can include details of the sale and the method of payment used (cash, cheque or card), the price and VAT (if applicable).

The default bank account is automatically set at 1235. You need to check your Cash Register settings in your Bank Default menu. From the Menu bar, click Settings and then Bank Defaults. Here, you can select the sales nominal code for your Cash Register takings, which automatically defaults to 4000 (you can change this code). When using a cash register, you may find that discrepancies exist between the cash register and actual takings. If so, use the Discrepancy account to balance the books – the default code is 8206 (which you can also change, if you wish). This screen also includes a tick box to confirm whether your cash takings are VAT inclusive or not.

For further help in using the Cash Register function within Sage, click Help on the main toolbar and select Contents and Index. Click the Search tab and enter the words 'Recording Cash Till Takings'. Sage presents you with a list of helpful reports; double click on any of these reports to help you fully understand how to use the Cash Register facility.

Managing the company credit card (1240) and credit card receipts (1250)

You can set up a bank account for each individual credit card and manage these accounts as normal bank accounts – reconciling them, for example, with your credit card statements. See the 'Paying the Credit Card Bill' section, later in this chapter, for further details about the mechanics of processing credit card transactions.

If you accept payment by credit card, keep a separate bank account for these transactions. You deposit batches of credit card vouchers into your account in the same way that you deposit a cheque. Use the Customer option if you receive money against a customer invoice. The credit card company then deposits the real cash into your nominated bank account, and you can make a transfer between that and the Credit Card Receipts account. You then receive a statement detailing all the transactions, including a service charge, which can be reconciled.

Tracking Bank Deposits and Payments

Your business earns money (which is a good thing, and much better than the reverse!). You need to keep track of how much money you put in the bank and Sage helps you do that in the Bank module. You may also have to make payments to the bank – wages, interest charges, loan payments and dividend payments, for example. Sage makes it as easy to process a bank payment as it does a receipt.

For both types of transactions, start from the Task pane within the Bank module:

- ✔ For **receipts**, click Bank Receipts. Alternatively, click the Bank Receipts icon.
- ✔ For **payments**, click Bank Payments or use the Bank Payments icon.

In both cases, a new window appears and, although the screens are different, they ask you for the same basic information whether you're recording a receipt or payment. Use the Tab key to move across the screen and enter the details that Sage asks for:

- ✔ **Bank:** Make sure that you select the correct bank account, using the drop-down arrows. Sage automatically defaults to account 1200, which is normally the Bank Current account.

✔ **Date:** As usual, Sage defaults to today's date, so ensure that you change this detail to match the date of the transaction.

✔ **Reference (Ref):** If you've a cheque number, payslip reference or BACS (Bankers' Automated Clearing Services) reference, enter it here as it proves useful when you come to reconcile your bank account.

When making a payment, be aware that the reference you enter appears on the audit trail in the Reference (Ref) column for that transaction, so use notation that you can understand – *DD* for direct debit or *SO* for standing order, for example. If you paid by cheque, enter the cheque number here.

✔ **Nominal Code (N/C):** Using the drop-down arrow, select the appropriate nominal code. You can create a new nominal code here if you need to.

✔ **Dept:** Enter the department, using the drop-down arrow. Ignore this field if you don't use departments.

✔ **Details:** Record any details that may help you with reconciling your account or identifying the transaction.

✔ **Net:** Enter the net amount of the transaction before VAT.

If you aren't VAT registered, put the gross amount here and tax code T0, or T9 if you don't want it to appear on a VAT Return report.

If you only have the gross amount of your receipts or a payment, you can enter this number and then click Calc Net (at the bottom of the Bank Payments/Receipts box) and, provided that the tax code is set correctly, Sage calculates the net and VAT amounts for you.

✔ **Tax Code (T/C):** Use the drop-down arrow to select the appropriate tax code.

✔ **Tax:** Sage calculates the amount of VAT for the transaction based on the net amount and the tax code selected.

Whatever your business type, all businesses receive monies that have nothing to do with their customers, such as bank interest or grants. Post these payments using the Bank Receipts option.

You can continue to enter receipts or payments in a batch. Figure 8-1 shows a Payment Batch Entry screen. As you enter new transactions, the total in the bottom-right corner of the screen increases. Check the batch total that you calculated against the total that Sage reached in the Total box in the top right of the screen.

The boxes at the top of the screen show which bank account the receipt is going to, what the nominal code is and the tax rate. A Total box that subtotals all the lines of information in the batch also shows.

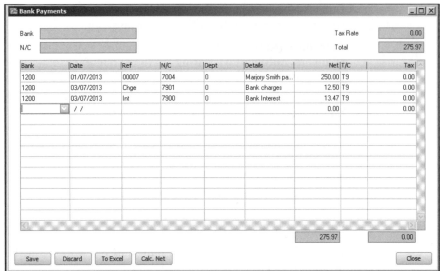

Figure 8-1:
A Payment
Batch Entry
screen.

When you're happy that the details on the screen are correct, click Save at the lower left of the screen to post payments to the appropriate nominal accounts and bank accounts. If you aren't happy with the information on your Batch Entry screen, simply click Discard and the information clears. To exit the Payment Batch Entry screen, click Close.

Transferring Funds between Accounts

Just as big banks move money around, you may occasionally want to move money from one account to another. For example, when you pay off your company credit card each month, you make a payment from your current account to your credit card account. Create a bank transfer between the two accounts to process this transaction easily.

To process a bank transfer, follow these steps:

1. **From Bank, click Bank Transfer in the Task pane (or click the Bank Transfer icon).** The Bank Transfer window opens.

2. **Select the bank account you want to transfer the money from, using the drop-down arrow.**

3. **Select the account you want to transfer the money to, again using the drop-down arrow.**

4. **Complete the information on screen:**

   - **Date:** Enter the date of the transaction. You need to overtype this date, as the system uses today's date.

   - **Reference (Ref):** Enter a reference relating to the transaction.

   - **Description:** You have up to 60 characters to describe the transaction.

   - **Dept:** Select a department, if applicable.

   - **Amount:** Enter the amount of the transaction.

5. **Click Save if you're happy with the information you entered.**

   Sage updates both bank accounts. If you aren't happy, click Discard and the screen clears.

6. **Click Close to exit the Bank Transfer screen.**

Repeating Recurring Entries

Designating recurring entries is extremely useful. Doing so speeds up the processing of data and saves time because you enter the information only once, at the set-up stage, and then process all future transactions with the click of a button. You don't have to re-enter the full details of those transactions again!

You can treat many different transactions as recurring items, although they're typically direct debits and standing orders. The next sections give you an explanation of the different types of transactions you can set up as recurring.

Going for consistency with your bank entries

You probably make regular payments into and out of your Bank Current and Credit Card accounts, as well as doing transfers between accounts on a monthly basis. To set up any of these types of transactions as recurring, follow the steps below.

To view existing recurring entries, from the Bank module on the navigation bar, click Recurring Items on the Links list or click the Recurring Items icon in the Bank module.

1. **From Bank, click New Recurring Transaction from the Task pane (or click the Recurring Items icon and then click Add).**

   Doing so opens the Add/Edit Recurring Entry box.

2. Fill in the Recurring Entry From/To section.

The information you're asked for includes:

- **Bank A/C:** Select the bank account that the transaction is coming from or going to.

- **Nominal Code:** Enter the nominal code for the transaction.

3. Enter details of the recurring entry.

These details include:

- **Transaction Type:** Choose from Bank/Cash/Credit Card Payment, Bank/Cash/Credit Card Receipts, Bank/Cash/Credit Card Transfer, Customer Payments on Accounts, Journal Debits, Journal Credits or Supplier Payments on Account.

- **Transaction Ref:** Enter a reference here. Note that Sage already uses DD/SO (direct debit/standing order), which may be sufficient, but you can change it as necessary.

- **Transaction Details:** Enter details of the transaction. In the example in Figure 8-2, I set up a recurring building insurance payment.

- **Dept:** Enter a department, if applicable.

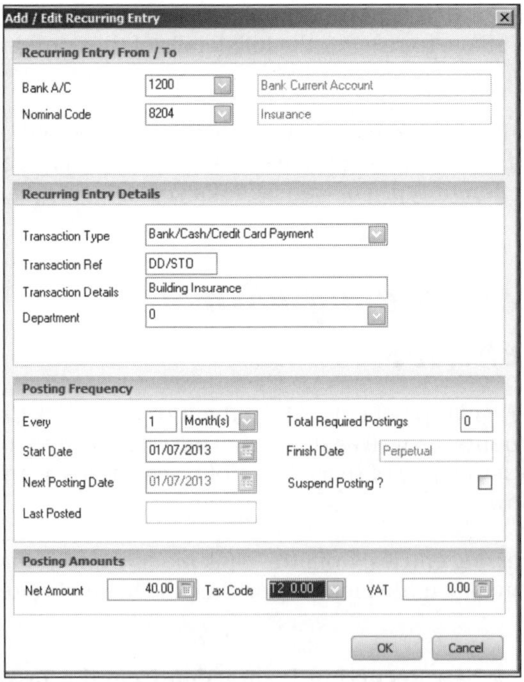

Figure 8-2:
Creating a recurring bank payment.

4. **Determine posting frequency.**

   Make selections about frequency:

   - **Every:** Enter the posting frequency here – daily, monthly, weekly or yearly.

   - **Total Required Postings:** If you know the exact number of postings to be made, enter the number here. The finish date automatically updates.

   - **Start Date:** The date that you want the recurring entry to start (obviously!). The system automatically defaults to today's date, but you can overtype it with the correct date.

   - **Finish Date:** If you haven't updated the total number of postings, then this date is blank. This means that the recurring entry continues until you choose to suspend posting or delete the recurring entry.

   - **Last Posted:** This selection shows the date of the last posting made. You can't change this date.

   - **Suspend Posting?** Tick this box if you don't wish to continue posting the recurring entry. The box can be un-ticked after you decide to resume posting.

5. **Type in the posting amount.**

   Break the amount down as follows:

   - **Net Amount:** Enter the net amount of the transaction.

   - **Tax Code:** Select the appropriate tax code, using the drop-down arrow.

   - **VAT:** This displays the VAT amount, determined by the net amount and tax code selected.

6. **To save the recurring entry, click OK. To exit without saving, click Cancel.**

Repeating customer and supplier payments

If a customer pays you regularly (and I hope they do!) or you pay your suppliers regularly (ditto!), set up these recurring payments as follows, particularly if the amount's the same each time (although it doesn't have to be):

1. **From Bank, click New Recurring Transaction from the Task pane or click the Recurring Items icon.**

2. **Enter the requested account information.**

   Fill in the following:

   - **Transaction Type:** Select Customer Payment On Account for a customer payment or Supplier Payment On Account for a supplier payment. Notice that the Recurring Entry To/From box changes to accept the Bank A/C and Customer or Supplier A/C details.

   - **Bank Account:** Select the account that the payment is to be deposited into, or the account that it's to be paid from if you're making a supplier payment.

   - **Customer/Supplier Account:** Choose the relevant account, using the drop-down arrow.

   - **Transaction Ref:** Enter a reference for your recurring transaction here.

   - **Department:** Select a department, if required.

3. **Select the posting frequencies as in Step 5 in the preceding section.**

4. **Enter the posting amount.**

5. **If you're happy with the information supplied on the screen, click OK to save the recurring entry.**

   If you click Cancel, you're asked if you want to save the changes. Click No to return to the main screen.

If you use this method to post payments on account to both suppliers and customers, allocate the receipts or payments to the specific invoices as a separate exercise. I don't tend to use this type of recurring option often because I find it quicker to process directly to the invoice in one step: it takes two steps to process a payment on account and then allocate that payment. But every business has different needs and different sets of circumstances, so this recurring option may well appeal to you.

Making regular journal entries – if you dare

This option is useful if you have to make an adjustment to the accounts where only a journal is possible. For example, if you make regular payments on a loan, rather than just setting it up as a bank payment, you can set it up as a journal and record both the payment and the interest (the specific journal depends on how the loan has been set up).

Only use a journal if you're confident with double-entry bookkeeping. If you aren't competent with your bookkeeping, doing so is dangerous territory! (I offer a brief explanation of double-entry bookkeeping in Chapter 12.)

1. **From Bank, choose New Recurring Transaction from the Task pane.**

   The Add/Edit Recurring Entry box appears.

   Although you enter your debit and credit transactions separately, you need to ensure that your journal entries balance, otherwise you get an error message. So, for every debit entry, you need to make a credit entry of the same amount.

2. **Enter the transaction information in the boxes.**

   You need to enter:

   - **Transaction Type:** Select Journal Debit or Journal Credit.

   - **Nominal Code:** Using the drop-down arrow, select the nominal account to use. The name of the nominal account appears in the box next to the code selected.

3. **Complete the transaction details, posting frequency and amounts fields, as shown in Steps 4 to 6 in the previous section, 'Going for consistency with your bank entries'.**

4. **Click OK if you're happy with the journal details or Cancel if you're not.**

Your newly created recurring entry now appears on the Recurring list.

Processing and posting recurring entries

After you've set up recurring entries, every time you start up Sage, you're asked if you want to process your recurring entries. Generally, you need to answer No at this stage, as processing them in a controlled manner is better.

You can turn off this reminder by selecting the No Recurring Entries At Start Up check box in the Parameters tab of Company Preferences (click Settings and then Company Preferences).

You normally process your recurring entries just prior to reconciling your bank account so that they're ready and waiting to be reconciled.

To process your recurring transactions, you need to:

1. **From Bank, click Recurring Items in the Links list.** The Recurring Entries window opens.

2. **Select the entry that you wish to post and click Process.**

   The Process Recurring Items box displays the message: Show recurring entries up to:.

3. **Enter the date you want to process recurring entries up to.**

   Normally, use the month-end date. For example, if you're about to reconcile the bank account to 30 April 2013, put in that date.

   After you enter the date, Sage shows you the recurring entries due to be posted up to the chosen date.

4. **Click Post.**

Sage doesn't post recurring entries with a zero value. Cancel the Posting screen and go back and edit the recurring entry so that a value is entered or choose to suspend the item. Sage doesn't process recurring entries if it can't find balancing debits and credits, so you must post your recurring journal entries correctly.

Dealing with Petty Cash

Petty cash, funds kept in the office for incidental expenses, can often be an absolute pain to administer. Normally a company has a petty cash tin, which usually contains a small amount of cash and is stuffed full of receipts. As members of staff are given money from the petty cash fund, they exchange the money for a receipt. If you count up the amount of cash and receipts, the total of both should equal the value of the petty cash float. Unfortunately, you may find that some people request £20 from petty cash to buy stationery, return with the receipt, but forget to return the change! The following sections tell you how to keep the petty cash tin in order.

Funding petty cash

Normally, you write out a cheque for petty cash or take the cash out of the bank and put it into the petty cash tin. To account for this arrangement within Sage, you can easily show this transaction as a bank transfer.

To do a bank transfer, follow the instructions in the 'Transferring Funds between Accounts' section earlier in this chapter. Make sure that the Bank Current account is selected as the *account from* and the Petty Cash account is selected as the *account to*. If you wrote out a cheque for petty cash, you can use the cheque number as a reference.

Making payments from the tin

Make one person solely responsible for the petty cash tin. They can then ensure that if someone returns and doesn't have the correct change and receipts, at the very least an IOU goes into the tin for the money owed. That individual must get the money returned to the tin as soon as possible.

When a payment is made from the petty cash tin, make sure that a receipt replaces the money or use a petty cash voucher to record where the money has been spent. Doing so ensures that all payments are correctly recorded and should also ensure that the petty cash tin balances to the agreed float amount.

To record a payment made from petty cash in Sage, follow the instructions for bank payments in the previous 'Tracking Bank Deposits and Payments' section, but select the Petty Cash account instead of the Bank Current account.

Reconciling the petty cash tin

Periodically, you need to reconcile the petty cash tin. The best time to do this reconciliation is when you decide to top it up.

To reconcile the petty cash tin, follow these steps:

1. **Extract all the petty cash receipts, batch them up and total them.**

2. **Give this batch a unique reference number, such as PC01 – you can use PC02 for the next batch and so on.**

   You can use this reference in the Reference field for recording the petty cash bank payments.

3. **Count the remaining petty cash.**

   The sum of the actual cash added to the total from Step 1 should equal the petty cash float.

   If the petty cash float doesn't balance, check to see whether anyone is holding back any petty cash receipts or whether anyone has been given cash to do something and hasn't returned all the change or the receipt.

4. **Write a cheque for cash for the value of the receipts and use this cheque to top up the petty cash float.**

   For all you techies out there, this method is known as the Imprest system – you only replenish what you've spent.

Paying the Credit Card Bill

Many businesses use credit cards as a convenient way to purchase goods and services. And, just like other financial accounts, you need to include credit card payments in the monthly processing of transactions – after all, they can amount to quite significant amounts of money.

Making payments

After you receive the credit card statement, you need to match up the invoices and receipts with the statement:

- **Invoices:** If you paid a supplier using your credit card, you received an invoice, which you've probably already entered and filed away. In order to process this payment, ensure that you select the Credit Card bank account, and then click the Supplier icon (refer to Chapter 7), but make sure that you insert a reference to the method of payment somewhere. For example, in the Cheque No. field, use the reference CC for credit card. Alternatively, use a unique reference number for each credit card statement, particularly if several employees have their own cards. In this case, give the statement sheet for each individual its own unique reference number, such as CC001. Doing so makes it easier to find the supporting papers for a transaction.

- **Receipts:** You may not have a proper invoice, just a till receipt for something purchased using the company credit card. In this instance, attach the receipt to the credit card statement and record the transaction as a bank payment. Make sure that you select the Credit Card account as the account from which the payment is to be made. Also, make sure that you're careful with the VAT element of the payment; the amount of VAT attributable to a transaction isn't always obvious.

Reconciling the credit card statement

After you enter all the transactions from the credit card statement onto Sage, you're then in a position to reconcile the Credit Card account in the same way as a normal bank statement. (Chapter 11 talks about reconciling your bank account if you need a reminder.)

The only thing to remember when entering the credit card statement balance is that this balance is a negative figure, because it's money that you owe the credit card company.

The statement is usually paid via a direct debit from your bank account on a monthly basis, and you can treat it as a bank transfer between the Bank Current account and the Credit Card account, as described in the 'Transferring Funds between Accounts' section earlier in this chapter. You can reconcile the statement in the same way as any other bank account. Provided you enter all the transactions and set the statement balance to a negative figure, you can't go too far wrong!

Chapter 9

Maintaining and Correcting Entries

. . . .

In This Chapter

▶ Doing file maintenance

▶ Locating transactions

▶ Searching for records

▶ Performing backup and restore routines

. . . .

*E*veryone makes mistakes. Sage understands this fact of life and makes it easy for you to correct them. You can completely delete an item, change elements of a transaction, such as the date or tax code, or find an item in order to check something.

In this chapter, I show you how to make changes to your data and correct mistakes where necessary.

Checking and Maintaining Your Files

You need to explore the file maintenance options. From the Menu bar, click File and then Maintenance. A Sage warning message opens saying that you must close all windows before proceeding. Click Yes. The File Maintenance box appears, as shown in Figure 9-1.

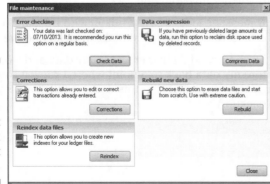

Figure 9-1: File maintenance options let you check and correct your data.

The File Maintenance screen may look a little daunting, but you probably need to use only the Check Data and Corrections options with any regularity. I look at each function in the following sections.

Checking data

This Error Checking facility allows you to check your data to make sure that that data is not corrupt. If your computer switches off in the middle of using Sage, using this facility is a good idea. Power cuts aren't unusual, and if you don't have an alternative power supply, Sage closes without being shut down properly, which can sometimes lead to corruption of data.

To check that no errors are present, perform a Check Data routine, following these steps:

1. **From the Menu bar, click File and then Maintenance.**

2. **Click Check Data.**

    The system checks each file, and if no problems are evident, gives you a message confirming that it has no problems to report.

3. **Click OK to return to the File Maintenance screen.**

4. **Click Close to exit the File Maintenance screen.**

Interpreting messages

If Sage finds any problems with your data, it brings up a box with several tabs that you can click for more information:

- ✔ **Comments:** The least serious messages, Comments simply alert you to the fact that your data may have inconsistencies. The Comments tab shows you which accounts you need to look at. Comments are usually insignificant and don't require data correction.

- ✔ **Warnings:** These messages are similar to Comments, in the sense that they often don't require data correction, Warnings alert you to problems that may require further investigation.

- ✔ **Errors:** An Error message indicates a problem with the data. You have the facility to fix an error, but you must make a backup before you do so.

    Personally, I'd be concerned if I had errors in my data and would be tempted to restore my data back to a point where I knew it was fine. (The 'Restoring Data' section later in this chapter tells you how to restore from a backup.)

The 'How to fix errors and warnings in your Sage data' link goes to a Sage website that guides you through resolving any errors or warnings in your data.

Fixing data

You can correct most data problems showing errors via the Fix option. However, the corrective action used to rectify problems can be quite complex. If you're uncertain about the consequences of running the Fix option, seek help from Sage Customer Support, using the telephone number given to you when you took out SageCover (see Chapter 1 for details of SageCover).

Making corrections

Probably the most used of the file maintenance options, the Corrections button is a godsend to anyone who makes the odd mistake (including yours truly!).

Be warned that all actions you take are recorded in the audit trail, so your accountant can see how many corrections you've made. From an audit point of view, transactions need to be traceable even if you've made mistakes. Unfortunately, any deletions or changes to data are highlighted in red on the audit trail, so if you make wholesale changes to your data they stick out like a sore thumb!

Sage makes corrections to the individual transactions themselves, so identifying the precise transaction that needs correcting is important. See the 'Finding Ways to Find Transactions' section, later in this chapter, for details on how to do this.

You can't correct journal entries using the File Maintenance method. You can only correct journal entries by using a reversing journal from within the Nominal Ledger module. Chapter 12 shows you how to do this.

To make a correction to a transaction, you can delete the whole transaction or correct a part of the transaction. Just follow these steps:

1. **From the File Maintenance screen, click Corrections.**

   Doing so brings up the Corrections screen. Essentially, this screen shows a list of all your transactions in transaction number order.

2. **Find the transaction that you want to correct.**

   You can click Find or use the up and down arrows to scroll through the data.

3. **Choose how to make the correction and make it.**

   You've the following two options:

   - **Edit Item:** Choosing this option opens a new window showing the details of that transaction. I've chosen a bank payment, as shown in Figure 9-2. The windows differ slightly, depending on the transaction type that you're editing. On the first screen, any item in black type can be changed. Click the Edit button to change greyed-out items. You then have the option of changing most other parts of the data. Make your changes and click Save. Sage asks Do you wish to post these changes? Click Yes to save or No to return to the original screen. Click Close and Sage asks Are you sure you wish to exit? Click Yes to return to the Corrections screen. Click Close and return to the Welcome screen.

Corrections

Number 30, Bank Payment

You can change details of all grouped items at once by using the fields below, or select individual transactions in the list to amend a specific item.

Bank Payment Details

Bank	1200		
Reference	00007		
Description	Marjory Smith payroll	Posted by	MANAGER
Created on	01/07/2013	☐ Bank rec. on	
Posted on	08/10/2013	VAT Rec. Date	/ /
Net	250.00	Paid	250.00
Tax	0.00		

No	N/C	Details	Net	T/C	Tax
30	7004	Marjory Smith payroll	250.00	T9	0.00

To edit details of a specific item on this Bank Payment, highlight the item and click 'Edit'.   Edit

How will this affect my data?   Save   Close

Welcome to Sage Instant Acco...   Corrections

Figure 9-2:
Editing
a bank
payment.

   - **Delete Item:** If you know that you want to delete an item, highlight it and click the Delete Item icon. The Deleting Transactions window appears. You can click the View button to see more of the transaction. If you're happy to delete it, click Delete. A confirmation message appears asking if you wish to delete the transaction. Click Yes to continue the deletion and No to take you back to the Deleting Transactions window. You can then click Close to return to the Corrections screen. Click Close again to go back to the Welcome screen.

That's how easy it is!

Re-indexing data

Sage recommends using the Re-indexing option only under the guidance of Sage Customer Support. When Sage recommends this course of action, the problem is usually pretty serious! I've never had to use this option myself, so I can only emphasise what Sage says: contact Customer Support if this need arises.

Compressing data

Compressing data files is also pretty serious stuff and outside the scope of this book. Briefly, this function basically constructs a new set of data files while removing deleted records, thereby reducing the file sizes. The files are compressed to create more disk space. As the compression procedure is irreversible, you need to take data backups beforehand, just in case any problems occur.

Rebuilding data

You need to tread carefully when using this part of the system because you can end up wiping all the data off your machine! (Mind you, if you take backups, which I explain in the 'Backing Up Data' section later in this chapter, you can restore it all fairly easily.)

You can choose to create new data files for all or part of the Sage Accounts system.

Click the Rebuild button, and the Rebuild Data Files window opens, with all the boxes ticked. A tick indicates that you don't want to create new data files for that part of the system. Removing the ticks tells Sage which parts of your software you want to create new data files for.

If you type **rebuild data files** into the Help menu, Sage guides you through the process. However, have Sage Customer Support on standby, just in case anything goes wrong, so that they can talk you through the steps.

Use the Rebuild tool with extreme caution and always take a backup prior to attempting to use this function.

Finding Ways to Find Transactions

Sometimes you need to find a transaction in order to correct or delete it. To find a transaction, you can use the Financials module, the Bank Reconciliation screen or the Corrections screen (in File Maintenance).

I demonstrate from the Financials module. Follow these steps:

1. **Using the Navigation bar, click Company and then choose Financials from the Links list.**

2. **Click the Find button at the bottom of the Financials screen.**

   Doing so brings up the Find box, shown in Figure 9-3, which, plainly enough, is what you use to find the transaction.

Figure 9-3:
The Find box.

Find	
Find What:	[ ]	Find First
Search in:	Transaction Number	Find Next
Match:	Any ☐ Case sensitive	Cancel

3. **Enter details into the boxes.**

   Tell Sage what to find and where to look:

   • **Find What:** The information entered here is dependent on what's shown in the Search In field (see the next point). For example, in Figure 9-3 the Search In field reads `Transaction Number`. So the entry in this Find What field should be a transaction number.

   • **Search In:** A drop-down box gives you different variables to search with. The default variable is Transaction Number, but you can choose other alternatives. Your other choices are: Account Reference, Reference, Details, Date, Net Amount, Bank Account Reference, Nominal Account Reference, Ex Reference, Tax Amount, Amount Paid, Date Reconciled and Late entry date.

   • **Match:** You don't have to search using the exact data; you have the option to select how close a match you can make.

     Any: Finds all transactions that contain the details you entered anywhere in the field you're searching on. For example, if you're searching for an account reference and you enter RED, Sage finds references such as RED, REDMOND and CALLRED.

Whole: Finds the transaction that contains the exact details you enter in the Find What field. In this instance, when searching for account references, it brings up the RED account transactions.

Start: Finds all transactions that begin with the details you enter. So, in the example, Sage would find transactions beginning with RED, such as RED or REDMOND, but it doesn't find CALLRED.

- **Case sensitive:** Check this box if you want Sage to find transactions that contain exactly the same upper and lower case letters as those entered in the Find What field.

4. **Click Find First.**

   If a transaction is found, Sage highlights it in blue. If this isn't the transaction that you're looking for, click Find Next.

   Note: You may need to cancel the Find box in order to see the transaction properly.

   If no transactions are found, a message to that effect appears. Click OK to return to the Find window so that you can enter new search details.

Searching For Records

You can search for records on Sage using the Search button in the Customers, Suppliers, Company, Products, Projects and Financials modules. The Search button is simply another method of tracing transactions.

I tend to search from the Financials module, as Sage performs a search on all the transactions from this module. If you search from the other modules, Sage limits the search solely to the information in that one module – which may be precisely what you want to do; in which case, choose that specific option.

To perform a search from Financials, follow these steps:

1. **From Financials, click Search.**

   The Search box opens.

2. **Choose the variables to perform the search.**

   Your choices are:

   - **Join:** From the Join drop-down list, choose the Where option, which is the only option available. (And as Sage doesn't explain the connection between Join and Where, don't expect me to. Just one of Sage's mysteries!)

   - **Field:** Click the Field column and select the variable you want to search by. In Figure 9-4, Total Amount Paid is selected.

- **Condition:** Click the Condition column and choose a condition, such as is equal to or is greater than.

- **Value:** Enter the value you want to search for.

  You can enter *wildcards,* which are special characters you can use to represent a line of text or an individual character. Click F1, the Help function key, while in the Search box, and Sage explains how to use wildcards.

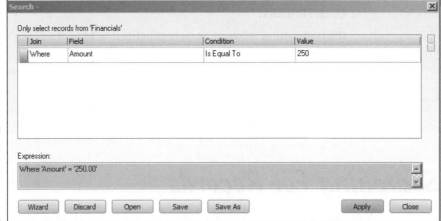

Figure 9-4:
Searching
for – and
finding! –
£250.

Figure 9-4 shows a search for a transaction for the amount of £250.

3. Click Apply.

   Sage identifies all transactions that meet the conditions you selected. If Sage can't find a transaction, nothing comes up.

 You can save a search so that you can find records with the same criteria later. Just follow the first two steps in the preceding list and then click Save instead of Apply. Enter a suitable filename and then click Save again. To access this saved file, open up the Search box, click Open and select the chosen file.

Backing Up Data

 Performing regular backup routines is extremely important. If your data becomes corrupt or you need to reinstall Sage for whatever reason, you then have a backup that you can restore onto your computer, allowing you to continue working with the least amount of disruption.

To back up your data, follow these steps:

1. **From the Menu bar, click File and then Backup.**

   A message asks whether you want to check your data. Sage recommends that you check your data, which normally takes a matter of seconds, depending on how may records you have. Click Yes to check or No to continue with the backup.

2. **Make adjustments on the Backup window that comes up.**

   The Backup window contains three tabs:

   - The Backup Company tab, shown in Figure 9-5, displays the filename SageAccts, followed by your company name, today's date and the .001 file extension.

     You can change the filename to one that has meaning for your business. For example, the filename 'Jingles accounts end of day 2013-11-23.001' indicates a backup of the Jingles card company's data as at close of business on 23 November 2013.

     Choose a location that you can find easily if you need to restore the data. Use the Browse button to change the location if you're not happy with the location Sage chooses.

Figure 9-5: The Sage Backup screen.

- The second tab, Advanced Options, allows you to choose how much you back up. For example, you can include only data, or data plus reports, templates and so on. At the very least, back up your data files.

- The Previous Backups tabs holds – you guessed it! – previous backups.

3. **Click OK.**

The backup starts. When the process is complete, you receive a confirmation message saying that the backup was successful.

Make sure that each backup has a different name. Sage makes doing so easy by adding the date to the file name, but if you perform more than one backup in a day, you have to change the name slightly or a backup with the same name overwrites the first set of data.

Take backups at the end of every day, at least, but if you're doing a large amount of processing, you may want to back up more often so that if you have to restore data you don't have to reprocess too much information. Many people use a different disk, CD or pen drive for each day of the week, naming the backup disk Monday, Tuesday, Wednesday, Thursday, Friday. You can then restore information back to any day in your current week.

Restoring Data

Restoring data means that you erase the current data on the computer and replace it with data from your backup disks.

Hopefully you won't need to run this function, but if you do, follow these steps:

1. **From the Menu bar, click File and then Restore.**

Sage tells you that it can't run this function without closing windows. Click Yes, and the Restore window appears.

2. **Click Browse and select the file that you want to restore.**

3. **Click OK.**

A message appears saying that you're about to restore and that the process overwrites any data currently on the computer. Click Yes to continue or No to exit.

After successfully restoring your data, use the Check Data facility in the File Maintenance screen to check for errors. Refer to the 'Checking data' section earlier in this chapter for advice on how to do this.

Chapter 10

Keeping Track of Your Products

. . . .

In This Chapter

▶ Recording a stock take

▶ Adjusting stock levels

▶ Checking stock availability

. . . .

A lot of money is often tied up in stock, and having proper control over your stock procedures makes good business sense. In this chapter, I give you the tools to manage your stock.

Sage Instant Accounts Plus offers an easy-to-use stock facility. Sadly, this facility is not available with Sage Instant Accounts (the entry-level program) – so if you have this version, you can happily skip this chapter.

Taking Stock

Every business should undertake a stock take periodically – once a year at the least – so that the year-end accounts show an accurate stock position. However, actually carrying out a stock take can prove a logistical nightmare, particularly if you've a vast array of products.

Usually, recording a stock take is best undertaken when the factory or office is closed for normal business. Many a time, I've rolled out of bed on a Saturday to help do stock takes! While Sage doesn't allow you the luxury of a weekend lie-in, it does help you organise your stock take methodically.

Prior to running the Stock Take option in Sage, you should run one of the Stock Take reports to assist you with the physical stock count. An example of one of these reports can be seen in Figure 10-1.

I have chosen the Stock Take Report (by Stock Category) and you can see that Sage helpfully provides the quantity of stock as recorded in Sage followed by a blank box, where you can record the actual stock quantity.

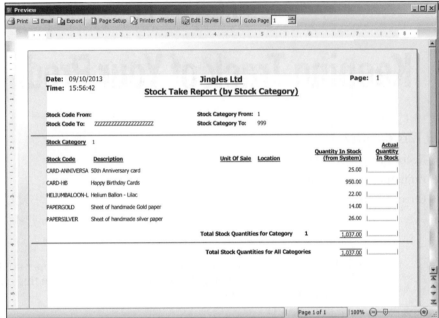

Figure 10-1:
An example
of a Stock
Take report.

When you've completed your physical stock check, you can then begin the steps of adjusting the data in Sage (only where you have stock differences).

You cannot run a stock take for service or non-stock items. To record any stock differences in Sage found during the physical stock take, follow these steps:

1. **From the Navigation bar, click Products.**

   Ensure that the screen is displaying the Products view and not the Products dashboard (which shows graphs). Use the Change View button to switch the display if necessary.

2. **Select the products for which you want to amend the stock as a result of the stock take.** Click Stock Take, which opens up the Stock Take window. Using the drop-down arrow, select each product where you need to make a stock adjustment, and amend the quantities in the Actual column. Sage then calculates an adjustment figure in the Adjustment column, as shown in Figure 10-2.

   If you want to select all product for the stock take, then click swap from the Products list page, and then click the Stock take icon. All the products then appear.

   Figure 10-2 shows a sample Stock Take window.

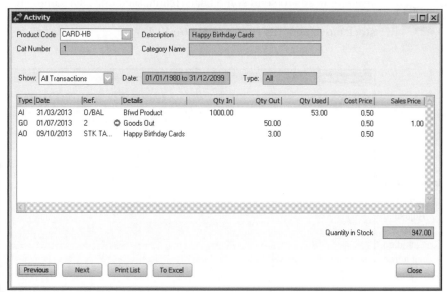

Product Code	Details	Date	Ref	Actual	Cost Price	In stock	Adjustment
CARD-HB	Happy Birthday Cards	09/10/2013	STK TAKE	947.00	0.50	950.00	-3.00
PAPERGOLD	Sheet of handmade Gol...	09/10/2013	STK TAKE	15.00	0.47	14.00	1.00
		/ /		0.00	0.00	0.00	0.00

Figure 10-2: Showing stock take adjustments for Jingle Ltd.

3. **When you're happy with the stock adjustments on screen, click Save. Close the Stock Take Window and you see the new stock quantities displayed on the product main screen.** You can see the adjustments that have been made by selecting a product and clicking the Activity icon. (As shown in Figure 10-3.) Any adjustments that have been made contain the default STOCK TAKE reference. The adjustments shown have an AI transaction for Adjustments In or AO for Adjustments Out.

Type	Date	Ref.	Details	Qty In	Qty Out	Qty Used	Cost Price	Sales Price
AI	31/03/2013	O/BAL	Bfwd Product	1000.00		53.00	0.50	
GO	01/07/2013	2	Goods Out		50.00		0.50	1.00
AO	09/10/2013	STK TA...	Happy Birthday Cards		3.00		0.50	

Figure 10-3: Showing the stock adjustment for Happy Birthday Cards.

Adjusting stock levels

Sage helps you to adjust stock levels. For example, you may need to return some goods to stock without generating a credit note – a *stock in* movement – or record the fact that you sent some stock out to potential customers as samples – a *stock out* movement. As you're not processing credit notes, you need to change the stock numbers manually to reflect the movement in stock.

To make a stock adjustment, follow these steps:

1. **From the Product window, select the product that you want to make an adjustment to. Click Adjustments In to put stock back into your stores, or click Adjustments Out to remove items.**

   The Stock Adjustment In/Out window appears, depending on which adjustment you've chosen.

2. **Enter the adjustment details, using one line per product.**

   Entering a reason for the adjustment in the Reference column is a good idea. You've 30 spaces to enter a description.

   The cost price and sale price automatically appear from the stock record.

3. **To save the details entered, click Save.**

   The stock is automatically adjusted.

Jeanette needs to send some Lilac Helium balloons as a sample to prospective customers, so she creates an Adjustment Out of stock to account for this stock movement (as shown in Figure 10-4).

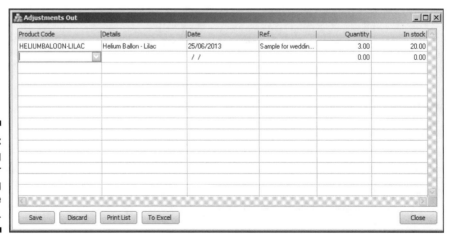

Figure 10-4:
Adjusting stock for sending out a free sample.

When Jeannette has saved her adjustment, Sage automatically recalculates the amount of stock shown in the stock activity.

Figure 10-5 shows the new stock level of 17 units and also shows the Adjustment Out of stock, with the reference Sample against it.

If you want to check on stock, simply highlight the product and click the Activity icon. You can see a history of all stock movements for that product item, as well as the current quantity held in stock.

Checking stock activity

You can look at a product's activity and view stock movements. The Activity screen records all movement of stock in and out as well as the quantity held in stock.

To check product activity, follow these steps:

1. **From Products, select the product that you want to view.**

2. **Click Activity.**

   The Activity screen opens, showing all movements of stock.

3. **You can print a list of activities or click Close to exit this screen.**

   You return to the Products list.

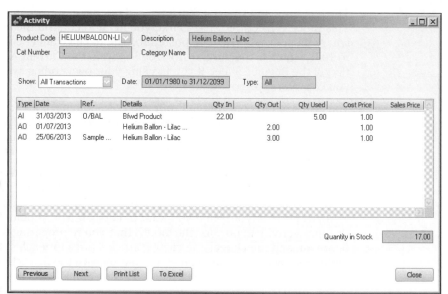

Figure 10-5:
Newly adjusted account for Lilac balloons.

Adjusting your Opening and Closing Stock

By now, you should have created your product records and entered opening balances for each stock record. Be aware, however, that this on it's own does not affect the stock figure shown in the Nominal Ledger. You need to have entered your opening Trial Balance correctly to show the opening stock figures at the start of the year.

Many companies that hold stock would like to account for the value of stock in their Balance Sheet on a more regular basis than at the end of each year. More than likely, they'll be checking their stock monthly. This means taking an opening and closing position of stock at the end of each month. Sage has made this simple to do – by creating a wizard to do the job for you!

By recording your opening and closing stock balances, Sage can accurately calculate the cost of sales figure within your Profit and Loss report. If you don't post your opening and closing balances, the cost of sales on the Profit and Loss report only includes your purchases, and not accurately record the true cost of goods sold.

To run the Opening and Closing Stock wizard, follow these steps:

1. **From Products, click Opening and Closing Stock from the Task pane.**

   Sage doesn't allow this option to run without closing windows, so say Yes.

2. **The Opening and Closing Stock wizard opens** (as shown in Figure 10-6.) This process has three steps. First, you need to confirm the accounts where the journals are to be posted to. The Balance Sheet code defaults to 1001, which is the normal stock code within the Current Assets section of the Balance Sheet. If you're using your own coding system, then you can over-type your code here.

   You also need to confirm the Profit and Loss nominal code (in the Purchase section of the Profit and Loss) for Closing stock. This defaults to 5201; you may change this if you've a different coding structure. When you're satisfied with the nominal codes that are to be used, click Next.

3. **The Enter Values window opens.** You must enter a date, reference and a description. Usually the date is the end of the month, and a suitable reference such as Closing Stock at April 2013 can be added. Sage calculates a stock figure for you, but if you want to check it, you should run the Product Activity Report for the month that you're preparing the stock figure for, and then check the closing stock figures for each stock item, multiplied by the cost price. If you're happy with the figure that Sage has given, then move to the Previous Closing Stock figure and enter the value. Then click Next.

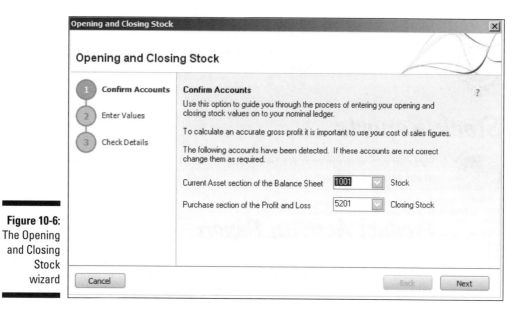

Figure 10-6:
The Opening
and Closing
Stock
wizard

4. **The final screen of the wizard shows you the double entry bookkeeping that Sage is about to complete for you** (as shown in Figure 10-7.) If you're happy to continue, click Post and Sage posts the appropriate journals.

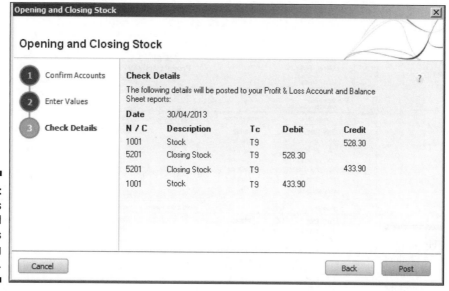

Figure 10-7:
The journals
to be posted
for Jingles
closing
stock.

That's it! You're done!

When you check your Balance Sheet, you can see that the Stock figure shown is the Closing balance figure that you've just posted.

Stock Reports

You can run various reports using Sage Instant Accounts Plus. Here are some of the more useful ones.

Product Activity Report

This shows the activity of each individual product line, including the quantity in stock. Please be aware that the quantity shown is the current quantity held in stock and may not be the same as the report dates that you've run. For example if you run the reports dated 30.04.13 and then move some stock out on 5 May, any reports printed at a date later than 5 May show the revised stock levels regardless of the dates chosen for the activity report.

Figure 10-8 shows a Product Activity report for Jingles Ltd at 30.04.2013.

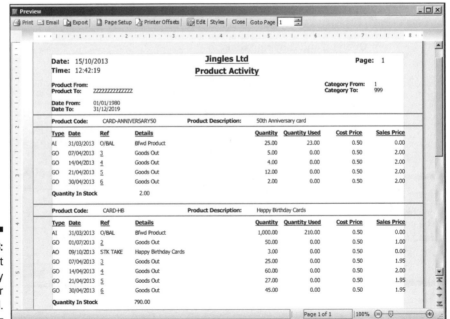

Figure 10-8:
A Product Activity report for Jingles Ltd.

The Product Activity report can be found by clicking on Products and then the Reports icon (or Reports from the Links List).

When the Product report window opens, you see a list of report categories down the left-hand side. The Product Activity report can be found within the Product Analysis category.

Product List

This is a straightforward list of products that you hold in stock. It gives you the stock code, description, sale price and nominal code, along with the nominal name. It does not give you the amount of stock held.

This report can be found within the Product Details category of the stock reports.

Product Profitability

This useful report shows you each product record and then the cost price and selling price for each. It then calculates the profit percentage. You can print the report percentage based on Cost Price or percentage based on Sales Price, whichever suits your needs.

Stock Take report

This report is extremely useful prior to running your physical stock count. You can see an example of this report in Figure 10-1 at the start of this chapter. There's space to amend the stock levels, should they need to be changed, on the face of the report.

This report can be found by clicking on the Reports icon within the Products module, or by clicking Reports within the Links List of the Products module and then clicking on the Stock Take category. You have a choice of printing the Stock Report by location, category or stock code.

Selling Stock

Obviously, when you've bought your stock, you hope to eventually sell it! Otherwise your business will not survive.

Sage Instant Plus makes it easy to keep a track of your stock that's sold.

Here's how Sage can help:

1. **When you're about to sell an item, highlight the product code and click the Sell Items icon within the Product module.**

2. **A new window opens, asking you to select which type of record you wish to create.** You've the option of creating a Sales Quotation or a Sales Invoice, as shown in Figure 10-9. Choose one or the other and then click Create.

3. **A Product Invoice or Quotation opens.** You can now complete the invoice/quotation as shown in 'Creating Invoices' in Chapter 6. When you update the invoice, the stock system is updated to reflect the products that you've sold.

While the products module within Sage Instant Accounts Plus is modest, compared to other Sage products, it more than adequately allows you to keep track of your stock, providing that you only require simple systems. If you want to start introducing Sales Order processing and Purchase Order processing, you need to upgrade your Sage software to Sage 50 Accounts Professional.

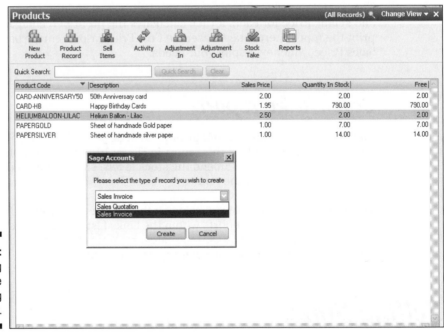

Figure 10-9:
Selecting an invoice when selling a product.

Part III
Running Monthly, Quarterly and Annual Routines

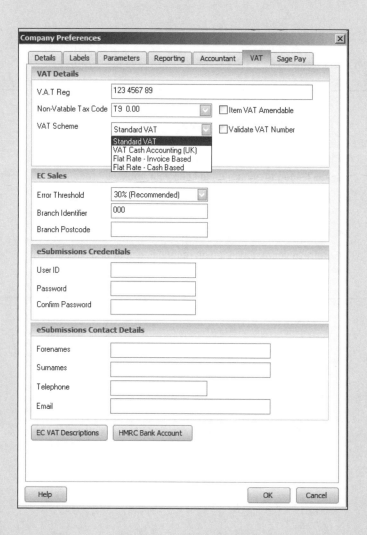

Go to www.dummies.com/extras/sageinstantaccountsuk for free online bonus content.

In this part . . .

✔ Get down with the deadlines: read up on the kinds of deadlines you'll need to adhere to, to keep your books in order.

✔ Keep the taxman happy: learn how to run your quarterly VAT Return.

✔ Get familiar with preparing your month end accounts.

✔ Refresh your knowledge on reconciling your bank account at month end.

Chapter 11

Reconciling Your Bank Accounts

In This Chapter

▶ Valuing the importance of bank reconciliations

▶ Preparing to do your bank reconciliation

▶ Reconciling your bank account

▶ Checking things out when things don't check out

▶ Clearing up items that haven't cleared

*I*f you like to know to the penny what's in your bank account, you're reading the right chapter! Reconciling your bank accounts normally forms part of your monthly accounting routine. Running through the bank reconciliation process gives you a thorough review of your bank statements and provides a good opportunity to investigate any unusual or incorrect transactions. As a result, you're fully aware of the financial transactions flowing in and out of your bank accounts.

Recognising Reasons to Reconcile

Performing a bank reconciliation requires you to check that you've matched all the bank transactions in Sage against the entries on your bank statements. Ultimately, you should be able to tick off every item on your bank statement against a corresponding entry in Sage.

Most businesses have at least one current account, a deposit account and possibly a business credit card, as well as a petty cash tin. Each one needs to have statements of one sort or another. Sage assumes that you have all these accounts and provides default accounts for each one, which you can rename or add to as required. (Refer to Chapter 3 for how to amend accounts.) Additionally, Sage includes a Building Society Account and Credit Card Receipts account as default accounts, as shown in Figure 11-1.

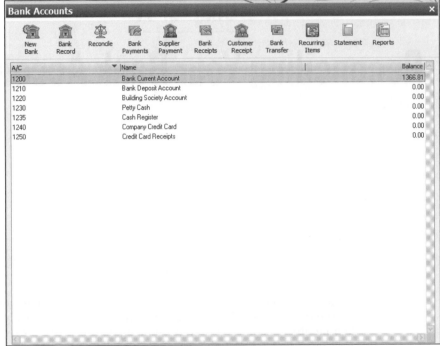

Figure 11-1:
The bank
accounts
that Sage
assumes
you to have.

After you reconcile the accounts, you can be sure that the data entered is accurate, as are any reports run from the information.

You need to reconcile all your bank accounts to ensure the accuracy of the accounting records. Reconciling all bank accounts is important, particularly if you're VAT registered, because in doing so you pick up all transactions that have VAT associated with them. Credit card transactions in particular can attract a lot of VAT. If you don't reconcile credit card statements, you can miss VAT-liable transactions and render both the accounts and the VAT return incorrect.

When you set up your bank records, you're given the opportunity to determine whether you want the bank account to be a reconciling one or not. If you don't want to reconcile an account, simply click the bank record and put a tick in the No Bank Reconciliation box, on the Account details tab. However, use this feature with caution! Most bank accounts need to be reconciled to ensure accuracy of information.

Doing your bank reconciliations on a regular basis not only guarantees the accuracy of your information, it also gives you the ability to run meaningful reports that help you manage your business and enable you to make sensible decisions.

Getting Ready to Reconcile

The aim of a reconciliation is to match transactions in Sage with your bank statement, so the process is easier if you've entered as many transactions as possible prior to looking at the bank statement. Before starting a reconciliation, make sure that you've accomplished the following tasks:

> ✔ **Entered all the payments from your cheque stubs for the period that you're reconciling.** Refer to Chapter 7 for a reminder on how to process supplier payments and Chapter 8 for all other payment types.
>
> ✔ **Entered the receipts from your paying-in book, up to and including the date to which you're reconciling.** Refer to Chapter 5 for help with processing customer receipts and Chapter 8 for recording other bank receipts.

Make sure that you enter the cheque numbers and payslip numbers in the Reference field so that you can easily identify those items on your statement.

Have a copy of your bank statements in front of you and check them for any other transactions that aren't yet in Sage but that you can input before the reconciliation. Items in this last-minute batch may include:

> ✔ Bank interest (both paid and received).
>
> ✔ Bank charges.
>
> ✔ Direct debits – to pay suppliers, for example
>
> ✔ Direct credits or BACS from customers
>
> ✔ Transfers between accounts

Tick off the items on your bank statement as you enter them onto Sage. This way, you can see whether you've missed anything that needs to be entered.

Doing the Actual Reconciliation

You need your bank statements in front of you as you work through the reconciliation process, so have them at hand (where they should be if you prepared properly according to the tips I offer in the preceding section).

If you mark each item with a tick as you enter it onto Sage, you can then put a line through the tick or use a highlighter pen to indicate that you've reconciled that item. Make your mark visible, so that you can easily spot anything that hasn't been reconciled. Figure 11-2 shows an example of a bank statement with marks for items entered and reconciled in this way. The payments are all entered onto Sage and reconciled; the receipts have been entered, but aren't yet reconciled.

BISI BANK LTD

Statement Period ended 30.04.13

Account No: 51235467   Sortcode: 21.45.85

		Payments	Receipts	Balance
01.04.13	Account Opened			£0
01.04.13	100001		£2000✓	£2000
01.04.13	Transfer	£100✗		£1900
15.04.13	100002		£200✓	£2100
23.04.13	100003		£52.87✓	£2152.87
30.04.13	Closing balance			£2152.87

Figure 11-2: A bank statement with the different types of ticks.

To begin the reconciliation process, follow these steps:

1. **From the Navigation bar, click Bank.**

   Make sure that your cursor is highlighting the bank account you want to reconcile. Sage defaults to account 1200, which is the Bank Current account, so move the cursor if necessary.

2. **Click Reconcile to bring up a Statement Summary, as shown in Figure 11-3.**

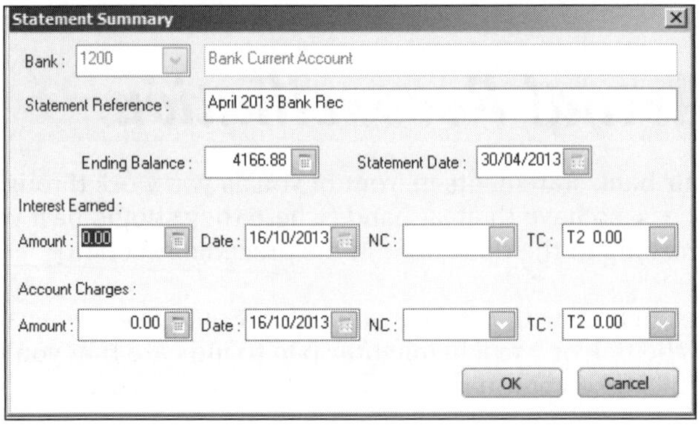

Figure 11-3: Statement Summary for bank reconciliation.

3. **Enter the Statement Summary information.**

   Your Statement Summary contains the following fields for you to fill in:

   - **Statement Reference:** Sage helpfully gives you a default reference, with the first four digits being the bank account nominal code and the remaining reference being today's date. You can easily over-write this reference and use one that may be more meaningful to you. Giving your statement a reference enables Sage to archive the reconciliation into History. Archiving the statement means that you can pull up a copy of that bank reconciliation at any point in the future. The reference is used to name the PDF document that's cre-ated when the reconciliation is archived.

   - **Ending Balance:** Enter the final balance shown on the bank state-ment for the period that you're reconciling.

   Most people reconcile to the end of the month, but I find it easier to reconcile a page at a time: you have fewer transactions to recon-cile, which means fewer transactions to check back through in the event of an error (yes, errors happen to the best of us!). To recon-cile by page, simply use the balance at the bottom of the statement page and reconcile each item on that single page.

   - **Statement Date:** Sage automatically defaults to today's date, so change this field to the date of the bank statement you're reconciling.

   - **Interest Earned:** If you've received any interest on the bank state-ment, enter it here. Alternatively, you can enter any interest as an adjustment in Step 6.

   - **Account Charges:** Enter any bank charges on this screen, or enter an adjustment on the Bank Reconciliation screen in Step 4.

4. **Click OK to bring up the Bank Reconciliation screen, shown in Figure 11-4.**

   If you click OK without changing any of the information on the statement summary, you still get the opportunity to change both the statement bal-ance and date on the actual Reconciliation screen itself.

   The screen is split into two parts. The top part shows all the transactions currently entered in Sage that need to be matched against the bank state-ment (up to and including the statement-end date, shown at the top of the screen). Items move to the bottom part of the screen after you match them against the bank statement. The bottom screen also shows any account charges or interest earned if you entered it on the statement summary, as well as showing you the last reconciled balance. If this occasion is the first time that you've performed a reconciliation, the last reconciled balance is zero. Otherwise, the balance from the previous reconciliation shows.

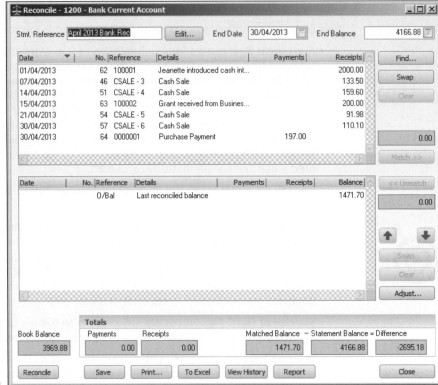

Figure 11-4:
The Bank
Recon-
ciliation
screen.

Sage only brings up transactions posted to the system up to the statement-end date that you enter on the Summary screen.

In Figure 11-4, the end date is 30 April 2013, so only items dated on or before that date appear. If you didn't specify a date on the Summary screen, Sage brings up *all* transactions posted to the system date, which is the current day's date, so you're looking at quite a few transactions!

You can change the statement-end balance and the date while in the Bank Reconciliation screen by overtyping the date and end balance at the top of the screen.

5. Match items on Sage against the bank statement.

Match each item on your bank statement against the same item in the top part of the Bank Reconciliation screen.

To match an item, double-click the item in the top box, or highlight it and click the Match Transaction button to the right of the screen. As soon as you match an item, it moves to the bottom part of the screen and the values of the Matched Balance and the Difference boxes at the bottom right of the screen change accordingly.

As you double-click each item in Sage, make a corresponding mark on the bank statement. If you ticked items on the statement, put a cross through the same tick or highlight the item. You can then identify anything that isn't reconciled at the end.

If you move a transaction to the bottom section in error, just double-click the transaction or highlight the transaction and click Unmatch Transaction, and it moves back to the unmatched items at the top.

The three boxes at the bottom-right corner of the screen keep track of the balance between the transactions you match and what your statement says. If you get everything to agree, the Difference box contains a zero.

6. **Click the Adjust button (above Difference at the bottom right of the screen) to make any adjustments.**

   You may find that you missed inputting an entry that's on the bank statement. See Figure 11-5 to see what you can adjust.

   When you're happy that you've completed any adjustments, move to Step 7.

Figure 11-5:
Adding an adjustment directly to your bank reconciliation.

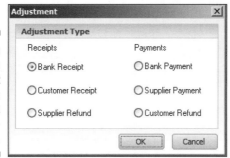

7. **Save the reconciliation.**

   Ideally, you work through the bank reconciliation until you've matched all your items from the bank statement. However, life isn't like that. Your phone may ring, or someone walks into your office for a chat. Save the work you've done so far by clicking the Save button, near the bottom left of the screen, and then click OK.

   When you're ready to continue reconciling, click the Reconcile icon. A pop-up screen asks whether you want to use the previously saved statement or discard it. Click the Use Saved button, and Sage takes you back to the point where you left off.

   Clicking Discard Saved wipes out your previous work, and you have to start your reconciliation again.

8. Reconcile your bank transactions.

All your transactions match, and the Difference box reads zero, so click the Reconcile button on the bottom left of your screen.

Sage saves your reconciled statement in a history file (using the reference you gave your reconciliation at the start of the reconciliation process), and you can review it later if you need to.

To access your archived reconciliations, click the Reconcile button and then click OK from the Statement Summary screen. Doing so opens up the Reconciliation screen, where you can then click the View History button at the bottom of the screen. A list of PDF files appears, displaying your historical bank reconciliations, as shown in Figure 11-6. Double-click the one you want to view, and the PDF file opens.

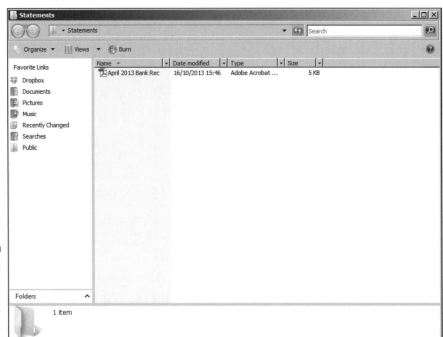

Figure 11-6:
View the historical bank reconciliations.

Troubleshooting when Your Account Doesn't Reconcile

Hopefully, your accounts always reconcile, especially because you've followed my recommendations to the letter. But, if they don't, try these suggestions:

- ✔ Check whether every item on your bank statement has been ticked off. You may have missed something, which is easy to do when you've lots of transactions on a page or lots of pages in a statement.

- ✔ Make sure that all the items left on the top part of the screen haven't yet cleared the bank account. On a bank statement several pages long, you can easily overlook a transaction, especially if you're going through the statement page by page.

- ✔ As a last resort, check off each item again, perhaps this time circling the items on the bank statement to differentiate your markings. You may have entered and ticked the same entry twice. If you have, double-click the offending item in the matched section of the Bank Reconciliation screen to unmatch it. You then need to find the transaction number of that item and delete it.

After you make sure that your difference is zero, you're in a position to save or reconcile.

If you reconcile a transaction by mistake, you can fix it by going into File Maintenance, clicking Corrections and finding that transaction. Click Edit Item, uncheck the Bank Reconciled box and save the changes. Click Yes to confirm the changes. The next time you open the bank reconciliation, that transaction appears.

Rounding Up Stragglers

You may find that even though the Difference box is zero, you still have a few unmatched items in the top part of the screen. Don't worry; this situation is perfectly normal. It just means that you've entered cheques or receipts that haven't cleared the bank account and therefore don't show on the current bank statement.

If you're preparing accounts to the end of March, you need to ensure that you've entered all cheques up to and including 31 March. However, the 31 March bank statement may not include cheques you wrote on 31 March – or even 30 March or 29 March – because they haven't cleared your bank yet. Your cheque may still be sitting on your supplier's desk, waiting for someone to take it to the bank.

Cheques that show on Sage but aren't yet on your bank statement are known as *un-presented cheques*. You may also have an *outstanding lodgement* or two – a deposit paid in toward the end of the month that doesn't appear on your bank statement because it hasn't cleared the banking system.

Listing un-presented cheques and outstanding lodgements

At the year-end, your accountant needs to perform a traditional bank reconciliation and has to know what the outstanding cheques and lodgements are. Figure 11-7 shows an example, using some of Jingles' figures.

Figure 11-7: The bank reconciliation that your accountant likes to prepare.

Bank Reconciliation as at 30th April 2013	
	£
Balance per Bank Statement	4168.88
Less unpresented cheques	(197.00)
Add back outstanding lodgements	250.00
Balance per Cash book	4221.88

You can print a list of un-presented cheques and outstanding lodgements at the end of any month. To do this, click the Report icon within the Bank module, (click on the small chevron to the right of Recurring Items to see the rest of the icons), scroll down the report headings listed on the left-hand side of the screen, and at the bottom, click Unreconciled Transactions. Click on the first report Bank Report – Unreconciled. If you click the preview icon, you can see that this report lists all the unreconciled items for the period selected.

The traditional bank reconciliation, as shown in Figure 11-7, is often done only at the year-end.

Remembering recurring entries

The Recurring Entries feature helps speed up the data-entry process, particularly where you have the same type of entries occurring every month. Set up the recurring entries and you no longer have the laborious task of entering them manually each month! Refer to Chapter 8 to find out how.

Entering recurring entries only works when the value is the same each month, but can be used for:

- ✔ **Regular supplier payment on account:** You may be paying off a large supplier balance in instalments. Set up a regular payment on account to that supplier by using recurring entries.

- ✔ **Customer payment on account:** You may have a customer who pays you a regular amount each month or week.

- ✔ **Bank receipts and payments:** You may have loans that go out of your account on a regular basis, for example car or equipment loans.

- ✔ **Bank transfers:** You may want to transfer a regular sum of money into a deposit account in order to put money aside for bills, such as VAT or PAYE.

- ✔ **Nominal journals (both debits and credits):** If you're confident with your double-entry bookkeeping, you may have regular journals for the same value that need to be done each month.

Chapter 12

Running Your Monthly and Yearly Routines

In This Chapter
▶ Discussing accruals, prepayments and depreciation
▶ Juggling journals
▶ Running month-end tasks
▶ Clearing stock and clearing the audit trail
▶ Carrying out year-end routines

The nominal ledger lists all the nominal codes that your company uses. These nominal codes, when grouped together, form the record of your company's assets, liabilities, income and expenditure. The codes are grouped together in categories identified in your Chart of Accounts, which I talk about in Chapter 2.

Sage uses the accounting principle of *accrual accounting*. Accrual accounting isn't just about accruals (bizarre as that may sound!); rather, accrual accounting is about recording sales and purchases when they occur, not when cash changes hands – you match revenue with expenditure. For example, if you're preparing the accounts for the month of June, you need to make sure that you enter all the sales invoices for June even if you haven't been paid for them yet. You also check that all the purchase invoices relating to June are posted, so that you get an accurate reporting position.

In this chapter, I talk about some of the journals available for you to create as part of your monthly routine.

This chapter comes with a health warning! Please do not attempt journals if you're not comfortable with double-entry bookkeeping. Leave that to your accountant!

However, if you're happy with posting journals, then you may want to read the upcoming sections on accruals, prepayments and depreciation. Sadly you don't get any fancy wizards to help you process these adjustments – you do get them if you upgrade to the Sage 50 accounts suite – but as long as you're a confident bookkeeper, you' won't have any problems!

The routines discussed in this chapter help you to produce timely and accurate reports for management decision making.

Adding Up Accruals

An *accrual* is an amount you know that you owe for a product or service you've received, but for which you haven't yet received the invoice. An accrual occurs for items that you pay in arrears, such as telephone bills. To maintain an accurate set of accounts, you post an accrual into your nominal ledger by using the appropriate journals. These journals increase the costs to the business and create an accrual for the value of the outstanding invoice. The accrual is treated as a liability within the accounts because the business owes money. As soon as you receive the bill, you can reverse the accrual.

Charging a monthly amount for a service that's normally paid in arrears has a smoothing effect on company profits. For example, a £3,000 telephone bill that's paid quarterly is accrued in the accounts for the three months prior to receiving the bill, and a charge of £1,000 is put through the accounts each month. Otherwise, the first two months of the quarter show artificially high profits and the third month shows artificially low profits when the full cost of the telephone bill hits the Profit and Loss account in one go. Obviously, the cumulative effect over the three months is the same, but the monthly effect can make the difference between a profit and a loss for that company. So reviewing your accruals and prepayments (which I talk about in the next section) is important for monthly reporting purposes.

If you're confident with your double-entry bookkeeping, you can post a debit to the Cost account and a credit to the Accruals account.

Using the telephone example above, if Jeanette knows that she's going to receive a £3,000 telephone bill, she can smooth the profit effect by creating an accrual in the accounts for the months leading up to receiving the bill. Each month, for the three months before she receives the bill, she can accrue £1,000 per month. The double-entry journal is:

Dr 7550 (Telephone Expenses)	£1,000
Cr 2109 (Accruals)	£1,000

By the end of the third month, Jeannette receives the actual telephone bill, which she codes to accruals (N/C 2109). This coding ensures that telephone costs are not double counted. The accrual account is debited by £3,000, thus reversing out the entire accrual, but ensuring that the Profit and Loss has been charged with the correct amount. Phew . . . .

Counting Out Prepayments

A *prepayment* is basically payment in advance for services you haven't completely received. For example, Jingles Ltd buys a year-long radio advertising campaign for £12,000, which is invoiced in March. The invoice is entered in March for the full value of the advertising campaign, which is clearly incorrect as most of this invoice relates to a future period of time. So Jeanette needs to create a prepayment for the 11 months of advertisements to come.

Here's the bookkeeping that Jeanette would need to do:

1. **Upon receipt of the invoice for radio advertising, Jeanette would code the whole value of the invoice, in this case £12,000 to prepayments (nominal code 1103).**

2. **Jeanette would create a nominal journal to be posted each month for the sum of £1000 (a twelfth of the total cost of the advertising) where she would:**

   Dr 6201 (Advertising)   £1,000

   Cr 1103 (Prepayments)   £1,000

   This journal would have the effect of putting a £1,000 charge to the Profit and Loss account each month, and at the same time reducing the overall prepayment that is sitting in the Balance Sheet. By the end of the twelfth month, Jingles Ltd would show the full charge of £12,000 in the Profit and Loss report and the Prepayment account would be zero (unless of course you've other prepayments relating to other things . . .).

As a Sage Instant Accounts user, you need to create a nominal journal if you wish to process Prepayments. The journal entry is debit the Prepayments code and credit the cost code, when entering the prepayment for the first time. You can then slowly release the prepayment and charge the Profit and Loss account with the appropriate amount each month as shown in the example for Jeanette and the radio advertising campaign.

Depreciating Fixed Assets

A *fixed asset* is an item likely to be held in the business for more than 12 months. Fixed assets are usually large and expensive items that have a long useful life, such as machinery, land, buildings, cars and so on.

Because fixed assets last so long, you can't charge the Profit and Loss account with their full value. Instead, you have to *depreciate* the asset, assigning a proportion of the asset to the Profit and Loss account and offsetting that amount against any profits you make.

Depreciation is an accounting method used to gradually reduce the value of a fixed asset in the accounts (otherwise known as *writing down your assets*). Depreciation applies a charge through the Profit and Loss account and reduces the value of the asset in the Balance Sheet.

Writing down your assets

As a Sage Instant Account user, you have to depreciate your assets manually by posting a nominal journal each month.

You can choose your method of depreciation, but after you have, you must use the same method consistently every year. This method becomes part of your Accounting Policy and is referred to in the Notes to the Accounts section of your year-end accounts if they're prepared by your accountant.

Your accountant can help you decide which of the methods I explain in the next sections is best for you.

Ruling on the straight line method

In *straight line depreciation*, the value of the asset is depreciated evenly over the period of its useful life. For example, an asset depreciated over a four-year period has a quarter of the value depreciated each year (25 per cent). The same amount of depreciation is charged each month. For example, an asset that cost £24,000 and is due to be depreciated over a four-year period is depreciated by £6,000 each year, which equates to £500 per month.

Counting down the reducing balance method

An asset is depreciated by a fixed percentage in *reducing balance depreciation,* but the calculation is based on the net book value (NBV) each year, so the NBV reduces each year. For example, a £12,000 asset with a four-year lifespan, depreciated at 25 per cent on the reducing balance basis, is depreciated as shown in Table 12-1.

Table 12-1	Depreciation on a £12,000 Asset over Four Years	
Year	*Net Book Value (NBV)*	*Depreciation Amount*
1	£9,000.00	£3,000.00
2	£6,750.00	£2,250.00
3	£5,062.50	£1,687.50
4	£3,796.88	£1,265.63

The *net book value* is the cost price of the fixed asset less the accumulated depreciation to date. So, at the end of year one, a £12,000 asset has depreciated by £3,000 (at 25 per cent), leaving the NBV as £9,000.

Using the reducing balance method means that the asset never fully depreciates. The amount of depreciation just gets smaller and smaller each year. You're actually likely to write off the asset as obsolete before the NBV is anywhere near zero.

Going for the one-time write-off

If you use the *write-off* method, you make a single posting to write off the remaining value of the asset in one go. You may choose to write off an asset if you disposed of it and need to remove the value from the books. Alternatively, if the asset is ancient and no longer worth the value shown in the books, you have a candidate for a write-off.

Posting assets and depreciation

As a Sage Instant Account user, you post your depreciation journals manually. The double-entry that you need to do is to debit Depreciation (an expense account in the Profit and Loss) and credit Accumulated Depreciation (a Balance Sheet account).

Jeanette has bought a company van, to assist with her business. The van cost £10,000. In order to account for this van correctly, Jeanette must first post the asset into Jingles Ltd accounts by following these steps:

1. **Upon receipt of the invoice for the purchase of the van, Jeanette posts the invoice into her purchase ledger and codes the invoice to nominal code 0050 which is the Motor Vehicles Fixed Asset account within the Balance Sheet.** The van now shows in the Balance Sheet at cost price, which is £10,000.

2. **Each month, Jeannette must process a charge in her Profit and Loss account for depreciation, to reflect the fact that the van is reducing in value over time, and a fair charge must be allocated to the accounts for the use of this asset.** She decides to adopt the Straight Line depreciation method as described in 'Depreciating Fixed Assets' earlier in this chapter. She decides that the useful life of the asset is going to be four years. Therefore she divides the cost of the asset by four to calculate the total amount of depreciation to be charged each year. This figure amounts to £2,500 (£10,000/4). The monthly amount needs to be £208.33 (£2,500/12). The journal that Jeanette needs to complete each month is as follows:

Dr 8000 (Depreciation)   £208.33

Cr 0051 (Accumulated Depreciation for Motor Vehicles)   £208.33

By the end of the fourth year, the Balance Sheet shows the Fixed Assets at Cost for Motor Vehicles of £10,000, but also the Accumulated Depreciation of £10,000, thus giving a net book value (Cost minus Accumulated Depreciation) of zero. The accounts have had the full charge of the depreciation posted through the books for the four-year period.

Entering Journals

You need to understand the principles of double-entry bookkeeping to make journal entries competently.

A *journal* is where you transfer values between nominal accounts. You can use journals to correct mistakes where something was posted incorrectly, but you don't use journals just for corrections. For example, you use journals to do your accruals and prepayments if you don't want to use wizards.

You use debits and credits to move values between nominal accounts. The journal must balance, so you need equal values of debits to equal values of credits, otherwise Sage is unable to post it.

Only use journals if you're confident with double-entry bookkeeping. You may need to update several journals on a monthly basis, including depreciation journals, wages journals and any other journals that you may require to correct items posted to the wrong account (cleverly known as *mispostings*).

To complete a journal, follow these steps:

1. **From the Company module, click Journal Entry from the Task pane or the Journal Entry icon.**

2. **Enter the necessary information in the Nominal Ledger Journal sheet.**

   You need to supply the following information:

   - **Reference:** For example, 'April 2013 depreciation'

   - **Posting Date:** The system uses the current day's date, so you need to specify the date on which you want to post the journal.

   - **Nominal Code:** Use the drop-down arrow to select the first nominal code for your journal.

     For example, using Jeanette's example of posting the depreciation for the company van, when posting the depreciation journal she would show a debit entry for Depreciation (Nominal Code 8000) for the sum of £208.33. The detail would read 'April 2013 Depreciation'. The corresponding credit entry would use the Accumulated Depreciation code for Motor Vehicles (N/C 0051) for the sum of £208.33, as shown in Figure 12-1.

   - **Name:** The nominal code name automatically comes up on the screen.

   - **Ex.Ref:** This column enables you to provide extra detail should you wish to.

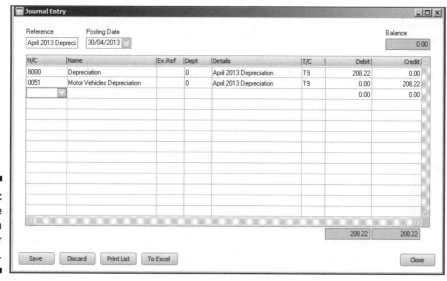

Figure 12-1: An example of posting a journal for depreciation.

- **Department:** Choose a department, if you need one.

- **Details:** Enter details of the journal to appear on the Nominal Activity report.

- **Tax Code:** The system defaults to T9, the code most often used, but you can change this code if you need to by using the drop-down arrows.

- **Debit or Credit:** Fill in the appropriate column according to whether you've a debit or a credit.

When you finish, the Balance box shows zero and the totals of the debits and credits are the same.

3. **Click Save if you're happy with the journal.**

Sage post the journal to the nominal codes shown.

Carrying Out Your Month-End Routine

When you're happy that you've entered all your transactions for the month, and that you've reconciled all bank accounts and posted all the necessary journals that you need to including accruals, prepayments and depreciation, you need to run the month-end process in Sage. You also get the opportunity to clear your customer and supplier month-to-date turnover figures. You can set a Lock Date, so that transactions cannot be posted prior to the date that you set.

If you're using Sage Instant Accounts Plus you can also clear the audit trail and remove stock transactions.

The month-end process gives you the opportunity to review your accounts and prepare for the next accounting period. After you post all the journals and run all monthly routines, you can start running reports (which I cover in Chapter 14).

Sage offers you a four-step wizard that can help you manage your month-end – an example can be seen in Figure 12-2.

You can click on each of the steps to reveal further sub-steps, which walk you through the month-end process.

I prefer to use my own checklist (see below), as I've found it works well for me. You've the option to use the Sage wizard, my checklist, or develop one of your own. The choice, as they say, is yours!

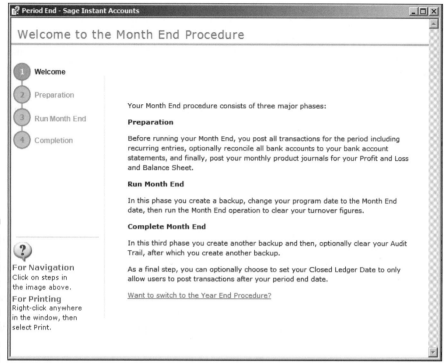

Period End - Sage Instant Accounts

Welcome to the Month End Procedure

1. Welcome
2. Preparation
3. Run Month End
4. Completion

Your Month End procedure consists of three major phases:

Preparation

Before running your Month End, you post all transactions for the period including recurring entries, optionally reconcile all bank accounts to your bank account statements, and finally, post your monthly product journals for your Profit and Loss and Balance Sheet.

Run Month End

In this phase you create a backup, change your program date to the Month End date, then run the Month End operation to clear your turnover figures.

Complete Month End

In this third phase you create another backup and then, optionally clear your Audit Trail, after which you create another backup.

As a final step, you can optionally choose to set your Closed Ledger Date to only allow users to post transactions after your period end date.

Want to switch to the Year End Procedure?

For Navigation
Click on steps in the image above.

For Printing
Right-click anywhere in the window, then select Print.

Figure 12-2:
Using the wizard to help you complete the month-end process.

Ticking off your checklist

Following a checklist is probably the easiest way to run the month-end in a controlled manner. Use this month-end checklist to ensure that you remember everything.

Prior to running the month-end, run through these tasks:

- ❏ Change your program date to the month-end (Settings➪Change Program Date).
- ❏ Enter all transactions for the current period.
- ❏ Process bank recurring entries for the month.
- ❏ Reconcile all bank accounts (including credit cards).
- ❏ Post all journals including prepayments, accruals, and depreciation.
- ❏ Post opening and closing stock journals (use Modules➪Wizards➪Opening Closing Stock Wizard, but only if you have Sage Instant Accounts Plus).
- ❏ Take a backup and label it. For example, 'April 2013 month-end'.

INSTANT ACCOUNTS PLUS ONLY

PLUS ✓

As you run month-end processes, be sure to cover these points, as necessary:

❑ Remove stock transactions, if required (only if you have Sage Instant Accounts Plus).

❑ Clear audit trail, if required.

❑ Take another backup entitled 'After month-end', together with the date.

As you work through the month-end processes, be sure to tick off each item, so that you can see which tasks are remaining.

Running the month-end

The month-end procedure enables you to clear down the month-to-date turnover figures on all your customer and supplier records. In clearing the month-to-date turnover figures, Sage zeroes down the sale or purchase values in the Month to Date field, which helps for reporting purposes. You can post transactions beyond the month-end date, and Sage designates them to the appropriate month. Even after you post the month-end, you can still post transactions to any previous accounting period. Sage just slots them into the appropriate month.

If you don't want anyone to be able to post items after your month-end date, you can enter a lock date when you're running the month-end. Doing so means that if you tick the Lock Date box and enter a specific date, and someone tries to post a transaction with a date prior to the Lock Date you've entered, they won't be able to. Using Lock Date helps control the accuracy of the reporting; for example, if someone requests reports with a prior period date, then the numbers in those reports should remain the same, and not be adjusted by late invoices being posted to prior periods.

To run the month-end, follow these steps:

1. **Click Tools⇨Period End⇨Month End from the Menu bar to bring up the Month End window.**

   Always check your data, to ensure that you don't have any errors. Click Check Data to do so.

2. **Ensure that you take a backup prior to running the Month End.** You take a backup just to ensure that you've a dataset to restore back to, should something go wrong.

3. **Enter the month-end date.**

4. **Enter a Lock Date** and prevent transactions with a prior month date being posted, then click the box to activate the Lock Date, and enter the appropriate Lock Date.

5. **Clear your turnover figures for customers and suppliers by checking the appropriate box to do so.**

6. **Click Run Month End** if you're happy with all the information you've entered. A confirmation message appears to say that the month-end has been completed.

Clearing stock transactions

Clearing stock transactions is a way of reducing the number of transactions that appear on your product activity ledger. You clear the transactions up to a date you specify. You may decide to clear stock transactions if your system is beginning to slow down as a result of the vast number of records it has to process. A year-end is often a good time to clear stock transactions. You don't have to clear the stock transactions, however, and many people prefer not to, as they like to be able to view a complete history of transactions.

You should print off your Product Activity reports prior to clearing your stock transactions.

When you run the Clear Stock option, it removes all individual product transactions from each product record, leaving Adjustment In (AI) and Movements In (MI) – records of stock movements – which are brought forward as opening balances.

To clear your stock, follow these steps:

1. **Take a backup before you run the Clear Stock option.**

2. **From the Menu bar, click Tools⇨Period End⇨Clear Stock. A confirmation message appears, asking if you're sure that you want to continue. Click Yes.**

3. **The Clear Stock window opens and confirms that this option permanently deletes stock from the Stock Transaction history. It also reminds you to take a backup prior to running this option.**

4. **Enter the date that you wish transactions to be deleted prior to. Then click OK.**

   Transactions prior to that date are permanently removed from stock transaction history.

Clearing your Audit Trail

The process of clearing your audit trail actually removes fully paid and fully reconciled transactions from the audit trail up to a date that you choose. You're left with fewer transactions on the screen, which makes it easier to work with and also speeds up the process of running reports and backing up your data. The process is usually done at year-end, and several criteria must be met before a transaction can be cleared. For example, transactions must be from a prior financial year, they must be fully paid and allocated, and all VAT and bank entries must be reconciled. If transactions don't meet these criteria, they won't be deleted.

Taking backups prior to running this process is absolutely essential. Clearing your audit trail is irreversible. Make sure that you print your audit trail, day-book reports, sales, purchase and nominal activity reports, and also any VAT return reports prior to running the Clear Audit Trail option.

You can look at the deleted transactions by clicking Company➪Financial Reports. When the Financial Reports window opens, select Cleared Audit Trail Reports, and you then see a variety of reports on the right-hand side of the screen. If you scroll down the list, you find the last report shows Removed Audit Transactions.

During the process of removing transactions, Sage posts journal entries to the nominal codes to which the transactions were linked. This posting ensures that the balances on the nominal accounts stay the same as before the Clear Audit Trail process was run. The journals are displayed with the detail Opening Balance and appear at the end of the audit trail when the Clear Audit Trail process is complete.

To run the Clear Audit Trail, follow these steps:

1. **From the Menu bar, click Tools➪Period End➪Clear Audit Trail. The Clear Audit Trail window opens. Sage prompts you to run several reports prior to this procedure. Click Next to continue.**

2. **Enter the date that you wish to clear transactions up to and including.** Back up your data by clicking the appropriate button and then click Next to continue.

3. **Confirm the date that you're clearing the audit trail up until by clicking Next.**

Doing a Year-End Routine

The year-end procedure is principally a financial accounting process. You must run your month-end for the last month of your accounting year, which takes care of the usual journal routines (although you're probably a little more careful at checking things like accruals and prepayments at the year-end).

The year-end procedure clears down the Profit and Loss accounts to zero and transfers any current-year profit or loss to the Retained Profit account. You carry forward the balances on the Balance Sheet to the new year and transfer any future-dated transactions into the relevant months for each nominal record.

As regards budgets, you transfer the actual values for the current to the prior year, so that you can make comparisons in the new financial year.

You must take a backup before you run this process (Sage recommends taking two, so that if one is lost or damaged, you always have another copy). You also need to check that you've run all the reports that you require for your accounts and that you've adjusted your system date to the same as your year-end date (Settings⇨Change Program Date).

Check that your Chart of Accounts doesn't contain any errors, although you should notice these sorts of mistakes when you run your Profit and Loss and Balance Sheets for the year.

To run your year-end, follow these steps:

1. **From the Menu bar, click Tools⇨Period End⇨Year End.**

   Click Yes to confirm that all other windows should be closed.

   The Year End window appears, which is essentially a checklist of things to do, prior to and during the year-end process.

   In the **Prepare for Year End** section, you're advised to check your data and check your Chart of Accounts before running backups. You're also given the option to archive your data, and have the chance to choose the location of that archive.

2. In the **Year End Options** section, you can choose to base next year's nominal or stock budgets on current year actual or budget data, by ticking the budget options box. This option opens the budget options window, where you can increase your budget by a percentage increase if you want to. You must also check the Year End Postings date and the Lock Date that Sage has suggested.

3. In the **Run Year End** section, Sage summarises the options that you've chosen. Check these details and if you're happy, click Run Year End box. A message appears asking you to confirm that you're happy to run the Year End. Click Yes if you are, or No to cancel.

4. If you click Yes, another message appears saying that processing the Year End applies to any existing layout of accounts. Click Yes to continue. The year-end process begins.

5. The Year End Report window opens, which asks you which method of output you require your year-end to be run. You can choose, Printer, Preview or File. I usually choose Printer. Click OK. The Print Year End report window opens and you can select your printer and the number of copies. Click OK.

6. A confirmation message appears saying that your year-end has now completed and gives you the dates of your new financial year.

You may want to take a backup and label it 'After the year-end'. You've now completed your year-end! Yay for you!

Chapter 13

Running Your VAT Return

In This Chapter

▶ Checking, analysing and adjusting your VAT return

▶ Matching your VAT transactions

▶ Sending in your VAT return

▶ Transferring your VAT

▶ Making a VAT payment or receipt

*T*he acronym VAT (which stands for Value Added Tax, of course) often has a profound effect on people – from turning grown men pale to inducing a state of panic when a VAT inspection suddenly looms! You can avoid all this hysteria by keeping proper accounting records with a system such as Sage and running your VAT returns in a systematic, methodical manner.

The actual running of a VAT return takes mere seconds as a result of the integrated nature of the Sage software.

In this chapter, I take you through the basics of running a VAT Return as well as highlighting the various VAT schemes that Sage offers.

Understanding Some VAT Basics

You only need to worry about VAT if your business is VAT registered. After you register, you can reclaim VAT on certain purchases, but you also have to charge and pay VAT on your sales.

Your company can voluntarily register for VAT and should if you can reclaim VAT on a significant proportion of your purchases. VAT registration is mandatory if you exceed certain VAT thresholds – currently, you must register if your annual sales reach £79,000 or above.

A basic knowledge of what you can and can't claim VAT on pays off (literally!). You can find many books on this subject, and the VAT office also provides plenty of publications for specific industries. A quick look on the HM Revenue and Customs (HMRC) website at `www.hmrc.gov.uk` gives you a list of all publications. You can find the main VAT rules and procedures in Notice 700.

Knowing your outputs from your inputs

VAT inputs and outputs have nothing to do with the Hokey Cokey. I wish they were that enjoyable!

Output VAT is just a fancy name for the VAT element of your sales. *Input VAT* is the opposite; it represents the VAT element of your purchases.

Basically, a VAT return compares the total of your VAT inputs and outputs, and subtracts one from the other. If the outputs exceed the inputs, you owe HMRC, and if the inputs exceed the outputs, then HMRC owes you a refund! Yes, it does happen . . .

Cracking the codes

When you enter invoices, credit notes or orders (whether for your customers or suppliers), you need to know which tax code to use. Sage automatically provides you with a list of UK tax codes, or T codes:

- ✔ **T0:** Zero-rated; VAT isn't payable on zero-rated supplies. Examples include books, children's clothes and certain items of food.
- ✔ **T1:** Standard rate; currently 20 per cent.
- ✔ **T2:** Exempt from VAT. For example, postage stamps.
- ✔ **T4:** Sales to customers in the European Union (EU).
- ✔ **T5:** Lower-rate VAT, usually 5 per cent. For example, this rate applies to the purchase of energy-saving materials and reclaiming VAT on DIY building work.
- ✔ **T7:** Zero-rated purchases from suppliers in the EU.
- ✔ **T8:** Standard-rated purchases from suppliers in the EU.
- ✔ **T9:** Transactions not involving VAT. For example, wages.

For unexplained reasons, Sage doesn't use T3 or T6, but you have eight other codes to use.

Comparing Sage's VAT accounting methods

Sage supports three types of VAT schemes: the standard VAT accounting scheme, VAT cash accounting and, more recently, the flat rate VAT scheme. HMRC provides helpful information about the VAT schemes available on its website; if you want to find out more, go to www.hmrc.gov.uk.

Set up your accounting method before you enter any transactions onto Sage. The Active Setup wizard I talk about in Chapter 1 includes the accounting method as one of its steps. If you're not sure which method you chose, click Settings➪Company Preferences and then click the VAT tab. In the VAT Details box, you can find the VAT scheme that you selected. Use the drop-down arrow to view the other VAT schemes available for you to use (see Figure 13-1). The next sections explain the three methods.

Figure 13-1:
Checking
your VAT
scheme.

Setting the standard scheme

In the standard VAT scheme, Sage calculates the amount of VAT based on when an invoice is issued. Therefore, as you raise each invoice, you're liable to pay the VAT on it when your next VAT return is due. However, you can reclaim the VAT on invoices sent to you from your suppliers, regardless of whether you've paid them or not.

Considering cash accounting

VAT cash accounting calculates the VAT based on when your customer pays an invoice and when you pay your supplier. You benefit if your customers are slow to pay, as you don't need to pay the VAT until they pay you.

Figuring out the flat rate VAT scheme

The flat rate VAT scheme allows you to pay VAT as a fixed percentage of your VAT-inclusive turnover. You don't claim VAT back on any purchases, making it a simple system to operate. The actual percentage you use depends on what type of business you're in.

You can only join the flat rate scheme if your estimated VAT taxable turnover (excluding VAT) in the next year is £150,000 or less. You can then stay on the scheme until your business income is more than £230,000.

Sage enables you to set up both invoice and cash-based flat VAT rate schemes.

Running the VAT Return

Running a VAT return in Sage is remarkably easy, *but* – and it's a big but – you have to check your VAT return before you send it in.

To access the VAT ledger, from Company, click Manage VAT from the Task pane. You can see the VAT Return icon here; this ledger provides you with both detailed and summary reports of the VAT on both sales and purchases, and calculates what you owe to HMRC or how much you're due to be refunded.

Sage also includes within the VAT ledger icons to help you submit returns, produce EC Sales Lists, produce a Reverse Charge sales list, run VAT reports and view submission receipts to the HMRC.

When working out your VAT, an appreciation of what items VAT is charged on and what types of items you can reclaim VAT on helps. If you're unsure, contact your accountant or HMRC for help.

I find keeping a checklist of all the things that need to be done prior to and during a VAT return helpful to focus my mind on the job in hand. Table 13-1 shows the checklist I use. Feel free to copy this checklist and use it yourself. Place a tick in the empty column as you accomplish each task.

Table 13-1	VAT Return Checklist
Task	*Accomplished*
Post scale charges if you have company cars.	
Calculate and print the VAT return for the appropriate quarter.	
Check the VAT return:	
Print the Detailed VAT report.	
Print the Nominal Transaction report for Sales and Purchase Tax control account.	
Make sure that the preceding reports are for the same quarter as the VAT return.	
If you use VAT cash accounting, print the necessary nominal, cash and bank daybook reports.	
Make any adjustments to your VAT return, as necessary.	
Reconcile your VAT transactions.	
Enter the details onto your hard copy of the VAT return or submit your VAT return online.	
Clear down your VAT control accounts.	
Make VAT payment/refund	

The sections throughout this chapter explain each task in the checklist.

Calculating your VAT

Before you start figuring out your VAT return, make sure that your books are up to date for that period. So, enter all sales invoices and purchase invoices and all receipts and payments, and reconcile all the bank accounts and credit card accounts to ensure that you've accounted for all elements of VAT.

The first step of running your VAT return is to calculate the amount owing or owed. The calculation is easy to do; just follow these steps:

1. **From Company, click Manage VAT in the Task pane to open up the VAT window.**

   Alternatively, you can click Financials from the Company Links list and then click VAT from the Financials screen.

2. **Click the VAT Return icon.**

   The VAT form opens up. This form looks like the manual VAT return that you get from HMRC.

3. **Enter the period that the VAT return relates to.**

   For example, 01.04.13 to 30.06.13.

4. **Click Calculate.**

   Sage tells you how many transactions it found for this VAT return, as well as how many transactions are dated before the specified period but haven't been reconciled. You can choose whether you want to include them or not. If you choose not to include them, they remain as unreconciled items in the audit trail and appear again when you do your next VAT return.

5. **Click OK to continue.**

   As soon as you click OK, the VAT Return fills with figures, and you can see how much Sage thinks you owe HMRC or vice versa.

Figure 13-2 shows a VAT return for Jingles. Sage calculates that Jingles owes £76.80.

VAT Return - NEW		
Jingles Ltd	For the period	01/04/2013
	to	30/06/2013
VAT due in this period on sales	1	151.80
VAT due in this period on EC acquisitions	2	0.00
Total VAT due (sum of boxes 1 and 2)	3	151.80
VAT reclaimed in this period on purchases	4	75.00
Net VAT to be paid to Customs or reclaimed by you	5	76.80
Total value of sales, excluding VAT	6	759.00
Total value of purchases, excluding VAT	7	375.00
Total value of EC sales, excluding VAT	8	0.00
Total value of EC purchases, excluding VAT	9	0.00
Calculate Adjustments Reconcile... Print Clear ☐ Include Reconciled		Close

Figure 13-2:
A standard VAT return for Jingles.

Checking Your VAT Return

You may think that the job is done after Sage calculates your VAT. However, the information is only as good as the person who entered it, so you need to check it against the information held in the nominal ledger. The checks are different depending on which VAT scheme you operate. I look at each scheme in turn and examine which reports you need to check to ensure the accuracy of your return.

Checking under the standard scheme

Your Sales Tax and Purchase Tax control accounts must agree with the boxes on the VAT return. To make sure that they do, print the VAT return, a detailed VAT report and the Nominal Activity report for both the Sales Tax control account and the Purchase Tax control account. These documents identify all elements of VAT on sales and purchases. Make sure that the Nominal Activity report is run for the same quarter period as the VAT return.

Printing out the VAT return and a detailed report

The main screen of the VAT return is the place to go to print VAT reports. Just click Print and a VAT Return Report window opens. Tick both the VAT Return and Detailed boxes and then click Run. Sage previews both reports on the screen, one behind the other. The screen behind the VAT return has a white background and has lost the green colour – don't worry, this change is normal. Print a copy of both reports.

The detailed VAT report provides a breakdown of all the transactions behind each number on the VAT return. And, if you use the VAT standard accounting scheme, the detailed VAT report shows each sales invoice and credit note, and every purchase invoice and credit note.

Sage groups the transactions on the report according to the box they belong in on the VAT return. For example, you can see each individual transaction contained within VAT box 1.

Getting a hard copy of the Nominal Activity report

You need to check that the net value of the Sales Tax control account and Purchase Tax control account on the Nominal Activity report agree with box 5 of the VAT return. To check, print the nominal activity for codes 2200 and 2201, the Sales Tax control account and the Purchase Tax control account.

If the net value of the tax control accounts doesn't agree with box 5, do the following checks:

✔ Make sure that you selected the same dates for the Nominal Activity report as you have for the VAT return. That way, you select data for the same period and it should agree, unless you've said Yes to any unreconciled items from a previous quarter.

✔ Check whether the VAT control accounts include any totals for tax codes that aren't included in your VAT return. For example, T9 by default isn't included in your VAT return.

✔ Check that your Clear Down journals have been correctly posted from the previous quarter. If you've used the VAT transfer button within the VAT Tasks window, Sage automatically posts the correct journals for you.

✔ See whether any journals were posted to the VAT control ledgers. Journals don't normally need to be posted to the control accounts, so if they are, you need to fix that error.

✔ Check the audit trail. You can check which items have already been reconciled by looking for *R* for reconciled in the V (VAT) column. Those with an *N* in the column haven't been reconciled and need checking as part of the current VAT return.

✔ If you still can't find the discrepancy, print the Customer daybook reports and the Supplier daybook reports and manually tick off each item to the tax control accounts. This last-resort check can be extremely time-consuming, but it does usually work.

✔ If you still have a discrepancy after all these checks, print the daybooks for your bank, cash, credit receipts and payments, and check these reports to find the error.

Checking with cash accounting

If you're operating the VAT cash accounting system and working from a cash-based system instead of an invoice-based one, you need to print several reports. First, print your detailed VAT report as described in the 'Printing out the VAT return and a detailed report' section earlier in this chapter. Then follow these steps:

1. **From the Navigation bar, click Company⇨Financials from the Links list.**

   The Financials window opens.

2. **Click the Audit Trail icon and select Detailed. Click Run.**

   The Criteria box opens.

3. **Select the same quarter period as your VAT return and then click OK.**

   Your report appears in Preview format. Click Print to obtain a hard copy.

4. **Make sure that you use the same date range as your VAT return to print nominal reports.**

On the couch: Analysing your VAT return

After you calculate your VAT return, you can analyse it.

If you look at your green stripy VAT return, you can see the numbers 1 to 9. Each number represents a line on the VAT return. By clicking each box with a pound value in it, you can drill down the VAT return and obtain a breakdown of all entries made to each tax code, indicating whether each entry is a sales invoice, credit note,

journal, receipt or payment. You can also see any manual adjustments that have been made.

If you want even more detail, you can double-click any of the numbers on the VAT Breakdown screen and view all the transactions that make up that total. You can click Print List to obtain a detailed VAT breakdown. Click Close to return to the VAT Breakdown screen and Close again to exit the screen.

The reports you print are:

- **Nominal Ledger Daybook reports:** From the Navigation bar, click Company, click the Reports icon and double-click Daybook Reports. Select Day Book: Nominal Ledger and the Criteria Value box opens. Select the same dates as your VAT quarter and click OK.

- **Customer Receipts and all other daybook reports:** Print these reports from Bank reports; they're all bank and cash accounts. (If you're using the Republic of Ireland VAT accounting scheme, you don't need to print the Supplier Payments report.)

- **Supplier Payments and all other Daybook reports:** Print these reports from Bank reports.

5. **Make sure that your VAT return is correct by checking it against all the reports you print in Steps 2, 3 and 4.**

Making Manual Adjustments to Your VAT Return

Sometimes you miss something from your VAT return from a previous quarter and you need to make an adjustment. In the past, you had to get your pen and calculator out and make an adjustment on the face of your VAT return prior to sending it to HMRC, but now you can do it within Sage. Just follow these steps:

1. **From the VAT Return window, click Adjustments.**

   The VAT Manual Adjustments screen opens, as shown in Figure 13-3.

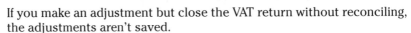

VAT Manual Adjustments

To adjust the box values, follow the link alongside the existing adjustment value, or press F3:

Box	Description	Calculated (£)	Adjustment (£)	Reported (£)
1	VAT due in this period on sales	151.80	0.00	151.80
2	VAT due in this period on EC acquisitions	0.00	0.00	0.00
3	Total VAT due (sum of boxes 1 and 2)	151.80	0.00	151.80
4	VAT reclaimed in this period on purchases	75.00	0.00	75.00
5	Net VAT to be paid to Customs or reclaimed by you	76.80	0.00	76.80
6	Total value of sales, excluding VAT	759.00	0.00	759.00
7	Total value of purchases, excluding VAT	375.00	0.00	375.00
8	Total value of EC sales, excluding VAT	0.00	0.00	0.00
9	Total value of EC purchases, excluding VAT	0.00	0.00	0.00

Close

Figure 13-3:
Making manual adjustments on your VAT return.

2. **Click the grey arrow in the Adjustments column, and, in the screen that appears, enter text describing why you're making the adjustment.**

   For example, your notation may be something like, 'prior quarter adjustment'.

3. **Click Save.**

   You return to the previous summary screen, where you can now see your adjustment.

4. **Click Close.**

   The VAT Return screen appears. The total amount owed to HMRC has now been revised for the manual adjustment that you just made. Sage posts the manual adjustments to the nominal default code 2204.

   If you make an adjustment but close the VAT return without reconciling, the adjustments aren't saved.

5. **Click Close again to return to the Financials screen.**

Reconciling Your VAT Transactions

After you're happy with the information in your VAT return, you need to flag each individual transaction for VAT so that an 'R' appears in the VAT column of the audit trail and it doesn't appear again in future returns, unless you ask to include previously reconciled transactions. This process is known as *reconciling your VAT return*.

To do the reconciliation, you must first calculate the VAT return for the correct VAT quarter. When you can view the VAT Return screen, click Reconcile. A confirmation message appears, asking whether you want to flag the transactions for VAT. Click Yes. Sage then processes the VAT return and then the VAT Tasks window opens, as shown in Figure 13-4.

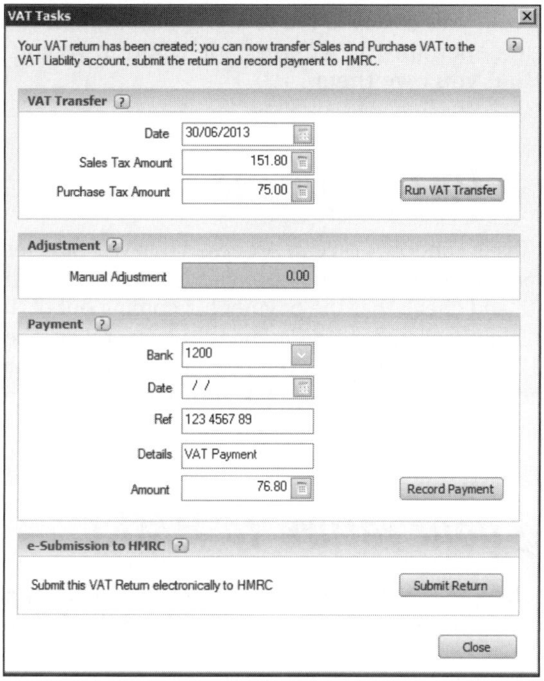

Figure 13-4:
The VAT
Tasks
window.

The VAT Tasks window makes it really easy to do the VAT housekeeping chores when the VAT return has been completed. The first task is to complete the VAT transfer.

VAT Transfer

This process is sometimes known as 'clearing down your VAT'.

If you're wondering what on earth *clearing* is all about, don't worry as clearing is quite straightforward. Essentially, clearing is transferring the values from your Sales Tax and Purchase Tax control accounts to your VAT Liability account.

The balance created in your VAT Liability account should agree with the amount due to HMRC, or, in the case of a reclaim, it should equate to the refund due.

After you make the VAT payment or refund (and post it to the VAT Liability account), the balance on the Liability account becomes zero.

Luckily Sage makes this process really easy. All you need to do is click the Run VAT Transfer button. When clicked, a big green tick appears against the VAT Transfer box.

From the same screen, you can also make a VAT adjustment or make a VAT payment or receipt, depending on whether the HMRC owe you, or in the more likely event that you owe them!

Recording a VAT payment

Still within the VAT Tasks window, you can process your VAT payment. Sage has helpfully pre-filled some of the reference boxes for you, so all that's left is to complete the date and check that the payment is coming out of the correct bank account. Then simply click Record Payment button and another green tick with the word Paid appears. Sage posts the payment automatically for you and you can see the transaction if you check your Financials page within the Company module.

Submitting your return to HMRC

Finally, still within the VAT Tasks window, you can electronically submit your VAT return (provided that you've set up Sage to submit the return).

When you've completed all your VAT Tasks, you can close the window, where you'll be taken back to the VAT main screen. Here you can now see that a line has appeared on the screen detailing the VAT return that you've just completed.

You can view a saved return by highlighting the one you want to view from the VAT ledger and clicking View. If you want to, you can delete the VAT return from Sage by highlighting the return and clicking Delete. However, you more than likely want to keep a copy of your VAT return on Sage. I recommend that you keep a hard copy of all your VAT returns and put them somewhere safe.

You should keep hold of your VAT returns for at least six years, in case of possible VAT inspection.

From April 2012, all VAT-registered businesses (with the exception of a small minority) have to submit their VAT return online. The exceptions to submitting your VAT Return online, are if you are subject to an insolvency procedure or if HMRC is satisfied that your business is run by practising members of a religion whose beliefs prevent them from using computers.

You must also pay electronically, and this change works in your favour as you actually get seven extra calendar days to pay your VAT liability.

Sending your VAT submission later

Assuming that you don't want to send your VAT Return straight away, you can wait until you're ready and then follow these steps:

1. **From the VAT Ledger screen, highlight the VAT return you want to send.**

   The return's status must be pending or partial.

2. **Click Submit Return.**

Assuming that your VAT preferences and eSubmissions credentials are set up correctly, the Sage Internet Submissions wizard guides you through the process.

You must have a Government Gateway account to make e-VAT payments. Go to www.hmrc.gov.uk for details on how to obtain one.

You must also enable e-VAT submissions on your VAT preference settings. To do so, click Settings⇨Company Preferences⇨VAT tab and complete your eSubmissions credentials and contact details.

Alternatively, if you'd prefer to submit your VAT return manually via the HMRC website, go to section 'Submitting your VAT return manually via HMRC'.

Submitting your VAT return manually via HMRC

This method of VAT submission requires printing out all your reports so that you can enter them into the HMRC system.

1. **From the VAT ledger, highlight the VAT return you want to submit and click View.**

   The VAT return opens up.

2. **Print the VAT return and keep a hard copy in your file.**

   Your VAT return is archived after you've reconciled, so you also have an electronic copy.

3. **Access the HMRC website (`www.hmrc.gov.uk`) and click the Online services button.** Using the login details you were given when you registered to use the Online services, access the VAT Return service.

4. **Submit the figures from the VAT report in Sage into the relevant boxes on the HMRC website.** Follow the online instructions to submit your VAT return, and print out a copy of the confirmation that the VAT return has been submitted. File this confirmation with your hard copy of the VAT Return.

   If the value in box 5 is negative, then you have a VAT reclaim, and HMRC actually owes you money! If the figure is positive, this amount is what you owe the HMRC.

Part IV
Using Reports

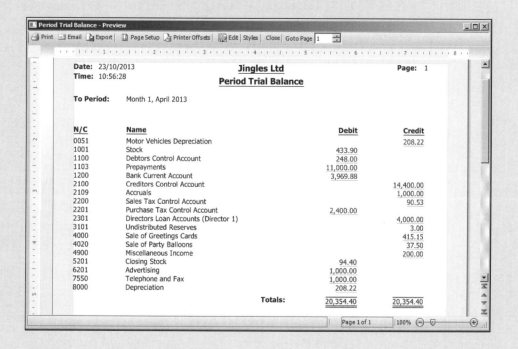

In this part . . .

✔ Get the most out of the reports run on Sage Instant Accounts and read up on which ones are most useful - particularly at month end.

✔ Easily track your finances by making use of the Profit and Loss Report, the Balance Sheet, the Trial Balance and Prior Year and Budget reports.

✔ Transfer data to your accountant the quick way by exporting data to spreadsheets and using the Accountant Link facility.

Chapter 14

Running Monthly Reports

In This Chapter

▶ Using the Sage standard reports

▶ Using the Chart of Accounts to check report layouts

▶ Running a Trial Balance

▶ Creating a Profit and Loss account

▶ Printing your Balance Sheet

▶ Viewing the audit trail

▶ Writing and designing your own reports

*T*his chapter concentrates on the reports that you can produce at the end of the monthly accounting procedure. I assume that you've run the month-end procedure and processed all the necessary journals, as I tell you how to do in Chapter 12. Now you need to provide meaningful information to the managers of the business. The reports must be easy to understand and use headings that are meaningful to the business.

Running reports is an opportunity to see how well your business is progressing: if the business is meeting set targets, if you're bringing in as much revenue as you'd projected and how actual costs compare to the budgeted or forecasted expenditures.

Making the Most of Standard Reports

Whenever possible, use the standard reports provided by Sage, as they're simple to run and provide most of the information you need.

Each ledger contains its own reports. For example, you go to Customer and then Reports to see the Aged Debtors or Customer Activity reports, or you go to Bank and then Reports to see copies of un-presented cheques. The

Financials module houses the Profit and Loss report and Balance Sheet – the key financial reports that tell you how the business is doing. You find these reports by clicking Company and then Financials (on the Links list), and then selecting the appropriate icon on the Financials screen. You can find more information about these reports and how to run them later in this chapter.

Whenever you select a report, you're given five choices of what to do with the data:

- ✔ **Preview:** This choice gives you the opportunity to preview the layout of the report on the screen, and you can check that it's providing you with the information you require. You can then print, export or email from this screen.

- ✔ **Print:** You can print a hard copy of the report straightaway without previewing.

- ✔ **Export:** You can save the file in a different format, such as PDF or CSV, as well as a variation of other file types.

- ✔ **Export to Excel:** This choice sends the contents of the report into an Excel document, which you can save and amend as necessary.

- ✔ **Email:** Depending on how your email system is configured, you can send the report as an attachment or link to your email software and send the report directly.

Usually at a month-end or year-end, the accountant prepares a set of management reports to present to the owners and managers of the business. I explain these reports in upcoming sections.

Checking the Chart of Accounts First

You must check the Chart of Accounts (COA) for errors before you run financial reports because errors in the COA can affect the accuracy of the reports. (Refer to Chapter 2 for more information on the COA.) If you try to run a Balance Sheet without checking, you're likely to get a message stating that errors exist in the COA and that the reports may be inaccurate as a result. And no one likes being told they're wrong by a machine!

To check the COA for errors, click the Chart of Accounts icon from the Company module, highlight the COA you want to check, click Edit and then click the Check box. If no errors exist, Sage advises you of this fact. If you have errors, Sage allows you to print or preview them.

Figuring Out the Financial Reports

The reports that give you a view of the business-end of your business are the Trial Balance, Profit and Loss and Balance Sheet reports. You generally run each report at the end of the accounting period, whether that's every month, every quarter or annually. I cover each report in the following sections.

Trying for an initial Trial Balance

This report doesn't show up in a pretty layout – it's basically a list of numbers in nominal code order, and numbers are rarely lovely to look at – but the Trial Balance forms the basis of your Profit and Loss and Balance Sheet reports, so it's important.

In this report, you see a list of all debit or credit balances in nominal code order for the period you specify – you have to specify a month, and Sage presents the balance at that time. The report only shows nominal codes that have a balance, so any codes with a zero balance don't make the list. As the example in Figure 14-1 shows, the debits and credits are in separate columns with totals at the bottom of each. Because of the double-entry bookkeeping principles (mandating a debit for every credit), the two columns balance.

Figure 14-1: Jingles' Trial Balance for the period ended April 2013.

The following reproduces the report window shown in Figure 14-1:

Period Trial Balance - Preview

Print Email Export Page Setup Printer Offsets Edit Styles Close Goto Page 1

Date: 23/10/2013 **Jingles Ltd** **Page:** 1
Time: 10:56:28 **Period Trial Balance**

To Period: Month 1, April 2013

N/C	Name	Debit	Credit
0051	Motor Vehicles Depreciation		208.22
1001	Stock	433.90	
1100	Debtors Control Account	248.00	
1103	Prepayments	11,000.00	
1200	Bank Current Account	3,969.88	
2100	Creditors Control Account		14,400.00
2109	Accruals		1,000.00
2200	Sales Tax Control Account		90.53
2201	Purchase Tax Control Account	2,400.00	
2301	Directors Loan Accounts (Director 1)		4,000.00
3101	Undistributed Reserves		3.00
4000	Sale of Greetings Cards		415.15
4020	Sale of Party Balloons		37.50
4900	Miscellaneous Income		200.00
5201	Closing Stock	94.40	
6201	Advertising	1,000.00	
7550	Telephone and Fax	1,000.00	
8000	Depreciation	208.22	
	Totals:	**20,354.40**	**20,354.40**

Page 1 of 1   100%

Jingles is still quite a new company and doesn't have many transactions yet, nor does it use many nominal codes. As business increases, the number of codes – and hence the Trial Balance – increases in length.

In a Trial Balance, you can see at a glance the extent of your assets and liabilities and use it as an investigative tool. For example, if something seems out of whack, you can run more detailed reports to see where the numbers came from. Each of the numbers in the Trial Balance can be further drilled down, so if you want to look at the detail behind any of the figures, simply click on the number and Sage takes you to the Nominal Activity for that nominal code. You can see exactly which transactions make up that number.

To run a Trial Balance, follow these steps:

1. **From Company, click Financials from the Links list.**

   The Financials window opens.

   Alternatively, from the Menu bar, click Modules and then Financials.

2. **Click the Trial Balance icon.**

   The Print Output box opens.

3. **Select Preview and then click Run.**

   The Criteria box opens.

4. **Use the drop-down arrow to select the period that you want to view.**

   In the example in Figure 14-1, I use April 2013.

5. **Click OK.**

   The Trial Balance report appears.

6. **Click Print, Email or Export to send the report to the destination of your choice.**

7. **Click Close to exit the report and return to the Financials window.**

Accounting for profit and loss

Owners and directors of businesses really like the Profit and Loss report (or at least they should do) because it shows them whether they're making any money! The Profit and Loss report shows the total revenue (sales) that your company has made in the specified period and then deducts both direct costs and overheads for that same period to arrive at a profit or loss for the period.

The layout of the Profit and Loss report is a standard format, but you can use the COA function to rename headings and group together your nominal codes so that the Profit and Loss report appears with terminology suited to your business. (Refer to Chapter 2 to see how to edit your COA.)

To run your Profit and Loss report, follow these steps:

1. **From Company, click Financials from the Links list and then Profit and Loss.**

2. **Select the Print Output that you want and then click Run.**

   You have a choice to print, preview, send to a file or email. Previewing first is wise, so that you can see whether you're happy with the report criteria you chose.

   The Criteria box opens.

3. **Select the period for which you want to run the report by filling in the From and To dates.**

4. **Select the COA layout you want, using the drop-down arrow to select a COA layout other than the default. Then click OK.**

   Refer to Chapter 2 for information on adding new COA layouts.

   The Profit and Loss report appears. This report is split into two columns, one showing the current period and the other showing the year-to-date (YTD).

   Be aware that if you select a full year as your From and To dates, you end up with both columns showing the same figures. If you choose a single month (for example, April) in the criteria, the Period column then differentiates the current period (April) from the YTD figures. Of course, the numbers for the first month of the year and the YTD numbers are the same!

5. **Choose to Print, Email or Export the report.**

   Perhaps your bank manager would appreciate timely receipt of monthly accounts via email!

In Figure 14-2, I selected the period from April 2013 to 30 April 2013. This date range represents the first month of trading, and goes some way to explaining why the business made a loss; all down to low sales and large advertising and telephone costs. You can also see that the Period and YTD columns contain the same data. As the year progresses, these figures cease to be the same and you'll see useful data appearing.

Date: 23/10/2013	Jingles Ltd	Page: 1
Time: 10:58:27	**Profit and Loss**	

From: Month 1, April 2013
To: Month 1, April 2013

Chart of Accounts: Default Layout of Accounts

	Period		Year to Date	
Sales				
Shop Sales	452.65		452.65	
Other Sales	200.00		200.00	
		652.65		652.65
Purchases				
Stock	94.40		94.40	
		94.40		94.40
Direct Expenses				
Sales Promotion	1,000.00		1,000.00	
		1,000.00		1,000.00
Gross Profit/(Loss):		(441.75)		(441.75)
Overheads				
Telephone and Computer charges	1,000.00		1,000.00	
Depreciation	208.22		208.22	
		1,208.22		1,208.22
Net Profit/(Loss):		(1,649.97)		(1,649.97)

Figure 14-2:
A Profit and Loss report for Jingles.

Comparing profit and loss

Sometimes, you require additional analysis from your reporting and the Comparative Profit and Loss report provides just that! With this report, you can choose to compare your current month values against budget and prior year data or both. You can also choose to include percentage variations too. The report shows current period values and also YTD values, so you've lot of information to digest.

To run the report:

1. **From Company, click Financials from the Links list and then Comparative Profit and Loss.**

2. **Select the Print Output that you want and then click Run.**

3. **The Criteria box opens.**

  - Select the period for which you want to run the report by filling in the From and To dates.

  - Using the drop-down arrows, select the appropriate COA.

  - You'll also notice that there's a Budget line and a Prior Year Values line. Click the drop-down arrow to determine whether you should show, not show, show as a variance or show as a variance with a percentage. Choose whatever variables you need, but be aware that if you choose them all, the report becomes more difficult to read!

4. **Finally, when you've made all your selections, click OK and the report generates in a preview format.** You then have the opportunity to adjust the variables if you're not happy or continue to print, export or email the document as you see fit. You can have a look at Figure 14-3 to see that Jeanette has printed out the Comparative Profit and Loss report for the month of April 2013, and has chosen to compare against budget but not prior year periods. Choosing not to show the Prior Year period figures (which in her case are nil anyway) has meant that the report is much easier to read, as fewer columns are displayed.

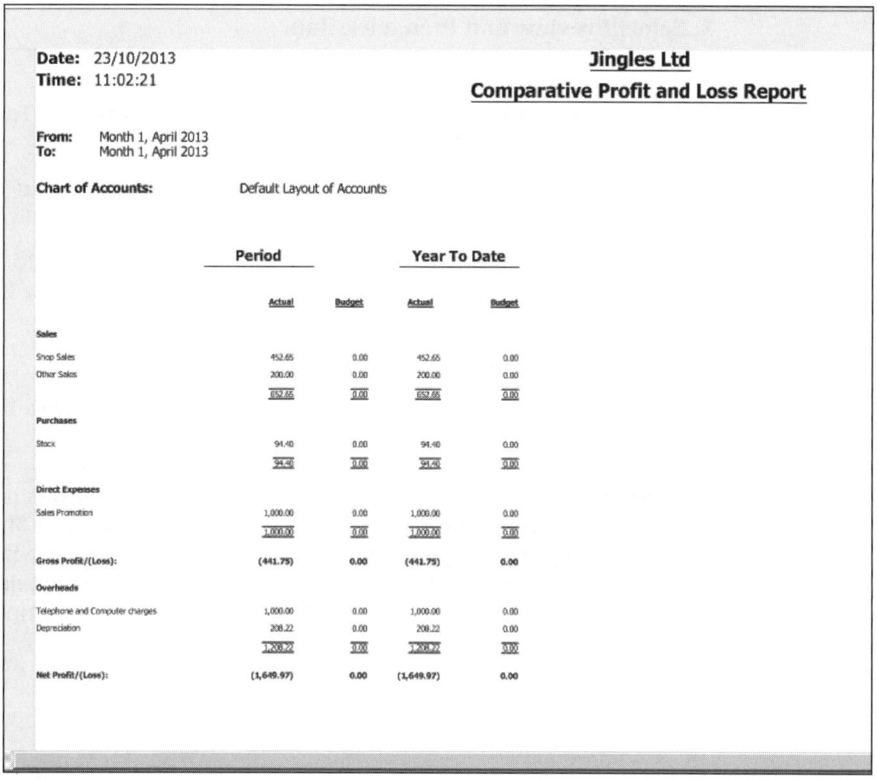

Figure 14-3: Comparative Profit and Loss Report.

Weighing the Balance Sheet

A Balance Sheet is a really useful tool for establishing the financial position of a company because it provides a snapshot of the business at a point in time. The Balance Sheet shows the assets and liabilities and the sources of funds that helped finance the business. From a Balance Sheet, you can see how much money is owed to the business and how much the business owes.

The Balance Sheet forms part of the management accounts of the business and is traditionally issued at the month-end, quarter-end and year-end. Some people prefer to issue just one set of accounts at the year-end, but others prefer a more regular source of information and require monthly accounts.

Follow these steps to run a Balance Sheet:

1. **From Company, click Financials from the Links list.**

   Alternatively, click Modules and then Financials from the Menu bar.

2. **Click Balance Sheet to open the Print Output box.**

3. **Select Preview and then click Run.**

   The Criteria box opens up.

4. **Use the drop-down arrow to select the period From and To that you want to view.**

   If you've more than one COA layout, select the one that you want to preview. Refer to Chapter 2 for details on setting up additional COA.

   The Jingles example in Figure 14-4 uses the period 1 April to 30 April 2013 to demonstrate the Balance Sheet layout. Because the first month has been selected, both columns show the same data.

5. **Click OK to open up the Balance Sheet.**

   As in the Profit and Loss report, the Balance Sheet shows a Period column and a YTD column.

Make sure that you understand the component parts of the Balance Sheet. For example, can you match your debtors figure in the Balance Sheet to an Aged Debtors report? Do you understand what transactions are included in the accruals and prepayments? You can check all figures by looking at your COA and determining which nominal codes represent each section of the

```
 ' ' ' I ' ' ' I ' ' 1 ' ' ' I ' ' ' 2 ' ' I ' ' ' 3 ' ' I ' ' ' 4 ' ' I ' ' ' 5 ' ' I ' ' ' 6 ' ' I ' ' ' 7 ' ' I ' ' ' 8 '
```

Date: 23/10/2013	Jingles Ltd		Page: 1
Time: 11:10:18	Balance Sheet		

From: Month 1, April 2013
To: Month 1, April 2013

Chart of Accounts: Default Layout of Accounts

	Period		Year to Date	
Fixed Assets				
Motor Vehicles	(208.22)		(208.22)	
		(208.22)		(208.22)
Current Assets				
Stock	(94.40)		433.90	
Debtors	48.00		248.00	
Prepayments	11,000.00		11,000.00	
Bank Account	2,498.18		3,969.88	
VAT Liability	2,309.47		2,309.47	
		15,761.25		17,961.25
Current Liabilities				
Creditors : Short Term	14,203.00		14,400.00	
Accruals	1,000.00		1,000.00	
		15,203.00		15,400.00
Current Assets less Current Liabilities:		558.25		2,561.25
Total Assets less Current Liabilities:		350.03		2,353.03
Long Term Liabilities				
Creditors : Long Term	2,000.00		4,000.00	
		2,000.00		4,000.00
Total Assets less Total Liabilities:		(1,649.97)		(1,646.97)
Capital & Reserves				
Reserves	0.00		3.00	
P & L Account	(1,649.97)		(1,649.97)	
		(1,649.97)		(1,646.97)

Figure 14-4:
Balance
Sheet for
Jingles as
at 30 April
2013.

Balance Sheet. You can review any of the numbers, by clicking directly on the number in the Balance Sheet and Sage provides details of the transactions behind those numbers using a Nominal Activity report.

Viewing the Audit Trail

The *audit trail* is a list of all the transactions that have ever occurred in Sage, including those subsequently deleted. So when you make a complete mess of something, rest assured that you can never escape it. The mess is there for all to see – even your accountant and the auditor, who may use it at year-end!

Sage lists the transactions in the audit trail chronologically and each has a unique transaction number. This number is used alongside a search tool to find a particular transaction, which is useful if you need to correct a specific transaction.

You can clear the audit trail periodically to remove the details of the transactions, but the balances are kept and carried forward so that the accounts remain accurate. You can find an explanation of this routine in Chapter 12. However, Sage has the capacity to hold 2 billion transactions in the audit trail, so you don't actually ever have to clear it down if you don't want to.

You access the audit trail through the Financials module. You can click the Audit icon to explore further. The Audit reports are available in brief, summary, detailed and deleted transactions. The first three reports show the transactions in varying levels of detail; the last shows exactly what it says – transactions you deleted from the system. The report lists a line per transaction, so if you've thousands of transactions, the whole report can be extremely long!

To run the audit trail, follow these steps:

1. **From Company, click Financials and then the Audit Trail icon.**

   The Audit Trail report window opens.

2. **Enter your choice of audit report – brief, summary, detailed or deleted transactions. Then choose the method of output and click Run.**

   The Criteria box opens.

3. **Choose the criteria required for this report.**

   Sage recommends that you run this report on a monthly basis, so enter the current month dates.

4. **Click OK to generate the report.**

   If you choose to preview the report, providing you're happy with the way it looks, you can print, export or email it from this screen.

5. **Click Close to exit the report and return to the Financials screen.**

You usually print off the audit trail at the end of each period, and it provides a hard copy of all business transactions. Often, businesses tend to print it at the year-end to provide a copy for the auditors, but how regularly you decide to print it is up to you; obviously the longer the period, the longer the report.

Figure 14-5 shows an extract from a brief Audit Trail report for Jingles.

Date:	23/10/2013				**Jingles Ltd**			Page:	1
Time:	11:15:21				**Audit Trail (Brief)**				

Date From:		01/01/1980				Customer From:		
Date To:		30/04/2013				Customer To:		ZZZZZZZ

Transaction		1				Supplier From:		
Transaction To:		99,999,99				Supplier To:		ZZZZZZZ

Exclude Deleted Tran: No

No	Items	Type	A/C	Date	Ref	Details	Net	Tax	Gross
1	1	SI	ANYTOW	31/03/2013	O/Bal	Opening Balance	200.00	0.00	200.00
2	1	PI	DAGENHA	31/03/2013	O/Bal	Opening Balance	197.00	0.00	197.00
3	1	JC	1100	31/03/2013	O/Bal	Opening Balance	200.00	0.00	200.00
4	1	JD	9998	31/03/2013	O/Bal	Opening Balance	3.00	0.00	3.00
5	1	JD	2100	31/03/2013	O/Bal	Opening Balance	197.00	0.00	197.00
6	1	SI	PETE	21/04/2013	1	Happy Birthday	40.00	8.00	48.00
35	1	JD	1001	31/03/2013	O/Bal	Opening balance	528.30	0.00	528.30
36	1	JD	1100	31/03/2013	O/Bal	Opening balance	200.00	0.00	200.00
37	1	JD	1200	31/03/2013	O/Bal	Opening balance	1,471.70	0.00	1,471.70
38	1	JC	2100	31/03/2013	O/Bal	Opening balance	197.00	0.00	197.00
39	1	JC	3101	31/03/2013	O/Bal	Opening balance	3.00	0.00	3.00
40	1	JC	2301	31/03/2013	O/Bal	Opening balance	2,000.00	0.00	2,000.00
41	5	SI	CASHSALE	07/04/2013	3	50th Anniversary	111.25	22.25	133.50
46	1	SR	CASHSALE	07/04/2013	CSALE - 3	Cash Sale	133.50	0.00	133.50
47	4	SI	CASHSALE	14/04/2013	4	50th Anniversary	133.00	26.60	159.60
51	1	SR	CASHSALE	14/04/2013	CSALE - 4	Cash Sale	159.60	0.00	159.60
52	2	SI	CASHSALE	21/04/2013	5	50th Anniversary	76.65	15.33	91.98
54	1	SR	CASHSALE	21/04/2013	CSALE - 5	Cash Sale	91.98	0.00	91.98
55	2	SI	CASHSALE	30/04/2013	6	50th Anniversary	91.75	18.35	110.10
57	1	SR	CASHSALE	30/04/2013	CSALE - 6	Cash Sale	110.10	0.00	110.10
58	1	JD	5201	30/04/2013	April	Closing Stock at	528.30	0.00	528.30
59	1	JD	1001	30/04/2013	April	Closing Stock at	528.30	0.00	528.30
60	1	JC	5201	30/04/2013	April	Closing Stock at	433.90	0.00	433.90
61	1	JD	1001	30/04/2013	April	Closing Stock at	433.90	0.00	433.90

Figure 14-5:
An extract
from the
Audit Trail
report –
the brief
version.

Designing Reports to Suit Yourself

Sometimes you need to personalise one of the many standard reports that Sage offers. You can change the existing layouts to suit yourself by using Report Designer.

Designing reports is a huge topic, and Sage used to have a separate reference book just to deal with report writing. Here, I just scratch the surface by showing you how to take an existing report and tweak it slightly.

The easiest place to start is by finding a report that almost matches your needs, but not quite. You can take this report, save it under a different file name and then reconfigure it with information that suits your business needs.

To reconfigure a report, follow these steps:

1. **Find the report you want to amend by choosing the report icon from whichever module you require, and preview the report.**

2. **When the report is in preview mode and you can check to ensure that this report is indeed the one that you wish to adapt, click Edit, at the top of the preview screen.** Doing so opens up Report Designer module.

Figure 14-6 shows a Sales Invoice that has been tweaked to show the new Jingle's logo.

Notice the helpful box on the left-hand side, which asks you what you would like to do next.

Jeanette decides that she wants to add a logo to the sales invoice, so she opens her Sales Invoice report from within Customers and then clicks Edit at the top of the screen to open Report Designer. She then clicks the Add an Image or Logo button located at the top of the screen. A cross appears where the cursor is, and Jeanette then draws a box on the face of the invoice, where she'd like the logo to appear. When she has drawn this box, a Choose Your Image box appears. She finds the appropriate file and follows the screen instructions to select her logo image. The image is resized on screen to fit the invoice.

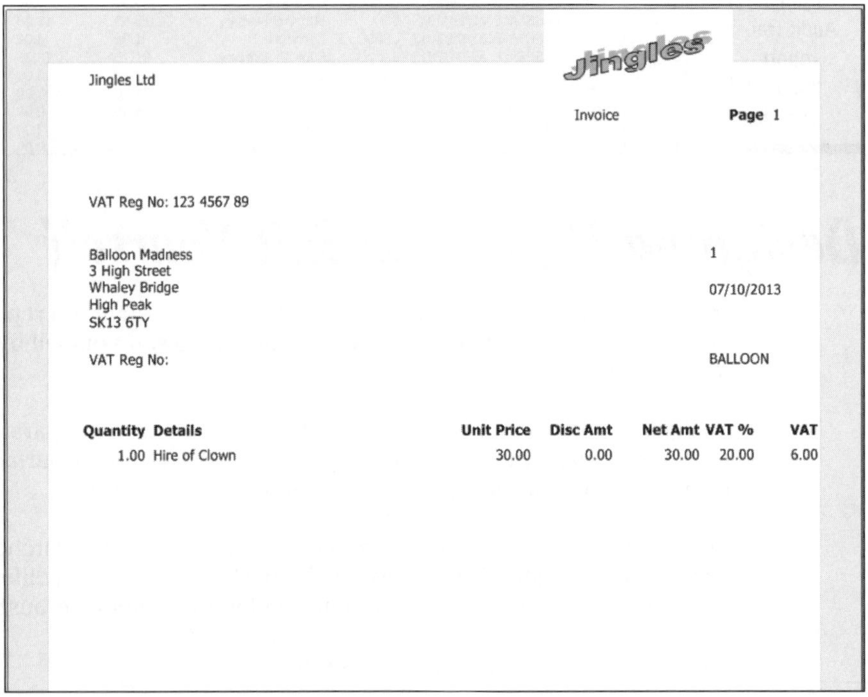

Figure 14-6:
Jeanette has tweaked the existing layout of her Sales Invoices.

Jingles Ltd

Invoice   **Page** 1

VAT Reg No: 123 4567 89

Balloon Madness   1
3 High Street
Whaley Bridge   07/10/2013
High Peak
SK13 6TY

VAT Reg No: BALLOON

Quantity Details	Unit Price	Disc Amt	Net Amt	VAT %	VAT
1.00 Hire of Clown	30.00	0.00	30.00	20.00	6.00

3. **If you want to change something else on the report you've chosen, select the type of change you want to make and follow the online screen instructions.**

   Don't forget you can open the Help menu if you get stuck, or if you have SageCover, you can give them a ring for any help or advice.

4. **When you've made the necessary changes, click File from the Menu bar and then Save as from the drop-down list. Choose an appropriate file to save the document into.**

   Take a note of where Sage saves the report that you've changed to make sure that you can find it again! Make sure that you save it as one of your Favourites as soon as you're happy with the layout.

   Jeanette adds the words 'with logo' against the invoice name, to ensure that she finds her amended version easily.

   A few of the other changes you can make include:

   - **Insert text:** Click **Toolbox⇨Text Box**. Use the mouse to drag and insert a text box in the appropriate part of the screen.

   - **Insert new variables:** Click **View⇨Variables**. A list opens up on the left side of the screen for new variables. You can drag and drop suitable variables into the main body of the report.

   Variables are the different possibilities for categorising something.

   If you press your F1 key while in Report Designer, you access the Report Designer help module, which is useful.

5. **Click Save.**

   You return to the Report Designer screen.

   Just play around with the report format until you find something that you can work with.

6. **Click File from the Menu bar and then click Exit when you're happy with the report design.**

   When you try to print a new report, you'll find your new report on the layouts list of reports. Select it as a new favourite and you can easily access it whenever you want it! See figure 14-6 to see the invoice where Jeanette has added a logo.

You have to be patient and prepared to spend time playing around with the format of your reports. But if you persist, you can come up with some useful and personalised reports. For the lazy among us (myself included), Sage still has plenty of standard reports to use!

Chapter 15

Tackling the Complicated Stuff

. . . .

In This Chapter

▶ Sending data out

▶ Bringing data in

▶ Using the Accountant Link

▶ Banking electronically

. . . .

*W*hen you're confident that you've got to grips with the day-to-day mechanics of the Sage system, you can tackle some of the more advanced options that Sage offers.

The extras I explain in this chapter include the ability to extract data from Sage to Microsoft Excel, Word and Outlook. You can also discover how to relay information to your accountant with minimum disruption to your data and your day-to-day workings with it.

I also look at the impact of using e-Banking to speed up the processing of banking transactions and making electronic payments to suppliers. Becoming competent with any of the techniques discussed in this chapter will make you justifiably proud of yourself – so get to it!

Exporting Data

You can send data from Sage to Microsoft Excel, Word or Outlook, and the next sections tell you how.

Sending spreadsheet stuff

The list of information you can send to Microsoft Excel is too long to provide here, so to find out whether you can extract what you want, press the F1 key and type **file export** into the Help field to get a list of the reports you can extract from each module.

The idea of sending information from Sage to Microsoft Excel is that you can mess about with the data in a spreadsheet to your heart's content without affecting the data held within Sage. You may want to edit the data and design specific reports and what-if scenarios to suit the purposes of your business.

To send information from Sage to Microsoft Excel, from the window you want to export, click File from the main toolbar, then Office Integration, and then Contents to Microsoft Excel.

All the standard reports that you print can be exported to Microsoft Excel. Simply choose the Export to Excel floating icon when you wish to print the report.

Transferring Microsoft Outlook contacts

You can send customer and supplier contact information from Sage Instant Accounts to Microsoft Outlook. This option is an excellent time-saving device, as it means that you don't have to type the information in twice.

The option creates a contact record within Microsoft Outlook for customers and suppliers who have a name entered on their customer or supplier record.

If you've two accounts with the same name, Sage creates two contact records in case the two contacts are two different people; for example, two John Smiths may be listed.

You can also make changes in Sage and then send those changes to Microsoft Outlook with the amended contact details.

To export account information to Outlook, follow these steps:

1. **From the Sage Menu bar, click File⇨Microsoft Integration⇨Microsoft Outlook Import/Export Wizard.**

2. **Select Export Contacts To Outlook.**

   You can choose the other destinations if you prefer.

3. **Follow the instructions on the wizard, clicking Next to continue on to each screen.**

When you've completed the transfer of information, a confirmation message appears, stating that the transfer has been successful. If a different message comes up, follow the advice on the screen. It may be that the folder to which you're trying to send information doesn't allow access, and Sage then suggests alternatives.

The following information can be copied from your customer and supplier records to Microsoft Outlook:

✔ Contact name and address

✔ Telephone and fax number

✔ Website and email address

Exporting to Microsoft Word

You can also send data to Microsoft Word from Sage. You can send information to a new or existing document or even as a mail-merge. For example, you can send a list of customer records to Microsoft Word and mail-merge the contact details with a standard letter from Microsoft Word.

Exporting to Word can be helpful, for example, if you run a sales promotion and want to contact all your customers to make them aware of it. You can produce a leaflet or a letter within Microsoft Word and send the customer contacts from Sage across to Word so that the names and addresses can be merged into your Word document. You save time as you don't have to type in the individual names and addresses for all your customers.

To merge customer contact details with a Microsoft Word document, follow these steps:

1. **From Sage, select the items from which you want to export data and click File from the Menu bar.**

2. **Click Microsoft Integration⇨Contents to Microsoft Word and the option that suits you.**

   Your choices are:

   • **New Document:** You can create a new Microsoft Word document to hold the information extracted from Sage.

   • **Open Document:** You can open an existing Microsoft Word document, for example a promotion letter. You can insert merge boxes, allowing you to personalise the promotion document with the customer details.

   • **Run Mail Merge:** You can use the selected data extracted from Sage in a mail-merged document.

Linking to Your Accountant

How would you like to reduce your accountant's bill? Well, by using Accountant Link within Sage you can, as long as your accountant has access to Sage 50 Client Manager. You can save untold amounts of time for both you and your accountant.

Normally, you employ an accountant to help you with quarterly VAT returns, and probably with the year-end accounts and tax computations, too. At some point after the year-end, the accountant requests your data files and takes them away to work on. This task often takes months, and you're left unable to use Sage because the accountant has a copy of the dataset and hasn't finalised the year-end.

But with Sage Version 11 and onwards, this wasted time is a thing of the past: clients and their accountants can exchange data in a speedy and accurate fashion.

Essentially, you send data from the company to the accountant, and the accountant can process adjustments while you continue to work on the data. The accountant can then send the adjustments back to you to apply them to your data. The Accountant Link keeps a log of any changes made to the data in the intervening period and both users keep one another informed of those changes.

The Accountant Link is a wizard that guides both you and your accountant through the different stages of the process. To access the wizard, from the Menu bar, click Modules⇨Wizards⇨Accountant Link. The wizard is split into two parts: one part exports data to the accountant, the other part allows the accountant to import the user's data, record adjustments and export the adjustments to a file and send it back to the client, ready for the company to apply those changes.

When you use the Accountant Link wizard, you're first asked whether you want to export your data to your accountant or import your accountant's adjustments. I cover both options in the next sections.

Ensure that your accountant's information is up to date, by clicking Settings, then Company Preferences followed by Accountant from the Menu bar.

Sending accounts to your accountant

If you select the wizard's Export option, you're guided through the process of exporting your file in a secure password-protected file to your accountant via email.

From the moment you export the data, Sage begins to record changes made. You can print a list of material changes and, if necessary, show it to your accountant before you import the records back into your system. The kinds of changes that Sage considers to be material are wide-ranging, but include transactions like deleting customer records, restoring data and creating a nominal account.

When you export your data, Sage generates an export file with an .sae extension. You're given two options, to navigate to the filename that Sage has given, or to email the file. You must select one of the options and then click exit.

If you click Navigate to file, Sage takes you to the folder where you saved the data to.

If you click Email file, Sage creates an email and attaches a copy of the export file.

Managing material changes

Once your data has been exported, Sage begins to record any changes that are made to the dataset. Any amendment to the data is considered a material change. You know when the system is recording changes, because the word Recording appears in red type at the bottom of the screen.

You can view any of these material changes by clicking on View, then Material changes from the Menu bar. The Accountant Link Material Changes window opens. From here, you can view the adjustments that anyone has made to the data. You can also print the changes if you wish. You also have the opportunity to add comments to the material changes file before you email the file to your accountant.

Finally, if you think that you need to restart the export process, you can stop recording material changes by clicking the Cancel button. Sage flags up a confirmation message asking whether you're absolutely sure that you want to cancel the material changes, as any changes made will be lost. Click Yes or No as appropriate. If you click No, the material changes stop recording, and the recording message at the bottom of the screen disappears.

Getting back adjustments and narratives

Your accountant makes the adjustments and sends the file back to you, for you to apply the adjustments and bring the accounts up to date. The adjustments fall into two categories:

- ✔ **Adjustments:** You can apply these to the accounts automatically from the Comments and Adjustments window. Examples include journals, journal reversals, bank payments and receipts.

- ✔ **Narratives:** Instructions that your accountant sends for changes, which you need to make to your records. You must change the data manually according to your accountant's instructions.

The last section of the wizard helps you to import the adjustments that your accountant made to your data.

To import the file that your accountant has sent you, (which should have an .saa extension), from the Menu bar, click Modules⇨Wizards⇨Accountant Link⇨Import. You need to locate the file and enter your password, then click Import. You can select to view the comments and adjustments now or later. You can then click the Adjustments tab, click Begin and then OK. The adjustments are processed in the order that they appear.

Allow plenty of uninterrupted time to complete the import process!

You can find further details about the Accountant Link by using the Help system within Sage. Press F1 and type in **accountant link** to get more information if you need it.

Trying e-Banking

How do you fancy a seamless interface between your bank account and Sage? Well, that can be a reality with the use of e-Banking. It allows you to pay your suppliers directly from your bank account by using electronic payments. You can also check your online bank statement against the bank statement generated by your Sage program, as well as import transactions sent by your bank so that you can reconcile those bank transactions within Sage.

Before you can start using this wonderful product, contact your bank and ask for the necessary software. After you set up the banking software, you can then enable the e-Banking options within Sage.

Check out the web page `https://my.sage.co.uk/public/sage-ebanking/compatible-banks.aspx`. It provides a helpful list of compatible banks for e-Banking purposes.

The e-Banking features available may be limited by your bank and the account type. Some banking products allow you to download statements, which helps with the bank reconciliation, but these products may not have the electronic payments option for your suppliers.

The benefits of making electronic payments include:

- ✔ **Fast:** No need to laboriously write out cheques; you click and type your way through invoice payment.

- ✔ **Good control of cash flow:** You know exactly when that payment clears your account – no waiting for cheques to arrive and no delays while the cheques are cashed.

- ✔ **Lower cost:** Online banking transactions are less expensive than clearing cheques and cash – sometimes they're free!

- ✔ **Secure:** No need to keep cash on the premises when you can pay all your debts electronically.

Getting your statements online brings benefits too:

- ✔ **Better cash flow management:** You can easily see what funds are available at any time.

- ✔ **Efficient:** Accounts can be kept up to date by seeing up-to-date information regarding interest payments, direct debits, bank charges and so on.

- ✔ **Environmentally sound:** No paper statements means saving trees and sparing the planet the chemicals used to make paper, ink and stamps.

- ✔ **Saving time:** You don't have to wait for statements to arrive by post; you can reconcile straight away.

Configuring your e-Banking

You need to make sure that Sage can interpret the file format required by your electronic banking system. So, before you can start using e-Banking, you need to configure your electronic banking facility.

To configure your e-Banking facility, follow these steps:

1. **From Bank, select the account that you want to configure.**

2. **Click Record and select the Bank Details tab.**

   Enter the sort code and account details. These must match the details that are to be imported from your bank.

Ensure that the Enable e-Banking box is ticked in the Bank Defaults box. (From the main toolbar, click Settings⇨Bank Defaults⇨Enable e-Banking.) If you don't enable this feature, the Bank Type field won't show on the Bank record.

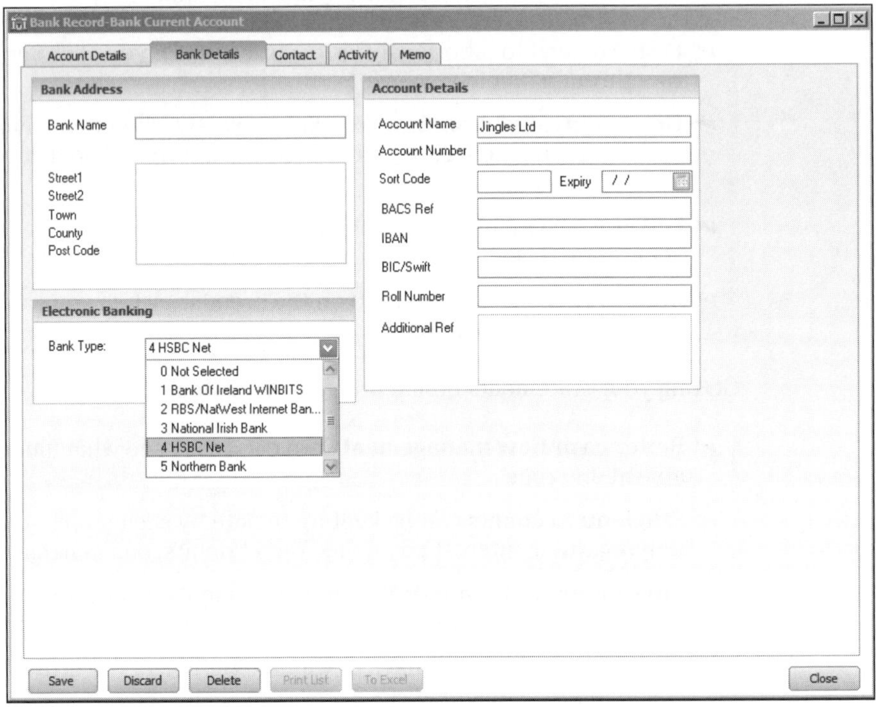

Figure 15-1:
Configuring
e-Banking
with Sage.

3. Select the bank type that you're going to use.

Some examples are RBS/Natwest and HSBC Net.

4. Click the Configure button.

The Sage e-Banking Configuration screen appears for your selected bank type.

5. Enter the information requested and click OK to save the changes you've made. Click Save in the Bank Details window to close the bank record and save the changes to the record.

You can now access the e-Banking options from the Bank Accounts window.

Opting for e-payments

As long as you have banking software that's compatible with Sage Instant Accounts and e-Banking is configured, you can use the e-Payments option and pay suppliers directly from your bank account using electronic payments (see Figure 15-2). You need to know the supplier's sort code, account number, BACS (Bankers' Automated Clearing Services) reference and account name. You also need to create the e-payments file by selecting the required bank account and then clicking e-Payments.

You may need to click the small chevron to find the e-Payments option.

Complete the payment processing window as required and click OK, then Save.

Make sure that each of your supplier records is set to allow online payments. To do so, tick the Online Payments box on the Bank tab of the supplier record.

To send payments via e-Banking, you need to enter your supplier payment by using the Bank Supplier Payment option. As long as you've activated that supplier to make online payments, the reference BACS automatically appears in the Cheque No. box when you make a payment. When you save the payment, it automatically transfers to the e-Payments window.

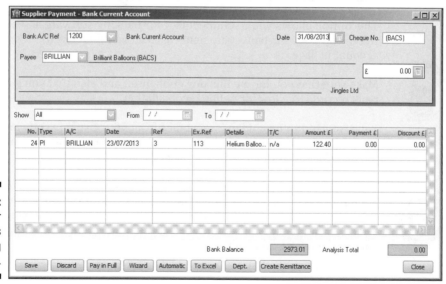

Figure 15-2: Supplier payments using e-Banking.

After you complete the supplier payment information, you can make the e-payment itself. Follow these steps:

1. **From Bank, select the bank account from which you want to make an e-payment. Click e-Payments.**

   The Send Payments window appears, showing details of all the outstanding supplier payments that you've set up to use online banking.

   You can restrict the number of transactions that appear by selecting a date range.

2. **Select the transactions that you want to send to your bank and click Send.**

   The transfer of information from Sage to your bank account begins. A confirmation message appears, showing the number and value of payments.

3. **Click OK to continue with the payments. To keep a record of this payment, click Print.**

If any problems occur with transferring your e-payments, you're prompted to view an error log. This log explains why the transfer hasn't been successful.

Reconciling electronically

This option allows you to connect to your banking software and see an electronic copy of your bank statement that you can then use to reconcile your account in Sage.

Make sure that you have e-Banking configured and also that you set up your bank records to allow for online reconciliation.

You also need to be able to import files from your banking software. Your banking software saves this data into a file on your computer. You use this file to reconcile your electronic bank statement to Sage.

If you accidentally reconcile a transaction, you can reverse the reconciliation process by using the Amend Bank Transactions option. From the Reconciliation screen, select Tools, and then, using the drop-down menu, select Amend Bank Transactions. Select the transaction that you want to amend and click Unreconcile.

Going automatic

First, you need to import your banking transactions. To do so, follow these steps:

1. **From Bank, select the bank account you want to reconcile and click e-Reconcile.**

   The Amend Bank Statement window appears.

2. **Enter the statement-end date and end balance and then click OK.**

   The Reconciliation From screen appears.

3. **Open the File menu and choose Import Bank Transactions. Browse to the required file and click** Open.

   The Open window for your selected bank appears. The left side of the window shows the files on your computer and the right side shows the bank statement files.

4. **Open the folder where your bank data is saved in the panel on the left.**

   The bank files for the selected bank account are now visible on the right panel.

5. **Select the bank file you want to import from the right panel and click Open.**

   The Reconciliation From window appears, showing your imported transactions. The imported transactions from your bank appear in the top part of the screen and the Sage account transactions in the bottom part of the screen.

6. **Select a method to match transactions.**

   Choose one of the three automatic matching buttons:

   - **Full Match:** Use this button to match items with the same reference and amount.

   - **Match Amount:** Click this option to match transactions of the same amount.

   - **Match Reference:** Use this option to match transactions that share the same reference as shown on the bank statement, such as 'British Gas DD'.

   If no transactions can be matched, a message appears and you can't reconcile your bank transactions with the automatic function. You need to click OK to go back to the Reconciliation screen.

If Sage finds more than one matching transaction, the Duplicate Transaction window appears. You must select the transaction you want to match by using the Confirm button. If you don't want to confirm the matching transactions but want to carry on with the automatic matching process, click Next. To close the window and not match any transactions, click Cancel.

Matching transactions then appear, highlighted in green. The Matched With column shows the number of transactions that have been matched.

7. **Click Confirm to verify the matched transactions and have them removed from the list.**

   You can view your confirmed transactions by clicking View and then Confirmed.

8. **When you're happy with your confirmed transactions, click Reconcile.**

   Sage marks the matched transactions as reconciled and they no longer appear on the Bank list or the Sage list.

Reconciling manually

Sage recommends that you use both the automatic and manual reconciling options. Use the automatic option first, to match the majority of the items, and then finish off the reconciliation with the manual reconciling option.

To do an e-reconciliation manually, follow these steps:

1. **From Bank, click e-Reconcile.**

   The Amend Bank Statements window appears.

2. **Enter the statement-end date and end balance details and then click OK.**

   The Reconciliation screen appears.

3. **Match transactions from the bank list or the Sage list by clicking Match Manual.**

   If the Automatically Confirmed Match Manual box is checked (the default setting), then the Match Manual button confirms the transactions. If you haven't ticked this check box, the transactions are highlighted in green and you must click Confirm before you reconcile those transactions. You can view the confirmed transactions by clicking View and then Confirmed.

4. **To finish the reconciliation, click Reconcile. If you aren't happy with the reconciliation, you can exit without reconciling by clicking Discard.**

5. **Click Yes to the confirmation message that appears or No to return to the Reconciliation screen.**

   The matched and reconciled transactions no longer appear on the Sage or bank transactions.

Chapter 16

Running Key Reports

In This Chapter

▶ Looking at your customer and supplier activity

▶ Working out who owes you money and who you owe money to

▶ Running simple management reports

▶ Searching for your top customers

*S*age produces so many reports that it can make your head spin just thinking about them. In this chapter, I pick out the reports I find most useful on a day-to-day basis – a selection of my favourites! I show you how to run each report, and use examples to demonstrate how to use them. I provide lots of lovely pictures – to whet your appetite like those in a recipe book – so that you can see what Sage *should* look like!

Sage contains lots of other useful reports; you just need to have a good root through and pick the ones that suit you.

Checking Activity through the Nominal Codes

The Nominal Activity report identifies transactions posted to specific nominal codes. It includes transaction types such as purchase invoices, sales invoices, bank payments/receipts and journals, to name but a few. I use this report on a daily basis, often just viewing the activity on-screen but sometimes printing out the information for further analysis.

This report is useful if you see a figure in the accounts that you want further information on, or if you simply want to know how much has been spent on an item for a specific time period.

Jeanette notices that £286 has been allocated to Party Gifts (N/C 5030) in May 2013 and wants to know the breakdown data for this expense item. Jeanette decides to run a Nominal Activity report for the nominal code 5030, which gives her more details (see Figure 16-1).

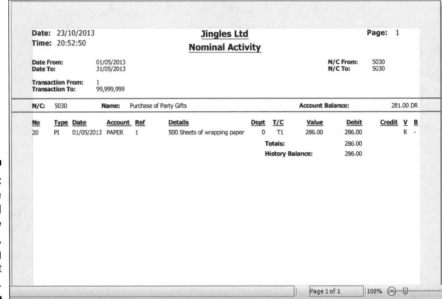

Figure 16-1:
An example
of a Nominal
Activity
report,
showing
party gift
expenses.

She can see by looking in the details column that the invoice is for paper that she purchased. Jeanette is now satisfied that she knows what the items are and is happy with the result of her investigation.

To investigate your own nominal codes, follow these steps:

1. **From Company, click the Reports icon to bring up the Nominal Reports window.**

2. **Click on Nominal Activity in the drop-down list on the left side of the screen. This selection displays a variety of report options shown on the right side of the screen. Highlight the activity report required and then click the Preview icon.**

   This preview brings up the Criteria Values box, as shown in Figure 16-2.

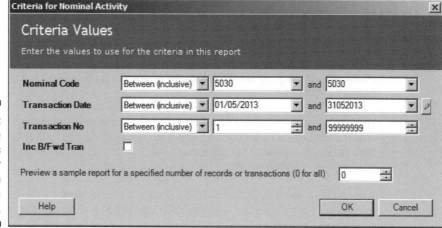

Figure 16-2:
Select the parameters for your report from the Criteria Values box.

3. **Select the nominal code for which you want to generate a report and the date range you want to look at.**

   If you can't remember the code, use the drop-down arrow to identify the nominal codes. You can run the report by using a range of transaction numbers, if you know them.

   If you don't put a code in the boxes, Sage uses the default codes 0010–9999. All nominal activities for all nominal codes then print. If you've lots of nominal codes, you're going to run out of paper before the report finishes!

4. **Click OK.**

   The report preview appears on screen, unless you've requested to print directly.

5. **Choose whether to print, email or export the report or just view it on-screen.**

   If you request print preview, you can scan the report on-screen to make sure that it has presented the information as expected. If you want to print the report, click the Print icon at the top of the Preview screen. This icon takes you into a Print Options box, where you can click OK to continue printing or Cancel to return to the report.

   In Chapter 15 you can find out how to export data from Sage into Excel.

6. **Close the report by clicking the black cross in the right corner or clicking Close at the top of the Preview screen.**

7. **Click Close to exit the Nominal Reports screen and return to the Nominal Ledger window.**

Looking into Supplier Activity

How often do you receive supplier statements that don't agree with the figure that you think you owe them? You need to be able to perform a quick reconciliation to make sure that the suppliers aren't charging you for things you haven't had.

You can print a supplier's Activity screen to show you the transactions entered onto the supplier's account within a specific period and compare that to the statement from your supplier. You can then instantly see whether you've any invoices missing.

You can also use a Supplier Activity report if you're keen to see how much you spend with a specific supplier. You can see the volume of transactions for a given period of time.

To run a Supplier Activity report, follow these steps:

1. **From Suppliers, click Reports from the Links list or the Reports icon.**

   This choice opens up the Supplier Reports window.

2. **Click Supplier Activity on the left side of the screen, then highlight the report of your choice, shown on the right-hand side of the screen**

   I recommend looking at the Supplier Activity (Detailed) report. When you've highlighted the report, click the Preview Icon. This icon opens the Criteria Values window, as shown in Figure 16-3. Double-clicking on the report you wish to view also opens up the Criteria Values box.

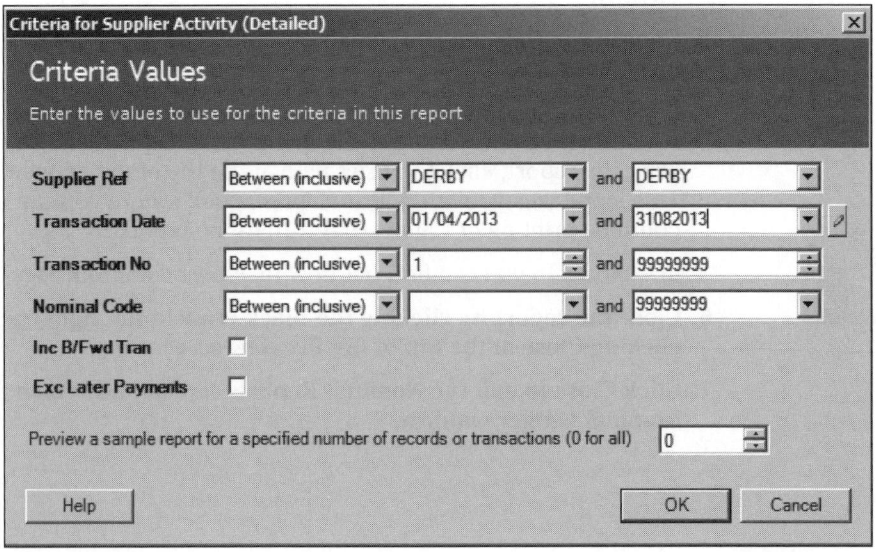

Figure 16-3:
Choose the criteria for your Supplier Activity (Detailed) report.

3. **From the drop-down arrow in the Supplier Reference field, select the supplier you want to view and the transaction dates that you require.**

In Figure 16-3, Derby Wholesale Cards is my chosen supplier and 01.04.13 to 31.08.13 are the specified dates.

4. **Click OK, and the report is displayed in preview format.**

Figure 16-4 shows the Supplier Activity (Detailed) report for Derby Wholesale Cards.

After you preview the report, you can choose to print, export or email from the toolbar on the report.

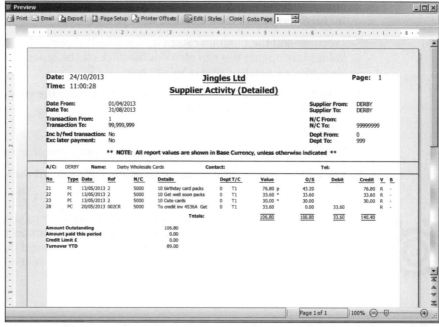

Figure 16-4: A Supplier Activity report for Jingles' supplier, Derby Wholesale Cards.

5. **Print the report if you want to and then click Close to exit.**

6. **Click Close again to close the Reports screen and return to the Supplier window.**

Tracking Customer Activity

You may be keen to look into the activity of one of your customers for a variety of reasons. Business may have tailed off a little with a customer and you want to see how much the decrease is. You may want to see what types of goods someone has been ordering from you to get an idea of what other products you can suggest. Viewing the Customer Activity report shows you the transactions with a customer for a specified period of time. You can view all transactions, including invoices, credit notes, payments and payments on account.

You generally want a hard copy of a report, so follow these steps:

1. **From Customers, click Reports from the Links list or click the Reports icon.**

   The Customer Report window opens.

2. **Click on Customer Activity on the left-hand side of the screen and choose a report option from the right-hand side of the screen, by highlighting it and then clicking the Preview icon.**

   I recommend the Customer Activity (Detailed) report. The Criteria Values box opens. You can also double-click on the report you wish to view to open up the Criteria Values box.

3. **Select the customer you want to look at and enter the range of transaction dates you're interested in.**

4. **Click OK to run the report.**

   When the report's done, choose whether to print, email or export it.

5. **Click Close or click the black cross at the right side of the screen to close the report.**

You can view customer activity on-screen if you don't want to print it by selecting the relevant customer and then clicking the Activity icon. The top half of the split screen that appears shows all transactions and the bottom part shows a breakdown of the item highlighted in the top section of the screen.

Checking Numbers with Supplier Daybook Reports

You can find daybook reports in the customer, supplier and nominal ledgers. I use the supplier daybook reports regularly to check the invoice number on the last invoice I posted. I always like to double-check to ensure that the last filed invoice is in fact the last invoice that was posted on the system. Starting off a numbering sequence for your new batch of supplier invoices only to find that you've duplicated your numbers is annoying – correcting these kinds of mistakes is time-consuming, and you have better things to do!

A *daybook* provides a list showing the items entered on the system in the same order that they were input. It shows transaction numbers, transaction types, account references, details of the transaction and the net, VAT and gross amount. Detailed reports often show the nominal code and the department that the transaction has been allocated to. A daybook is important because it allows your accountant to prove that the original source documents, such as sales and purchase invoices, cheque stubs, paying-in slips and electronic payments, have been entered onto the computer.

You can choose from a number of different daybooks. Using Sage, you can print daybooks for all invoices, paid invoices, credit notes and discounts.

To find the last invoice number, choose the Supplier Invoices (Detailed) option from Daybooks. This report clearly shows the invoice reference, so if you scroll down to the bottom of the report you can see the last invoice reference, which is the last invoice posted.

Just make sure that the invoicing sequence runs in order, and you've definitely got the last posted invoice number.

To run a Supplier Daybook report, follow these steps:

1. **From Suppliers, click Reports from the Links list or click the Reports icon.**

   The Supplier Report window opens.

2. **Click on Daybook Reports on the left-hand side of the screen. Highlight your chosen a report option from the right-hand side of the screen and click the Preview icon.**

   The Criteria Values box opens. Specify your criteria in the relevant sections.

3. **Click OK to run the report.**

   Don't specify any dates if you want the report to list all invoices.

If you're looking for the last invoice number, scroll to the bottom of the report and check the Invoice Reference column. Check that this number agrees with the last invoice filed. If it does, you can start the next batch of invoices with the subsequent number.

Finding the Customers Who Owe You

The saying, 'cash is king' is certainly true in business. A business can make huge losses, but until it runs out of cash, it can still struggle on. If your business is running short of cash because customers aren't paying you promptly, you can produce an Aged Debtors Analysis report to tell you who owes you money, how much and for how long. You can see instantly which customers need a polite kick up the proverbial to help get some cash across to your bank account.

An Aged Debtors Analysis report builds up a payment profile of your customers so that you can see who pays you within 30 days and who takes more than 90 days. You can use this information to determine who you prefer to continue working with. Selling to customers who don't pay you is pointless.

If you employ a credit controller, make sure that she creates an up-to-date report each month so that she can collect the debt as efficiently as possible.

Make sure that your bank is reconciled on a regular basis so that the reports are meaningful. You need to be sure that all the cash received has been correctly allocated to the customer accounts so that you've the most up-to-date information available.

The most sensible time to run off an Aged Debtors Analysis report is at the beginning of the month following the month you're trying to chase. For example, you can run the report for the period ended 30 June in the first week of July, when you know that all the sales invoices for June have been posted onto the system and you've had a chance to reconcile the bank up to the end of June. Obviously, you have to wait until you see the bank statements, which sometimes take up to a week to arrive following the month-end. Nowadays, however, with the advent of Internet banking, you can run off your bank statements online and don't have to wait until the end of the month before processing bank entries all in one go.

To run off an Aged Debtors Analysis report, follow these steps:

1. **From Customers, click Reports on the Link list, or click the Reports icon.**

   The Customer Report window opens.

   If you can't see the Reports icon, you may have to click the little chevron next to the Letter icon; you may have too many icons to view on the screen at one time.

2. **Click on Aged Debtors on the left-hand side of the screen and high-light the report of your choice from the right-hand side of the screen.**

   You're greeted with a raft of options – don't panic! You can run an Aged Debtors Analysis (Detailed) report (located about one-third of the way down the screen), which shows all the individual invoices/credit notes outstanding, or you can run a much shorter Aged Debtors Analysis (Summary) report (located approximately two-thirds of the way down the screen), which shows only the total debt outstanding from each customer. Both reports show the outstanding balance for each customer, and also age the debt. You can see the current-month debt as well as those debts that are 30, 60 and 90 days old, and older than 90 days.

   Highlight the report you want and then click the Preview icon; the Criteria Values box opens.

   You can also double-click on the report you wish to view to open up the Criteria Values box.

3. **Select the customers and dates for which you want to run an Aged Debtor Analysis report.**

   You normally select everyone, so leave the Customer Reference box as is. However, selecting the correct dates is important. You need to pick up all transactions outstanding, from day one to the end of the period for which you've decided to run a report, so the end date of the report is the most important one. Choose the end of a period – a month, a quarter and so on.

   If you're trying to run a debtors report to tie in with your accounts at a period end, you need to run the report to the period end, but then select Exclude Later Payments. You only need to make this selection if you've processed any bank entries after the accounting period that you're trying to reconcile to. For example, if you produce accounts to 30 June but continue to process sales receipts into July and then run the Aged Debtors Analysis to 30 June without checking this box, the current amount outstanding is updated by the July sales receipts and the overall balance of debts outstanding doesn't agree with the Balance Sheet as at 30 June. By checking the Exclude Later Payments, you can run the report to exclude the July receipts and the report then balances as at 30 June.

4. **Click OK to run the report.**

   Figure 16-5 shows a detailed report.

   You can print or email the report, or export it to Microsoft Excel.

5. **Click Close to exit the report.**

   You return to the Reports window. From here, click Close again to return to the Customers screen.

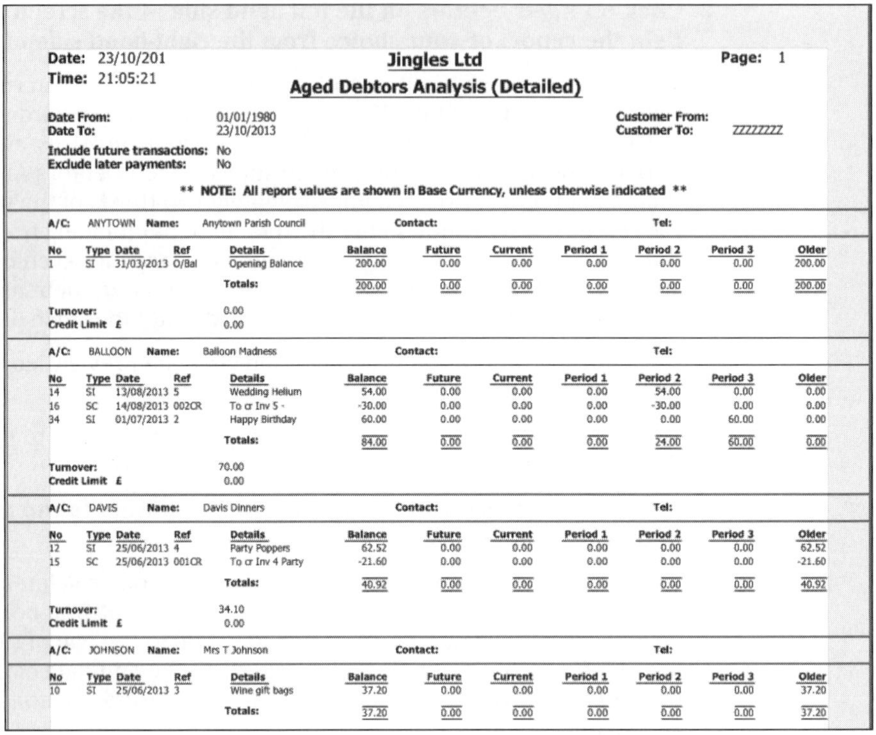

Date: 23/10/201
Time: 21:05:21

Jingles Ltd

Aged Debtors Analysis (Detailed)

Page: 1

Date From: 01/01/1980
Date To: 23/10/2013
Include future transactions: No
Exclude later payments: No

Customer From:
Customer To: ZZZZZZZZ

** NOTE: All report values are shown in Base Currency, unless otherwise indicated **

A/C: ANYTOWN Name: Anytown Parish Council Contact: Tel:

No	Type	Date	Ref	Details	Balance	Future	Current	Period 1	Period 2	Period 3	Older
1	SI	31/03/2013	O/Bal	Opening Balance	200.00	0.00	0.00	0.00	0.00	0.00	200.00
				Totals:	200.00	0.00	0.00	0.00	0.00	0.00	200.00

Turnover: 0.00
Credit Limit £ 0.00

A/C: BALLOON Name: Balloon Madness Contact: Tel:

No	Type	Date	Ref	Details	Balance	Future	Current	Period 1	Period 2	Period 3	Older
14	SI	13/08/2013	5	Wedding Helium	54.00	0.00	0.00	0.00	54.00	0.00	0.00
16	SC	14/08/2013	002CR	To cr Inv 5 -	-30.00	0.00	0.00	0.00	-30.00	0.00	0.00
34	SI	01/07/2013	2	Happy Birthday	60.00	0.00	0.00	0.00	0.00	60.00	0.00
				Totals:	84.00	0.00	0.00	0.00	24.00	60.00	0.00

Turnover: 70.00
Credit Limit £ 0.00

A/C: DAVIS Name: Davis Dinners Contact: Tel:

No	Type	Date	Ref	Details	Balance	Future	Current	Period 1	Period 2	Period 3	Older
12	SI	25/06/2013	4	Party Poppers	62.52	0.00	0.00	0.00	0.00	0.00	62.52
15	SC	25/06/2013	001CR	To cr Inv 4 Party	-21.60	0.00	0.00	0.00	0.00	0.00	-21.60
				Totals:	40.92	0.00	0.00	0.00	0.00	0.00	40.92

Turnover: 34.10
Credit Limit £ 0.00

A/C: JOHNSON Name: Mrs T Johnson Contact: Tel:

No	Type	Date	Ref	Details	Balance	Future	Current	Period 1	Period 2	Period 3	Older
10	SI	25/06/2013	3	Wine gift bags	37.20	0.00	0.00	0.00	0.00	0.00	37.20
				Totals:	37.20	0.00	0.00	0.00	0.00	0.00	37.20

Figure 16-5: Reviewing the Aged Debtors Analysis (Detailed) report for Jingles.

Paying Attention to Your Creditors

If you find going through your credit card bill terrifying, you probably won't like looking at the Aged Creditors report either! It shows a list of all monies owed to your suppliers.

This report is presented in a similar format to the Aged Debtors Analysis report (see the preceding section), and shows how much you owe, to whom and for how long. You can use this report to decide which suppliers to pay at the end of the month.

The Aged Creditors report is only useful if you've updated your bank account with all relevant supplier payments, whether Bankers' Automated Clearing Services (BACS) or cheque. Make sure that you reconcile your bank account before you prepare the Aged Creditors report.

Be sure to reconcile all bank accounts from which you're likely to make supplier payments, including credit cards! If you overlook some credit card payments to suppliers, your Aged Creditors Analysis report isn't accurate, and you can potentially end up paying a supplier twice by writing out a cheque and not realising that the debt was already paid by company credit card.

To run the Aged Creditors Analysis report, follow these steps:

1. **From Suppliers, click Reports on the Links list, or click the Reports icon.**

   The Supplier Report window opens.

2. **Click on Aged Creditors on the left-hand side of the screen and highlight the report of your choice from the right-hand side of the screen.**

   I usually select Aged Creditors Analysis (Detailed) from the raft of options. The Criteria Values box opens.

   You can save your regular reports as favourites. That way, you don't have to keep scrolling down the list of reports to find the one you want.

   Double-clicking on the report you wish to view also opens up the Criteria Values box.

3. **Select the supplier that you want to run an Aged Creditors report for.**

   I usually select all suppliers. If you leave the Supplier Reference fields alone, Sage automatically selects all suppliers. You must use the dropdown arrows if you want to select a specific supplier.

   Ensure that the Date From and To fields are correct. Also make sure that you tick the Exclude Later Payment box to tell Sage to ignore information beyond the *To* date.

4. **Click OK to run the report. Choose to print or email the report, or export it to the destination of your choice.**

   Figure 16-6 shows a detailed Aged Creditors Analysis (Detailed) report for Jingles.

5. **To exit the report, click Close.**

   You go back to the Reports window. Click Close again to exit the Reports window and return to the Suppliers window.

Date:	24/10/2013					**Jingles Ltd**						Page: 1
Time:	11:07:31					**Aged Creditors Analysis (Detailed)**						

Date From: 01/01/1980   Supplier From:
Date To: 24/10/2013   Supplier To: ZZZZZZZZ

Include future transactions: No
Exclude later payments: No

** NOTE: All report values are shown in Base Currency, unless otherwise indicated **

A/C: BRILLIAN   Name: Brilliant Balloons   Contact: Tel:

No:	Type	Date	Ref	Details	Balance	Future	Current	Period 1	Period 2	Period 3	Older
24	PI	23/07/2013	3	Helium Balloons -	122.40	0.00	0.00	0.00	0.00	122.40	0.00
				Totals:	122.40	0.00	0.00	0.00	0.00	122.40	0.00

Turnover: 102.00
Credit Limit £ 0.00

A/C: BT   Name: British Telecom   Contact: Tel:

No:	Type	Date	Ref	Details	Balance	Future	Current	Period 1	Period 2	Period 3	Older
75	PI	30/06/2013	5	Telephone bill	3,600.00	0.00	0.00	0.00	0.00	3,600.00	0.00
				Totals:	3,600.00	0.00	0.00	0.00	0.00	3,600.00	0.00

Turnover: 3,000.00
Credit Limit £ 0.00

A/C: DAGENHAM   Name: Dagenham Party Supplies   Contact: Tel:

No:	Type	Date	Ref	Details	Balance	Future	Current	Period 1	Period 2	Period 3	Older
27	PC	10/08/2013	001CR	To credit invoice	-6.00	0.00	0.00	0.00	-6.00	0.00	0.00
				Totals:	-6.00	0.00	0.00	0.00	-6.00	0.00	0.00

Turnover: -5.00
Credit Limit £ 0.00

A/C: DERBY   Name: Derby Wholesale Cards   Contact: Tel:

No:	Type	Date	Ref	Details	Balance	Future	Current	Period 1	Period 2	Period 3	Older
21	PI	13/05/2013	2	10 birthday card	106.80	0.00	0.00	0.00	0.00	0.00	106.80
				Totals:	106.80	0.00	0.00	0.00	0.00	0.00	106.80

Figure 16-6: Jingles' creditors and how much they're owed.

Handling Unreconciled Bank Transactions

After you reconcile your bank account, you probably have a few transactions that you can't reconcile. They may be unreconciled payments or unreconciled receipts.

You quite often have entries posted in Sage that haven't yet cleared the bank account (refer to Chapter 11 for more about reconciling). For example, you post cheques on Sage before they clear the bank account; these cheques are known as *un-presented cheques*. The same applies for receipts, which have the rather weird name of *outstanding lodgements*.

To print an Unpresented Cheques report, follow these steps:

1. **From Bank, click Reports from the Links list, or the Reports icon.**

   If you can't see the Reports icon, click the little chevron at the end of the row of icons to show the list of icons that aren't currently visible.

   The Bank Reports window opens.

2. **Scroll to the bottom of the list on the left-hand side of the screen and click Unreconciled Transactions.**

   You may need to scroll down the list of reports to see this option, as lots of bank reports are available (as shown in Figure 16-7).

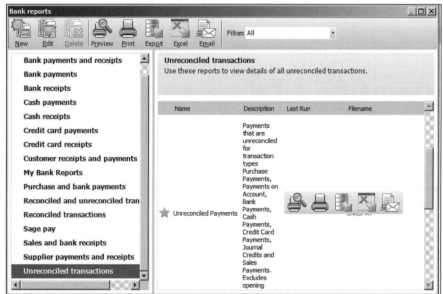

Figure 16-7:
The list of bank reports is long and varied.

3. **Highlight Unreconciled Payments, and then click the Preview icon.**

   The Criteria Values box opens.

4. **Enter the transaction dates that you require.**

   You usually print to the end of the month that you've just reconciled.

5. **Click OK to open the report.**

   You can print, email or export this report to your required destination.

6. Click Close to exit the report.

This selection returns you to the Bank Reports window. Click Close again to return to the Bank window.

Figure 16-8 shows an Unreconciled Payments report from 01.01.1980 to 30.04.2013. Using the default start date of 01.01.1980 ensures that Sage picks up all transactions, from day one to 30 April 2013. These dates are the correct ones to select if you've just performed a bank reconciliation to 30 April 2013. Notice that the report shows an entry cheque number 000001, dated 30 April 2013. This cheque is classed as an un-presented cheque; it was probably written out on the last day of the month and only posted that day, so it hasn't got as far as being paid into a bank account!

Figure 16-8:
Viewing the Unpresented Cheques report for Jingles.

To run an Outstanding Lodgement report, follow these steps:

1. Follow Steps 1 and 2 as for the Unpresented Cheques report.

2. Click Unreconciled Receipts.

The Criteria Values box opens.

3. Enter the transaction dates that you require.

You generally print to the end of the month that you've just reconciled.

4. **Click OK to open the report.**

   You can print or email this report, or export it to your required destination.

5. **Click Close to exit the report.**

   You go back to the Bank Reports window. Click Close again to return to the Bank window.

Your accountant probably requires a copy of your unreconciled bank transactions at the year-end, so don't forget to put a copy in with your data set to send to them. Any extra work that you can do saves on accountancy costs!

Ranking Your Top Customers

The Top Customers report can be a real eye-opener and is a useful management tool. You may think that you know who your top customers are, but this report may reveal some interesting results.

The report has a simple layout and shows you the customer account and name, contact details, when you last invoiced them, their credit limit and what the turnover was year-to-date (YTD) or month-to-date (MTD), depending on which you choose.

Here's the interesting bit: the customers are arranged in order of turnover, so you can see which customer is invoiced with the highest value, revealing where the bulk of your sales turnover is coming from.

You may find that your turnover is being generated by the top 5 customers, or you may find that you've 20 customers who spend slightly less individually with you. You may consider the second arrangement to be more beneficial as it spreads the risk across a wider customer base. If one customer disappears, you aren't going to feel the effect quite so dramatically.

To run the Top Customer report, follow these steps:

1. **From Customers, click Reports from the Links list, or click the Reports icon from the Customers screen.**

   The Customer Reports window opens.

2. **Click on Top Customers at the bottom of the left-hand side of the screen. Then highlight the Top Customer List – Year. Click on the Preview icon.**

   The report opens and you can print, email or export it.

You may find it quite useful to export this report and play around with the numbers in a spreadsheet. You can put the information into graphical format to send to managers.

If you run the Top Customer List – Month, you need to ensure that you complete regular month-ends and tick the Clear Turnover Figures in the Month-End window, otherwise the information is the same as the YTD report. Refer to Chapter 12 for more information on running your month-ends.

Part V

The Part of Tens

Go to www.dummies.com/extras/sageinstantaccountsuk for free online bonus content.

In this part . . .

✔ Familiarise yourself with the function keys, which act as short cuts to save you time when entering your data.

✔ Wise up on the Sage Wizards – a series of step by step hand-holding guidelines helping you carry out specific processes within Sage, such as setting up a new record or running the Opening/Closing stock routine.

Chapter 17

Ten (Okay, Eleven) Funky Functions

In This Chapter

▶ Getting help

▶ Finding out about shortcuts

▶ Opening programs

*I*f you want to wow your friends (or your boss) with a few neat tricks, then look no further than this chapter! Here, you find out how to use some of the function keys that give you great shortcuts – for example, the copy key (F6), which speeds up processing no end, and F7, which can get you out of a tight spot if you need to insert an extra line somewhere (particularly useful if you've missed a line of information from the middle of a journal). Read on to find out more.

Browsing for Help with F1

Pressing F1 launches the help system. The system is intelligent enough to know which part of the system you're working in and displays the Help screens most suited to your needs. In doing so, it saves you having to scroll through the Help index list to find the appropriate section. For example, if you're in the Batch Entry screen for suppliers, pressing the F1 key brings up a Help screen related to entering purchase invoices.

Calculating Stuff with F2

Having instant access to a calculator is pretty handy, particularly if you're in the middle of a journal and you need to add something up. Simply press your F2 function key, and a little calculator appears on the screen. You can quickly do your sums and then carry on processing information using Sage, without having to dive through your office drawers trying to find the calculator.

Accessing an Edit Item Line for Invoicing with F3

Pressing F3 displays the Edit Item line when you're entering invoices. You can add additional information and comments to your invoice, whether for a product or service.

Note: You need to enter some information first before the Edit box will open.

Finding Multiple Functions at F4

Pressing this button does different things depending on which screen or field you're in:

- In a field that has a drop-down arrow, press F4 to display the full list.
- In a Date field, press F4 to show the calendar, instead of clicking the Calendar icon.
- In a numeric field, press F4 to make a mini-calculator appear, instead of clicking the Calculator icon. (F2 opens a calculator in any screen; F4 opens one only if you're in a screen devoted to numbers.)

Calculating Currency or Checking Spelling with F5

The F5 key has two purposes:

- It shows the Currency calculator when the cursor is in a numeric box. (*Note:* You need to ensure that your currencies and exchange rates are set up for this purpose to function.)
- It brings up the spell checker when the cursor is in a text box.

Copying with F6

F6 is one of the best inventions ever! It copies entries from the field above, which is particularly useful when you're entering batch invoices (for both customers and suppliers). For example, if a batch of invoices all have the same date, you can enter the date once, and, as you enter each subsequent invoice, press F6 when you get to the Date field. Sage copies the date from the field directly above your line of entry and enters the same date into the invoice on the line of the batch that you're working on. You can use this function for any of the fields. So, if you're entering a mass of invoices from the same customer or supplier, you can use F6 to copy the details from one invoice to the next. This function has an amazing impact on the speed of data entry, and is an absolute godsend when you set up a new system, as you often have a lot of data entry to do.

Inserting a Line with F7

The ability to add a line may seem pretty mundane and boring, but is very useful when you're entering batches of invoices or journals. You can be halfway through entering a journal and realise that you've missed out a line. Instead of putting it at the bottom of the journal, you can press F7 to insert a line where you want it.

Deleting a Line with F8

F8 is one of my favourite function keys. Many a time, I've got to the bottom of a very long and laborious journal and been a bit carried away. Before realising it, I've started to enter an extra line of journal that shouldn't be there.

After you enter a nominal code, Sage expects you to continue to post that line of the journal and waits for you to enter a value. When you realise your mistake and try to save the journal with a zero amount on the last line, Sage doesn't allow you to post. Instead, it gives you a warning message stating No transaction values entered.

But click the line you want to delete, press F8 and it miraculously disappears, allowing you to save the journal with no further problems.

Many a student has told me that they've got to that point and, not realising what to do, have ended up discarding the original journal and retyping it all!

The F8 key can be used in other parts of the system, too, for example when you want to delete a line from an invoice or order.

Calculating Net Amounts with F9

When entering an invoice, Sage asks you for the net amount of the invoice, followed by the tax code. After you enter the tax code, Sage calculates the VAT. If you don't know the net amount of the invoice and only have the gross amount, you can type the gross amount in the Net field and press F9. Sage then calculates the net amount for that invoice.

Launching Windows with F11

F11 launches the Windows control panel. Having access to the control panel is useful, for example, if you accidentally send a report to the printer. To cancel the job, press F11. The control panel opens and you select the Printer icon. Double-click the printer where the job is waiting to print and delete the report from the queue. Click the black cross in the right corner to exit the control panel. Alternatively, you can configure this button to launch another program. Use the Help menu for instructions on how to configure this button.

Opening Report Designer with F12

F12 launches Report Designer, or you can configure this button to launch another program from your PC.

Report Designer is an additional feature of Sage that allows you to create your own reports or modify existing ones. If you can't find a standard report that produces the information in the way that you want, this feature enables you to design a report with exactly the details needed for your business. (I explain how to use Report Designer in Chapter 14.)

Chapter 18

(Not Quite) Ten Wizards to Conjure

In This Chapter

▶ Looking at how wizards can help you perform tricky transactions

▶ Investigating the more helpful wizards and how they work

Sage helpfully provides a number of *wizards*. No, I don't mean little characters with pointy hats and wands. By wizards, I mean step-by-step instructions on how to carry out specific procedures. Sometimes they can be a bit long and laborious to use, but at other times they provide some much needed expertise. For example, they can help you to complete complicated journal entries – even the most dedicated bookkeepers can do with a bit of help sometimes!

Here, I provide a brief summary of the most helpful wizards that Sage offers.

Creating a New Customer Account

Using the Navigation bar on the left side of your screen, click Customers and then New Customer in the Task pane. The New Customer wizard starts, taking you step-by-step through the seven-window process of setting up your customers. As the wizard can take a long time, I use the quicker method of clicking Customer and then Record, but you may prefer the wizard's guidance, so make sure that you grab a cuppa first!

To have a look at the type of questions that you're asked as you work through the wizard, press the F1 function key. The Sage Help facility describes in detail the type of information you need to enter in each of the seven windows.

Setting up a New Supplier

Using the Navigation bar, click Suppliers and then New Supplier in the Task pane. The New Supplier wizard walks you through the process of setting up your supplier records, just as the New Customer wizard takes you through setting up your customer records – wizards are handy, but not too imaginative. The seven windows you complete help you set up supplier names, addresses, contact details, credit details, bank details and settlement discounts, if applicable.

If you want to preview the types of information required to complete the wizard, have a look at Sage Help. Press the F1 function key and scroll up and down the screen to see for yourself.

You don't have to complete every field in the wizard to set up a supplier, but you do need to click through all seven windows to get to the end and save what information you've entered, so stick with it! You can always add information to your supplier record at a later date if you feel that you've missed anything out – simply open the supplier record, make your changes and click Save – it's that easy!

Helpfully, the final stage of both the customer and supplier wizards allows you to enter opening balances, so you need to remember that you've already done this task when you're reading Chapter 4.

Initiating a New Nominal Account

Use the Nominal Record wizard to create new nominal accounts to utilise in your Chart of Accounts (COA). You only need to work through two screens – what a relief! From the Navigation bar, click Company and then the New Nominal icon, which starts the wizard for you.

The wizard asks you to enter the name of your new nominal account and confirm what type of account it is – sales, purchase, direct expenses, overheads, assets, liabilities and so on.

Sage then asks you to enter your nominal category from within the COA – for example, product sales. It also asks you to type in your nominal code.

Save yourself some annoyance and decide on your nominal code before you start the wizard. At this point in the wizard, you don't have the option of searching your nominal code list to check whether your chosen code is suitable.

After you've clicked Next, the wizard asks whether you want to post an opening balance. Click the appropriate answer, and then click Create. New boxes appear asking you whether it's your balance is a debit or a credit and the date and the amount. Click Create and the new account is prepared.

Don't forget to check your COA for any errors after you enter new nominal accounts. You can find details on how to do this check in Chapter 2.

Creating a New Bank Account

The Sage New Bank Account wizard enables you to open new bank accounts. The first four windows ask for the usual bank details, such as bank name, sort code, account number and so on. The last window allows you to enter your opening balances.

From the Navigation bar, click Bank, and then click the New Bank icon.

Launching a New Product (For Sage Instant Accounts Plus Only)

Use the New Product wizard to create a new product record. The wizard asks you to enter descriptions of the product, selling price and cost price information, as well as nominal codes and supplier details. It also has a section on opening balances that allows you to enter these balances through the wizard.

To access the wizard, from the Navigation bar, click Products and then click the New Product icon. Alternatively, you can click New Product from the Task pane on the Navigation bar, instead of clicking the New Product icon.

Helping Out at Month-End: Opening/ Closing Stock (For Sage Instant Accounts Plus Users Only)

Click Modules from the Menu bar, and then click Wizards. Choose the Opening Closing Stock wizard, which forms part of the month-end routine and is a welcome method of recording your closing stock. The wizard records the amount of closing stock you have at the end of a period and then transfers it to the start of the next period. The theory is that, by recording your opening and closing stock figures, the cost of sales figures can be accurately calculated by the wizard for your Profit and Loss report. (Cost of Sales = Opening Stock + Purchases – Closing Stock.) If you don't post opening and closing stock figures, the cost of sales only reflects the purchase cost and doesn't reflect stock that you have left to sell.

The wizard asks you to confirm the closing stock nominal accounts in both your Balance Sheet and the Profit and Loss report. Sage asks you to enter the value of this month's closing stock and that of the previous closing stock. Sage then calculates the double-entry bookkeeping when you click the Calculate button and then posts those entries when you click the Post Transactions button.

Saving Time: Global Changes

The Global Changes wizard helps you make global changes to information in customer, supplier or product accounts without having to change each account individually. For example, you can raise the selling price of all your products by 10 per cent, as the sample business in Figure 18-1 did, just like that! (I don't recommend such an abrupt and significant change, however, lest you lose more than 10 per cent of your customers!)

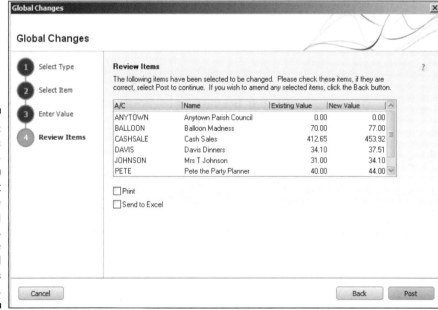

Figure 18-1: The results of applying a 10 per cent increase in selling prices, using the Global Changes wizard.

Work through each of the windows, selecting the appropriate boxes for your global change. When you're happy with the details and can see the results shown on screen, click Finish. Sage then activates the changes. How's that for a brilliant and simple way to save yourself time!

Keeping Others in the Loop: Accountant Link

The Accountant Link is a very useful facility that enables you to send a copy of your data to your accountant via email or post. In the past, if you sent data to your accountant, you had to stop work and wait for the adjustments to your accounts. Nowadays, the Accountant Link allows you to send the data to your accountant, but still continue to work on the data yourself in the meantime, minimising disruption within your business.

After you export the data to your accountant, Sage begins to record material changes that you make to the data. You can print a list of these changes, and your accountant may request a copy of them before sending the data back to you. Your accountant can send the data, with adjustments, back to you via a secure file, and you can then import those changes. The Accountant Link helps you apply the accountant's adjustments to your data to bring it up to date. At this point, the program stops recording material changes.

The Accountant Link wizard takes you through the exporting and importing process step by step (refer to Chapter 15 for more details).

Appendix

Glossary

Aged Creditors report: A report showing all balances owed to *creditors,* categorised into debts owed for 30 days, 60 days and 90 days or older.

Aged Debtors report: A report showing all outstanding balances owed to a business, categorised into amounts owed for 30 days, 60 days and 90 days or older.

Asset: Item that a business owns. (See *current asset; fixed asset.*)

Audit trail: A list of all the transactions that occur in Sage in chronological order. Each transaction is identified by its own transaction number.

Balance Sheet: A financial report that shows a snapshot of the financial status of a business at a point in time. It identifies the business's *assets* and *liabilities* and shows how these assets and liabilities have been funded through *retained profits* or invested *capital*.

Capital: Money invested into a business by owners or shareholders.

Cash flow: The amount of cash flowing in and out of the business.

Chart of Accounts: A list of all the *nominal accounts* used to analyse *assets, liabilities, income* and *expenses*. It drives the format of the Profit and Loss account and Balance Sheet.

Cost: Items of expense in the accounts, such as wages costs. See *direct costs*.

Credit: A bookkeeping entry that increases the value of a liability or income and decreases the value of an asset or expense. A credit is always shown on the right side of a journal.

Creditor: Person or company to whom a business owes money.

Creditor ledger: See *supplier ledger*.

Customer ledger: A ledger that holds all the individual customer accounts and their balances. Also known as the debtor ledger.

Current asset: An *asset* with a lifespan of 12 months or less. A current asset can be *liquidated* reasonably quickly.

Debit: A bookkeeping entry that increases the value of an asset or expense and decreases the value of a liability or income. Debits show on the left side of a journal.

Debtor: Person or company that owes a business money.

Debtor ledger: See *customer ledger*.

Depreciation: An accounting tool used to gradually reduce the value of a *fixed asset*.

Direct cost: A cost that can be directly attributed to the manufacturing of a product.

Double-entry bookkeeping: An accounting method that records each transaction twice. Every debit entry has a corresponding credit entry. Doing the two entries helps balance the books.

Expense: A cost incurred as a result of doing revenue-generating business activities.

Fixed asset: An item owned by the business that has a useful life longer than 12 months.

Gross profit: The difference between *revenue* less *direct costs*.

Income: The amount of money received for goods and/or services provided.

Liability: An amount the business owes. (See *long-term liability; short-term liability*.)

Liquidate: To redeem an *asset* for cash.

Long-term liability: A *liability* the business owes for a period longer than 12 months – a mortgage, for example.

Net profit: *Revenue* less *direct costs* and *overheads*, including depreciation and taxes. Also known as the bottom line.

Nominal account: An account to which every item of income, expense, asset and liability is posted. Individual nominal accounts are grouped into ranges and can be viewed in the *Chart of Accounts*. (See *nominal ledger*.)

Nominal journal: In years gone by, this journal was leather-bound. Nowadays, computers have replaced the traditional journal and a computerised journal entry screen is used to transfer values between nominal accounts by using *double-entry bookkeeping*.

Nominal ledger: The ledger that includes balances and activities for all the nominal accounts used to run the business. The nominal ledger contains all the transactions that the business has ever made.

Overheads: An *expense* that can't be directly matched to a product or service the business provides. Electricity and telephone costs are examples of overheads.

Outstanding lodgement: A deposit or receipt entered in the company's books that hasn't yet cleared the banking system.

Profit and Loss account: A financial statement that shows sales revenue less direct costs and overheads and arrives at the net profit or loss of the business.

Retained profit: *Profit* from a prior period reinvested in the business for future growth.

Revenue: See *sales revenue*.

Sales revenue: The net value of a business's sales invoices.

Short-term liability: An amount owed for a period of less than 12 months.

Supplier ledger: The ledger that holds all the individual supplier accounts and their balances. Also known as the creditor ledger.

Un-presented cheque: A cheque written out and entered into the book-keeping system that hasn't yet cleared the bank account. Un-presented cheques show as outstanding items remaining to be reconciled after a bank reconciliation is complete.

VAT: Value Added Tax. A tax due on purchases of most goods and services supplied by UK businesses and those in the Isle of Man. VAT is collected on business transactions, imports and acquisitions.

Index

• *Symbols and Numerics* •

* (asterisk)
  in Customer Activity tab, 102
  in Supplier Activity screen, 122
.001 file extension, 27, 151

• *A* •

About page, 31
account code (A/C)
  for payments, 123
  sorting nominal records by, 65
accountant
  audit trail viewed by, 145, 215
  bank reconciliation performed by, 174
  exchanging data with, 224–226, 261
  journals handled by, 36, 71, 177
  management reports prepared
    by, 208
  opening balances provided by, 76, 77
  Trial Balance provided by, 82–83
Accountant Link wizard, 224–225, 261
accounting methods
  accrual accounting, 177
  double-entry bookkeeping, 36, 264
accounts. *See also* bank accounts
  Accruals account, 178–179
  Accumulated Depreciation account,
    181–182
  Building Society account, 128
  cash account, 128
  Cash Register account, 129
  COA (Chart of Accounts). *See* COA
    (Chart of Accounts)
  control accounts, 29, 71
  Cost account, 178–179
  credit card account, 129, 130
  Current account, 129
  Deposit account, 129
  Depreciation account, 181–182
  double-entry rules for, 36

Mispostings account
  journals for, 182
  nominal codes for, 45
nominal account
  creating, 258–259
  described, 36, 264
  list of. *See* COA (Chart of Accounts)
  opening balances for, 88–89
  transfers between accounts. *See* journal
Petty Cash account
  described, 129, 138
  funding, 138
  making payments from, 139
Profit and Loss account, 263, 265
Suspense account, 45, 91
Accounts Installshield wizard, 10–11
accrual, 178–179
accrual accounting, 177
Accruals account, 178–179
Accumulated Depreciation account, 181–182
Activation, Tools menu, 30
activation key, 9, 15
Active Set-Up wizard, 14–20
Activity tab
  customer and supplier records, 59–60, 102
  nominal record, 67
  product record, 72, 90
add-on software, 30
Adjustment In (AI) record, 187
adjustments, from accountant, 226
Advanced Options tab, backups, 152
Aged Creditors report
  described, 263
  opening balances from, 77, 79
  running, 244–246
Aged Debtors report
  described, 263
  opening balances from, 77, 79
  running, 242–244
Ageing tab, customer or supplier defaults, 60
AI (Adjustment In) record, 187
amount, for invoices, 110

asset
  current asset
    described, 41, 263
    nominal codes for, 42
  described, 263
  fixed asset
    depreciation of, 180–182, 264
    described, 41, 180, 264
    NBV (net book value) of, 180–181
    nominal codes for, 42
asterisk (*)
  in Customer Activity tab, 102
  in Supplier Activity screen, 122
audit trail
  all transactions shown in, 145, 215
  clearing, 188
  described, 263
  running at month-end, 215–217

• B •

Backup, File menu, 27, 151
Backup Company tab, 151
backups
  after year-end processes, 189
  before clearing audit trail, 188
  before month-end processes, 186
  before year-end processes, 189
  creating, 27, 86, 150–152
  restoring data from, 15, 27, 152
Bad Debts, nominal codes for, 45
Balance Sheet
  Chart of Accounts for, 263
  described, 37, 263
  nominal code categories in, 38, 41–43
  running at month-end, 214–215
Balance Sheet tab, 38, 47, 50
bank account record
  creating, 68–70
  default, 67
  deleting, 70
  duplicating, 69
  opening balances for, 77, 84–85, 87–88
  renaming, 68
bank accounts
  Building Society account, 128
  cash account, 128
  Cash Register account, 129

creating, 259
credit card account, 128, 130
Current account, 129
Deposit account, 129
interest on, earning, 128, 169
nominal codes for, 42, 43
payments to, 130–132
Petty Cash account
  described, 129, 138
  funding, 138
  making payments from, 139
receipts, depositing, 130–132
reconciling
  archives of, accessing, 172
  electronically, 230–233
  importance of, 165–166
  no reconciliation option, 166
  performing, 167–172
  preparation for, 167
  problems with, resolving, 173
  unmatched items after, 173–175, 246–249
recurring entries
  for bank receipts or payments, 175
  for bank transfers, 175
  for customer payments, 135–136, 175
  for journals, 175
  processing and posting, 137–138
  setting up, 133–135
  for supplier payments, 135–136, 175
transferring funds between
  entering before reconciliation, 167
  processing, 132–133
  recurring bank entries for, 175
  types of, 128–129
Bank button, Navigation Bar, 32
Bank Charges & Interest, nominal
  codes for, 45
Bank Defaults, Settings menu, 29
Bank module, 68–69
Bank Payments icon, 130
Bank Receipts icon, 130
Bank Reconciliation screen, 169–170
Bank Report - Unreconciled report, 174
bank statement
  account charges, 169
  direct credits or debits, 167
  ending balance, 169
  interest earned, 169

marking while reconciling, 167–168, 171
reconciling, 165–173
reference for, 169
statement date, 169
transfers, 167
Bank tab, customer and supplier records, 60
Bank Transfer icon, 132
Barrow, Paul (author)
    Bookkeeping For Dummies, 36
Batch Credit icon, 120
Batch Credit Note icon, 98
Batch Invoice icon, 96, 118
Batch Report Converter, 30
bookkeeping, double-entry, 36, 264
Bookkeeping For Dummies
    (Kelly; Barrow; Epstein), 36
books and publications
    Bookkeeping For Dummies
        (Kelly; Barrow; Epstein), 36
Building Society account, 128
business (others)
    balances owed to. *See* Aged Debtors
        report
    suppliers. *See* supplier (creditor)
business (yours)
    address of, 16–17
    assets of, 263
    business type for, 16–17
    currency for, 18–19
    customising, 20–22
    existing, copying data from, 15
    financial year for, 18
    name of, 16–17
    new, setting up, 15–20
    VAT setup for, 18–19
buttons, Navigation Bar, 28, 32

● *C* ●

calculator, displaying, 253, 254
calendar, displaying, 254
Calendar Monthly Ageing, 60
capital
    described, 42, 263
    nominal codes for, 43
Capital & Reserves category, for nominal
        codes, 42, 43
carriage terms, for invoices, 112

cash account, 128
cash accounting VAT scheme, 194, 198–199
cash flow, 263
Cash Register account, 129
categories of nominal codes
    headings for
        adding, 48
        deleting, 49
        renaming, 47
    list of
        for Balance Sheet, 41–43
        in COA, 38
        for Profit and Loss report, 43–45
Change Password, Settings menu, 29
Change Program Date, Settings menu, 29
Change View menu, 24
Chart of Accounts. *See* COA
cheque number, for payments, 123
clearing down your VAT, 201–202
Close, File menu, 27
COA (Chart of Accounts)
    creating, 49–51
    default, 38–41
    Default Layout of Accounts, 40
    deleting, 51
    described, 35, 38, 263
    editing, 46–49
    errors in
        checking for, 51, 208
        resolving, 53
        viewing, 52
    multiple, by locations or segments, 49–51
    nominal code categories in, 38
    nominal codes in, 40–41
    partial, 49
    viewing, 39–41
codes
    nominal code (N/C)
        for bank receipts or payments, 131
        category headings for, modifying,
            47, 48, 49
        correct category for, ensuring, 46
        described, 37
        errors with, 53
        floating nominal, 46, 53
        for invoices, 119
        leaving gaps between, 45
        list of, 38, 41–45

codes *(continued)*
  mirroring, 45–46
  printing list of, 41
  viewing for each category, 41, 62
  viewing list of, 62
  product code
    in invoices, 109
    in product record, 71–72
  tax code (T/C)
    for bank receipts or payments, 131
    for invoices, 119
    list of, 97, 192
comments, 144
Comments tab, error messages, 144
Commissions, nominal codes for, 44
company. *See* business (others); business
    (yours); nominal ledger
Company button, Navigation Bar, 32, 41
Company Credit Card account, 130
Company module, 39
Company Preferences, Settings menu, 28
Comparative Profit and Loss report,
    212–213
compressing data, 147
Configuration Editor, Settings menu, 28
contacts, exporting to Microsoft Outlook,
    222–223
control account, 29, 71
Control Accounts, Settings menu, 29
control panel, Windows, 256
Convert Reports, Tools menu, 30
copying fields, 254–255
Corrections button, Navigation Bar, 32, 145
cost. *See also* expense
  described, 263
  direct cost (expense), 44, 264
Cost account, 178–179
Countries, Settings menu, 29
countries in EU, changing, 29
credit
  described, 263
  double-entry rules for, 36
credit card
  making payments from, 140
  paying statements from, 141
  reconciling statements from, 140–141
credit card account, 129, 130
Credit Card (Creditors), nominal codes
    for, 43

Credit Card (Debtors), nominal codes for, 42
Credit Card Receipts account, 130
Credit Charges, nominal codes for, 44
Credit Control tab, customer and supplier
    records, 59
credit note. *See also* refund
  for customers
    creating, 97–99, 113
    default settings for, 116
    deleting, 105, 116
    posting, 97–99
  from suppliers
    allocating, 122
    credit number for, 120
    posting, 120–121
creditor (supplier)
  balances owed to. *See* Aged Creditors
    report
  contact information, exporting,
    222–223
  credit note from
    allocating, 122
    credit number for, 120
    posting, 120–121
  described, 22, 263
  invoices from
    not yet received, 178–179
    paid in advance, 179
    paying with credit card, 140
    posting, 118–120
    receiving, 117–118
  payments to
    e-payments for, 227, 229–230
    processing, 123–124
    recurring bank entries for, 135–136, 175
  refunds, recording, 124–125
  returns, recording, 124–125
  write offs, recording, 124–125
creditor (supplier) ledger, 265
Creditors: Long Term, nominal codes for, 43
Creditors: Short Term, nominal codes for, 43
Currencies, Settings menu, 29
currency
  changing, 29
  setting up, 18–19
current (short-term) liability
  described, 42, 265
  nominal codes for, 43
Current account, 129

current asset
  described, 41, 263
  nominal codes for, 42
Current Assets category, for nominal
    codes, 41, 42
Current Liabilities category, for nominal
    codes, 42, 43
Custom installation, 11–12
customer (debtor)
  contact information, exporting, 222–223
  credit notes for
    creating, 97–99, 113
    default settings for, 116
    deleting, 105, 116
    posting, 97–99
  described, 22, 264
  invoices for
    creating, 108–113
    default settings for, 116
    deleting, 105, 116
    editing, 112, 254
    matching to a payment, 100–102
    not matched to a payment, 104
    posting, 95–97
    printing, 113–115
    product invoices, 107
    service invoices, 107
    updating ledgers for, 115–116
  payments from
    credit notes, allocating, 102–104
    customer receipts, allocating, 99–102
    matching to an invoice, 100–102
    not matched to an invoice, 104
    recurring bank entries for, 135–136, 175
  refunds, recording, 105–106
  returns, recording, 105–106
  write offs, recording, 105–106
customer (debtor) ledger
  described, 263
  updating, from invoices, 115–116
Customer Activity report, 239–240
Customer Dashboard view, 24–25
Customer Daybook report, 240–241
Customer Defaults, Settings menu, 29, 60
Customer List, as default view, 56–57
Customer module, 31–32, 33, 86
Customer Process map, 23–24
Customer Process screen, 23–25
Customer Process tab, 23
Customer Receipt icon, 100, 103, 104

customer record
  creating, 58–61, 257
  default settings for, 60
  deleting, 61
  opening balances for, 77, 79–81, 86–87
Customer Record icon, 56–57
Customers button, Navigation Bar, 32
Customers view, 24–25
customising reports, 217–219

• *D* •

data files
  backing up
    after year-end processes, 189
    before clearing audit trail, 188
    before month-end processes, 186
    before year-end processes, 189
    creating, 27, 86, 150–152
  checking for errors, 144–145
  compressing, 147
  corrections to, making, 145–147
  exchanging with accountant, 224–226
  exporting, 221–223
  fixing errors in, 145
  maintenance of, 143–148
  rebuilding, 147–148
  re-indexing, 147
  restoring from backups, 15, 27, 152
data to practice with
  Demo data, 24, 66
  Practice data, 26, 27
dates
  current, changing for reports, 29
  financial year, 9, 18, 29
  lock date, setting, 29, 186, 187, 189
daybook reports, 240–241
debit
  described, 264
  double-entry rules for, 36
debtor (customer)
  contact information, exporting,
    222–223
  credit notes for
    creating, 97–99, 113
    default settings for, 116
    deleting, 105, 116
    posting, 97–99
  described, 22, 264
  invoices for

debtor *(continued)*
  creating, 108–113
  default settings for, 116
  deleting, 105, 116
  editing, 112, 254
  matching to a payment, 100–102
  not matched to a payment, 104
  posting, 95–97
  printing, 113–115
  product invoices, 107
  service invoices, 107
  updating ledgers for, 115–116
  payments from
    credit notes, allocating, 102–104
    customer receipts, allocating, 99–102
    matching to an invoice, 100–102
    not matched to an invoice, 104
    recurring bank entries for, 135–136, 175
  refunds, recording, 105–106
  returns, recording, 105–106
  write offs, recording, 105–106
debtor (customer) ledger
  described, 263
  updating, from invoices, 115–116
Debtors, nominal codes for, 42
Default Layout of Accounts screen, 40
Defaults tab, customer and supplier
    records, 59, 96
deleting lines, 51
Demo data, 24, 66
department, for bank receipts or
    payments, 131
department, for invoices, 119
deposit, for invoices, 111
Deposit account, 129
Deposits & Cash, nominal codes for, 42
depreciation
  described, 180, 264
  methods of, 180–181
  posting, 181–182
Depreciation, nominal codes for, 45
Depreciation account, 181–182
designing reports, 217–219
desktop
  Customer Process screen, 23–25
  customising. *See* Options, Tools menu
  Menu Bar. *See* Menu Bar
  Navigation Bar, 26, 31–33

Welcome screen, 22–23
Work Area, 26
destination folder for installation, 11–13
Details tab
  customer and supplier records, 58–59
  invoices, 108, 113
  nominal record, 67
  product record, 71–72
Diary button, Navigation Bar, 32
direct cost (expense)
  described, 44, 264
  nominal codes for, 44
Direct Expenses category, for nominal
    codes, 44
Discount tab, invoices, 111
double-entry bookkeeping, 36, 264
drop-down arrows, displaying list
    of, 254

• *E* •

e-Banking
  configuring, 227–228
  described, 226–227
  e-payments, 227, 229–230
  online statements, 227, 230–233
Edit Chart of Accounts screen, 40
Edit menu, 27
electronic banking. *See* e-Banking
email
  for COA errors, 52
  for reports, 208
  sending, 27
  for transactions, 30
Email Defaults, Settings menu, 29
Epstein, Lisa (author)
  Bookkeeping For Dummies, 36
Equipment Hire & Rental, nominal codes
    for, 45
errors
  in COA, 51–53
  in data files, 144–145
  types of, 144
e-VAT payments, 203
example data
  Demo data, 24, 66
  Practice data, 26, 27
Example icon, 2

Excel, exporting data to, 221–222
Exit, File menu, 27
expense, 264. *See also* cost
Export Sales, nominal codes for, 44
exporting
  data, 27, 221–223, 225
  reports, 208

• *F* •

F1 function key, 253
F2 function key, 253
F3 function key, 112, 254
F4 function key, 254
F5 function key, 254
F6 function key, 254–255
F7 function key, 48, 51, 255
F8 function key, 51, 255
F9 function key, 256
F11 function key, 256
F12 function key, 256
Favourites menu, 30
File menu
  Backup, 27, 151
  Close, 27
  Exit, 27
  Import, 27
  Maintenance, 27, 143–144
  Microsoft Integration, 27, 222, 223
  New Report, 27
  Open, 27
  Restore, 27, 152
  Send, 27
files, data
  backing up
    after year-end processes, 189
    before clearing audit trail, 188
    before month-end processes, 186
    before year-end processes, 189
    creating, 27, 86, 150–152
  checking for errors, 144–145
  compressing, 147
  corrections to, making, 145–147
  exchanging with accountant, 224–226
  exporting, 221–223
  fixing errors in, 145
  maintenance of, 143–148

rebuilding, 147–148
re-indexing, 147
restoring from backups, 15, 27, 152
financial year
  start date for, 9, 18, 29
  switching to Sage at start of, 75–76
Financial Year, Settings menu, 29
fixed asset
  depreciation of, 180–182, 264
  described, 41, 180, 264
  NBV (net book value) of, 180–181
  nominal codes for, 42
Fixed Assets category, for nominal
    codes, 41, 42
flat rate VAT scheme, 194
floating nominal, 46, 53
footer details, for invoices, 112–113
Footer Details tab, invoices, 112
function key shortcuts
  F1 function key, 253
  F2 function key, 253
  F3 function key, 112, 254
  F4 function key, 254
  F5 function key, 254
  F6 function key, 254–255
  F7 function key, 48, 51, 255
  F8 function key, 51, 255
  F9 function key, 256
  F11 function key, 256
  F12 function key, 256
  website for, 3
Furniture & Fixtures, nominal codes for, 42

• *G* •

General Expenses, nominal codes for, 45
geographic location, multiple COAs
    for, 49–51
Global Changes, Tools menu, 29
Global Changes wizard, 29, 260–261
global terms, for invoices, 112–113
Government Gateway account, 203
Graphs tab
  customer and supplier records, 59
  nominal record, 67
gross profit, 264
Gross Wages, nominal codes for, 44

• H •

Heat, Light, & Power, nominal codes for, 44
Help menu, 31
help system, 253
HM Revenue and Customs (HMRC)
  reclaiming VAT, information about, 192
  submitting VAT Return to, 202–204
  VAT accounting schemes, 193

• I •

icons in Sage Instant Accounts
  Bank Payments icon, 130
  Bank Receipts icon, 130
  Bank Transfer icon, 132
  Batch Credit icon, 120
  Batch Credit Note icon, 98
  Batch Invoice icon, 96, 118
  Customer Receipt icon, 100, 103, 104
  Customer Record icon, 56–57
  New Bank icon, 69
  New Invoice icon, 108
  Nominal Record icon, 63
  Record icon, 55–56
  Sage Instant Accounts icon, 13, 14
  Supplier Payment icon, 122, 123
  Supplier Record icon, 56–57
icons in this book, 2
Import, File menu, 27
importing data
  from accountant, 226
  with Microsoft Integration, 27
income, 264
input VAT, 192
inserting lines, 48, 51, 255
installation
  Custom installation, 11–12
  destination folder for, 11–13
  operating systems supported, 8
  procedure for, 9–14
  requirements for, 9
  Standard installation, 11
interest earned, on bank account, 128, 169
Internet Options, Tools menu, 30

Internet resources
  e-Banking, 226
  function key shortcuts, 3
  HM Revenue and Customs (HMRC),
    192, 193
  for Sage Instant Accounts, 30
  Sage Services, 30, 32, 33
  for this book, 3
  Weblinks, 30
Invoice Defaults, Settings menu, 29
invoice number, 109
invoice reference number, 119
invoices
  for customers
    creating, 108–113
    default settings for, 116
    deleting, 105, 116
    editing, 112, 254
    matching to a payment, 100–102
    not matched to a payment, 104
    posting, 95–97
    printing, 113–115
    product invoices, 107
    service invoices, 107
    updating ledgers for, 115–116
  from suppliers
    not yet received, 178–179
    paid in advance, 179
    paying with credit card, 140
    posting, 118–120
    receiving, 117–118
item number, for invoices, 109

• J •

journal
  described, 182
  posting to, 183–184
  recurring bank entries for, 136–137, 175

• K •

Kelly, Jane (author)
  Bookkeeping For Dummies, 36

• *L* •

Labour, nominal codes for, 44
ledgers
 customer (debtor) ledger, 263
 nominal ledger
  described, 22, 37, 177, 264
  displaying, 39–40, 61–62
 supplier (creditor) ledger, 265
 updating, from invoices, 115–116
 VAT ledger, 194
liability
 current (short-term) liability
  described, 42, 265
  nominal codes for, 43
 described, 264
 long-term liability
  described, 42, 264
  nominal codes for, 43
Licence agreement, 10–11
Limited Company business type, 17
Links list, Navigation Bar, 31
liquidate, 264
location, multiple COAs for, 49–51
lock date, setting, 29, 186, 187, 189
Lock Date, Settings menu, 29
Long-term Liabilities category,
  for nominal codes, 42, 43
long-term liability
 described, 42, 264
 nominal codes for, 43

• *M* •

M Message Line product code, 109
main screen (desktop)
 Customer Process screen, 23–25
 customising. *See* Options, Tools menu
 Menu Bar. *See* Menu Bar
 Navigation Bar, 26, 31–33
 Welcome screen, 22–23
 Work Area, 26
Maintenance, File menu, 27, 143–144
Maintenance, nominal codes for, 45
material changes, 225
material purchases, 43

Memo tab
 nominal record, 67
 product record, 72
Menu Bar
 described, 26
 Edit menu, 27
 Favourites menu, 30
 File menu
  Backup, 27, 151
  Close, 27
  Exit, 27
  Import, 27
  Maintenance, 27, 143–144
  Microsoft Integration, 27, 222, 223
  New Report, 27
  Open, 27
  Restore, 27, 152
  Send, 27
 Help menu, 31
 Modules menu, 28
 News Feeds menu, 30
 Settings menu, 28–29, 60
 Tools menu
  Activation, 30
  Convert Reports, 30
  described, 29–30
  Global Changes, 29
  Internet Options, 30
  Opening Balances, 30, 78
  Options, 26, 30, 56–57
  Period End, 30
  Report Designer, 30, 217–219, 256
  Transaction Email, 30
 View menu, 28
 Weblinks menu, 30
MI (Movements In) record, 187
Microsoft Excel, exporting data to, 221–222
Microsoft Integration, File menu, 27, 222, 223
Microsoft Outlook, exporting contacts to,
  222–223
Microsoft Word, exporting data to, 223
Miscellaneous Expenses, nominal codes
  for, 44
Mispostings account
 journals for, 182
 nominal codes for, 45

Module buttons, Navigation Bar, 28, 32
modules
  Bank module, 68–69
  Company module, 39
  Customer module, 31–32, 33, 86
  list of, 28, 32
  Products module, 71, 161, 162
  Supplier module, 86
Modules menu, 28
Month End Procedure wizard,
      184–185, 186–187
month-end processes
  audit trail, clearing, 188
  backup prior to, 186
  checklist for, 185–186
  lock date, setting, 186, 187
  month-end date for, 186
  performing, 184–185, 186–187
  preparation for, 184, 185
  stock transactions, clearing, 187
month-end reports
  audit trail, 215–217
  Balance Sheet, 214–215
  checking COA before, 208
  Comparative Profit and Loss report,
      212–213
  customising reports, 217–219
  emailing, 208
  exporting, 208
  previewing, 208
  printing, 208
  Profit and Loss report, 210–212
  program date for, changing, 29
  Trial Balance report, 209–210
Motor Expenses, nominal codes for, 44
Motor Vehicles, nominal codes for, 42
Movements In (MI) record, 187

• N •

narratives, from accountant, 226
Navigation Bar, 26, 31–33
NBV (net book value), 180–181
N/C. *See* nominal code
net amount
  for bank receipts or payments, 131
  for invoices, 111, 256
net book value (NBV), 180–181

net profit, 264
New Bank Account wizard, 259
New Bank icon, 69
New Customer wizard, 57, 257
New Invoice icon, 108
New Product wizard, 71, 259
New Report, File menu, 27
New Supplier wizard, 57, 258
news feeds, 14, 30
News Feeds menu, 30
nominal account
  creating, 258–259
  described, 36, 264
  list of. *See* COA (Chart of Accounts)
  opening balances for, 88–89
  transfers between accounts. *See* journal
Nominal Activity report, 235–237
nominal code (N/C)
  for bank receipts or payments, 131
  category headings for
    adding, 48
    deleting, 49
    renaming, 47
  correct category for, ensuring, 46
  described, 37
  errors with, 53
  floating nominal, 46, 53
  for invoices, 119
  leaving gaps between, 45
  list of, 38, 41–45
  mirroring, 45–46
  printing list of, 41
  viewing for each category, 41, 62
  viewing list of, 62
Nominal Daybook report, 240–241
nominal journal
  described, 264
  posting depreciation of assets to, 180–182
  posting prepayments to, 179
nominal ledger. *See also* business (yours)
  described, 22, 37, 177, 264
  displaying, 39–40, 61–62
  updating, from invoices, 115–116
Nominal Ledger screen, 39–40, 61–62
nominal record
  creating, 63–64
  deleting, 67
  described, 37

renaming, 63
searching for, 65
viewing, 61–62, 66–67
Nominal Record icon, 63
Nominal Record wizard, 258–259

• *O* •

Office Equipment, nominal codes for, 42
online banking. *See* e-Banking
online resources. *See* website resources
Open, File menu, 27
Opening and Closing Stock wizard,
  158–160, 259–260
opening balances
  backing up data after entering, 86
  bank balances, 77, 84–85, 87–88
  checking for errors, 85–86, 90–91
  customer balances, 77, 79–81, 86–87
  default date for, 79
  described, 75
  entering
    manually, 86–90
    with wizards, 78–86
  nominal account balances, 88–89
  obtaining, 76–78
  product balances, 78, 89–90
  reversing, 81–82
  supplier balances, 77, 79–81, 86–87
  Trial Balance, 76, 82–83
  uncleared transactions, 84–85
Opening Balances, Tools menu, 30, 78
Opening Balances wizard, 78–86
operating systems supported, 8
Options, Tools menu
  default view, setting, 56–57
  described, 30
  process maps, switching off, 56
  Work Area, configuring, 26
order details, for invoices, 112
Order Details tab, invoices, 112
order number, for invoices, 109
orders, invoices for. *See* invoices: for
  customers
Other Sales, nominal codes for, 44
Outlook, exporting contacts to, 222–223
output VAT, 192
outstanding lodgement, 174, 246,
  248–249, 265

Outstanding Lodgement report, 248–249
overheads
  described, 44, 265
  nominal codes for, 44–45
Overheads category, for nominal
  codes, 44–45
owners
  capital invested by, 263
  Profit and Loss report for, 210–212

• *P* •

'p,' in Customer Activity tab, 104
partial COA (Chart of Accounts), 49
Partnership business type, 17
password
  for Accountant Link, 225, 226
  for accounts data, 29
  for Sage Services, 30, 33
paying-in slip, 100
Payment tab, invoices, 111
payments
  from customers
    credit notes, allocating, 102–104
    customer receipts, allocating, 99–102
    matching to an invoice, 100–102
    not matched to an invoice, 104
    paying-in slip for, 100
    remittance advice slip for, 100
  to suppliers, 123–124
Period Ageing, 60
Period End, Tools menu, 30
Period Trial Balance report. *See* Trial
  Balance report
period-end processes
  month-end processes
    audit trail, clearing, 188
    backup prior to, 186
    checklist for, 185–186
    lock date, setting, 186, 187
    month-end date for, 186
    performing, 184–185, 186–187
    preparation for, 184, 185
    stock transactions, clearing, 187
  month-end reports
    audit trail, 215–217
    Balance Sheet, 214–215
    checking COA before, 208

period-end processes *(continued)*
   Comparative Profit and Loss report,
     212–213
   customising reports, 217–219
   emailing, 208
   exporting, 208
   previewing, 208
   printing, 208
   Profit and Loss report, 210–212
   program date for, changing, 29
   Trial Balance report, 209–210
   year-end processes
     audit trail, clearing, 188
     performing, 189–190
     preparation for, 189
     program date for, changing, 29
     stock transactions, clearing, 187
Petty Cash account
   described, 129, 138
   funding, 138
   making payments from, 139
Plant & Machinery, nominal codes for, 42
Plus icon, 2
Practice data, 26, 27
prepayment, 179
price, for invoices, 110
printing
   COA errors, 52
   invoices, 113–115
   queue for, displaying, 256
   reports, 208
Printing & Stationery, nominal
    codes for, 44
process maps
   Customer Process map, 23–24
   switching off, as default, 56–57
product code
   in invoices, 109
   in product record, 71–72
Product Defaults, Settings menu, 29
product invoices, 107. *See also* invoices:
    for customers
product record
   creating, 71–72
   deleting, 73
   editing, 73
   opening balances for, 78, 89–90

Product Sales, nominal codes for, 44
products
   activity of, viewing, 157
   clearing, 30, 187
   closing stock, adjusting, 158–160
   creating, 259
   opening stock, adjusting, 158–160
   reports on
     Product Activity Report, 160–161
     Product List report, 161
     Product Profitability, 161
     Stock Take report, 153, 161
   selling, 161–162
   stock levels, adjusting, 156–157
   stock take for
     physical stock check, 153–154, 161
     recording differences from,
      154–155
Products button, Navigation Bar, 32
Products module, 71, 161, 162
Professional Fees, nominal codes for, 44
profit, retained, 265
Profit and Loss account, 263, 265
Profit and Loss report
   described, 37
   nominal code categories in, 38, 43–45
   running, 210–212
Profit and Loss tab, 38, 47, 50
Property, nominal codes for, 42
Purchase Charges, nominal codes for, 44
purchase invoices. *See* invoices: from
    suppliers
purchases. *See also* supplier (creditor)
   described, 43
   input VAT for, 192
   material purchases, 43
   nominal codes for, 44
Purchases, nominal codes for, 44
Purchases category, for nominal codes,
    43, 44
Purchases tab, supplier record, 59

quantity, for invoices, 110
Quick Print, for invoices, 115

• *R* •

rebuilding data, 147–148
Reconcile screen, 169–170
reconciling bank account
  archives of, accessing, 172
  electronically, 230–233
  importance of, 165–166
  no reconciliation option, 166
  performing, 167–172
  preparation for, 167
  problems with, resolving, 173
  unmatched items after, 173–175, 246–249
reconciling VAT Return, 200–202
Record icon, 55–56
Record tab, customer or supplier
  defaults, 60
records. *See also* transactions
  bank account record
    creating, 68–70
    default, 67
    deleting, 70
    duplicating, 69
    renaming, 68
  creating, 55–57
  customer record
    creating, 58–61, 257
    default settings for, 60
    deleting, 61
    opening balances for, 77, 79–81, 86–87
  nominal record
    creating, 63–64
    deleting, 67
    renaming, 63
    searching for, 65
    viewing, 61–62, 66–67
  product record
    creating, 71–72
    deleting, 73
    editing, 73
    opening balances for, 78, 89–90
  searching for, 149–150
  supplier record
    creating, 58–61, 258
    default settings for, 60
    deleting, 61
    opening balances for, 77, 79–81, 86–87

recurring bank entries
  for bank receipts or payments, 175
  for bank transfers, 175
  for customer payments, 135–136, 175
  for journals, 136–137, 175
  processing and posting, 137–138
  setting up, 133–135
  for supplier payments, 135–136, 175
reducing balance depreciation, 180
reference number
  for bank receipts or payments, 131
  for invoices, 119
refund. *See also* credit note
  to customers, recording, 105–106
  from suppliers, recording, 124–125
registration, Sage Instant Accounts, 15
registration number, VAT, 18–19
re-indexing data, 147
Remember icon, 2
remittance advice slip, 100
Rent & Rates, nominal codes for, 44
Report Designer, Tools menu
  customising reports, 217–219
  described, 30, 256
reports
  Aged Creditors report
    described, 263
    opening balances from, 77, 79
    running, 244–246
  Aged Debtors report
    described, 263
    opening balances from, 77, 79
    running, 242–244
  audit trail
    all transactions shown in, 145, 215
    clearing, 188
    described, 263
    running at month-end, 215–217
  Balance Sheet
    Chart of Accounts for, 263
    described, 37, 263
    nominal code categories in, 38, 41–43
    running at month-end, 214–215
  Bank Report - Unreconciled report, 174
  Comparative Profit and Loss report,
    212–213
  converting, 30

reports *(continued)*
creating, 27
Customer Activity report, 239–240
Customer Daybook report, 240–241
customising, 217–219, 256
exporting to Microsoft Excel, 222
favourites, 30
Nominal Activity report, 235–237
Nominal Daybook report, 240–241
Outstanding Lodgement report, 248–249
Product Activity Report, 160–161
Product List report, 161
Product Profitability, 161
Profit and Loss report
described, 37
nominal code categories in, 38, 43–45
running, 210–212
Stock Take report, 153, 161
Supplier Activity report, 238–239
Supplier Daybook report, 240–241
Top Customers report, 249–250
Trial Balance report, 209–210
Unpresented Cheques report, 247–248
Unreconciled Payments report, 247–248
reserves (retained earnings)
described, 42
nominal codes for, 43
Reserves, nominal codes for, 43
resources. *See* books and publications;
website resources
Restore, File menu, 27, 152
retained earnings. *See* reserves
retained profit, 265
returns
from customers, recording, 105–106
to suppliers, recording, 124–125
revenue, sales
described, 43, 265
nominal codes for, 44
RSS news feeds, 14, 30

• *S* •

S1 Special Product Item Tax Chargeable
product code, 109
S2 Special Product Item Zero Rated, 109
SA (sales receipt on account) transaction
type, 104
.saa file extension, 226

.sae file extension, 225
Sage 50 Accounts Professional,
162, 178
Sage 50 Client Manager, 224
Sage Instant Accounts
activation key for, 9, 15
add-on software for, enabling, 30
dates for
current, changing for reports, 29
lock date, setting, 29
described, 7
desktop
Customer Process screen, 23–25
customising. *See* Options,
Tools menu
Menu Bar. *See* Menu Bar
Navigation Bar, 26, 31–33
Welcome screen, 22–23
Work Area, 26
exiting, 27
installing
Custom installation, 11–12
destination folder for, 11–13
operating systems supported, 8
procedure for, 9–14
requirements for, 9
Standard installation, 11
Internet options for, 30
news feeds for, 14, 30
online services for
accessing, 32, 33
login and password for, 30, 33
operating systems supported, 8
password for, 29
registering, 15
serial number for, 9, 15
starting, 14
system and version information for, 31
updates for
criteria for, 30
RSS news feeds for, 14, 30
Sage Services for, 33
upgrades for
copying previous data for, 15
performing, 30
with SageCover Extra, 8
versions of, 7
Weblinks for, 30
when to start using, 75–76

Sage Instant Accounts icon, 13, 14
Sage Instant Accounts Plus
  clearing audit trail, 188
  described, 7
  New Product wizard, 71, 259
  Opening and Closing Stock wizard,
    158–160, 259–260
  Product Activity Report, 160–161
  Product List report, 161
  Product Profitability report, 161
  selling stock, 161–162
  Stock Take report, 153, 161
Sage Services
  accessing, 32, 33
  login and password for, 30, 33
Sage Services button, Navigation Bar, 32, 33
Sage System Checker, 9–10
SageCover, 8, 33
SageCover Extra, 8
sales. *See* customer (debtor)
sales credit (SC) transaction type, 100
sales invoice (SI) transaction type, 100
sales invoices. *See* invoices: for customers
Sales of Assets, nominal codes for, 44
Sales Promotion, nominal codes for, 44
sales receipt on account (SA) transaction
    type, 104
sales revenue
  described, 43, 265
  nominal codes for, 44
Sales Revenue category, for nominal
    codes, 43, 44
Sales tab, customer record, 59
SC (sales credit) transaction type, 100
screens (desktop)
  Customer Process screen, 23–25
  customising. *See* Options, Tools menu
  Menu Bar. *See* Menu Bar
  Navigation Bar, 26, 31–33
  Welcome screen, 22–23
  Work Area, 26
Send, File menu, 27
serial number, 9, 15
service invoices, 107. *See also* invoices:
    for customers
Settings menu, 28–29, 60
settlement terms, for invoices, 112
Share Capital, nominal codes for, 43
shareholders, capital invested by, 263

short-term (current) liability
  described, 42, 265
  nominal codes for, 43
SI (sales invoice) transaction type, 100
Software Licence agreement, 10–11
Sole Trader business type, 17
spell checker, displaying, 254
spreadsheets, exporting data to, 221–222
Standard installation, 11
standard VAT scheme, 193, 197–198
Statement Summary screen, 168–169, 172
Statement tab, customer or supplier
    defaults, 60
status bar, switching on and off, 28
stock
  activity of, viewing, 157
  clearing, 30, 187
  closing, adjusting, 158–160, 259–260
  creating a new product, 259
  levels of, adjusting, 156–157
  opening, adjusting, 158–160, 259–260
  reports on
    Product Activity Report, 160–161
    Product List report, 161
    Product Profitability, 161
    Stock Take report, 153, 161
  selling, 161–162
  stock take for
    physical stock check, 153–154, 161
    recording differences from, 154–155
Stock, nominal codes for, 42, 44
Stock Take report, 153, 161
stocktake list, 78
straight line depreciation, 180
supplier (creditor)
  balances owed to. *See* Aged Creditors
      report
  contact information, exporting, 222–223
  credit note from
    allocating, 122
    credit number for, 120
    posting, 120–121
  described, 22, 263
  invoices from
    not yet received, 178–179
    paid in advance, 179
    paying with credit card, 140
    posting, 118–120
    receiving, 117–118

supplier *(continued)*
  payments to
    e-payments for, 227, 229–230
    processing, 123–124
    recurring bank entries for, 135–136, 175
  refunds, recording, 124–125
  returns, recording, 124–125
  write offs, recording, 124–125
supplier (creditor) ledger, 265
Supplier Activity report, 238–239
Supplier Activity screen, 118
Supplier Daybook report, 240–241
Supplier Defaults, Settings menu, 29, 60
Supplier module, 86
Supplier Payment icon, 122, 123
supplier record
  creating, 58–61, 258
  default settings for, 60
  deleting, 61
  opening balances for, 77, 79–81, 86–87
Supplier Record icon, 56–57
Suppliers button, Navigation Bar, 32
support
  continuous, with SageCover, 8, 33
  temporary, with Sage Instant Accounts, 8
Suspense & Mispostings, nominal
    codes for, 45
Suspense account, 45, 91

• T •

T0 (zero-rated) tax code, 192
T1 (standard rate) tax code, 192
T2 (exempt from VAT) tax code, 192
T4 (sales to EU customers) tax code, 192
T5 (lower-rate VAT) tax code, 192
T7 (zero-rated purchases from EU
    suppliers) tax code, 192
T8 (standard rate purchases from EU
    supplieers) tax code, 192
T9 (transactions not involving VAT)
    tax code, 192
tabs
  Activity tab
    customer and supplier records, 59–60, 102
    nominal record, 67
    product record, 72, 90
  Advanced Options tab, backups, 152
  Ageing tab, customer or supplier
      defaults, 60
  Backup Company tab, 151
  Balance Sheet tab, 38, 47, 50
  Bank tab, customer and supplier
      records, 60
  Comments tab, error messages, 144
  Credit Control tab, customer and supplier
      records, 59
  Customer Process tab, 23
  Defaults tab, customer and supplier
      records, 59, 96
  Details tab
    customer and supplier records, 58–59
    invoices, 108, 113
    nominal record, 67
    product record, 71–72
  Discount tab, invoices, 111
  Footer Details tab, invoices, 112
  Graphs tab
    customer and supplier records, 59
    nominal record, 67
  Memo tab
    nominal record, 67
    product record, 72
  Order Details tab, invoices, 112
  Payment tab, invoices, 111
  Profit and Loss tab, 38, 47, 50
  Purchases tab, supplier record, 59
  Record tab, customer or supplier
      defaults, 60
  VAT tab, invoices, 111
Task pane, Navigation Bar, 31
tax code (T/C)
  for bank receipts or payments, 131
  for invoices, 119
  list of, 97, 192
Taxation, nominal codes for, 43
Technical Stuff icon, 2
technical support
  continuous, with SageCover, 8, 33
  temporary, with Sage Instant
      Accounts, 8
third-party integration, enabling, 30
Tip icon, 2
Tools menu
  Activation, 30
  Convert Reports, 30

described, 29–30
Global Changes, 29
Internet Options, 30
Opening Balances, 30, 78
Options
  default view, setting, 56–57
  described, 30
  process maps, switching off, 56
  Work Area, configuring, 26
Period End, 30
Report Designer
  customising reports, 217–219
  described, 30, 256
Transaction Email, 30
Top Customers report, 249–250
total, for invoices, 111
Transaction Email, Tools menu, 30
transaction type
  SA (sales receipt on account), 104
  SC (sales credit), 100
  SI (sales invoice), 100
transactions. *See also* records
all, in chronological order.
    See audit trail
corrections to, making, 145–147
deleting, 146–147
reconciling, 169–173
searching for, 148–149
un-reconciling, 173
transfers between accounts
bank accounts
  entering before reconciliation, 167
  processing, 132–133
  recurring bank entries for, 175
nominal accounts. *See* journal
Travelling & Entertainment, nominal codes
  for, 44
Trial Balance
checking against opening balance, 85,
  90–91
described, 76
entering, 82–83
opening Trial Balance, printing, 91
Trial Balance report, 209–210

• *U* •

un-presented cheque, 174, 246–248, 265
Unpresented Cheques report, 247–248
Unreconciled Payments report, 247–248
updates
criteria for, 30
RSS news feeds for, 14, 30
Sage Services for, 33
updating ledgers, 115–116
upgrades
copying previous data for, 15
performing, 30
with SageCover Extra, 8
user list, 28

• *V* •

VAT (Value Added Tax)
accounting schemes for, 18–19, 193
described, 191–192, 265
input VAT, 192
for invoices, 111, 119
output VAT, 192
quarters for, 76
rate for, 18–19
registerting for, 191–192
registration number for, 18–19
setting up, 18–19, 193
tax codes for, 97, 192
VAT Return for
  checking, 196–199
  examining, 199
  manual adjustments to, 199–200
  payment for, 202
  preparation for, 194–195
  reconciling, 200–202
  running, 195–196
  submitting to HMRC, 202–204
  VAT transfer (clearing) for, 201–202
VAT ledger, 194
VAT Liability, nominal codes for, 42, 43
VAT tab, invoices, 111
View menu, 28

• *W* •

Wages, nominal codes for, 43
Warning! icon, 2
warnings, 144
Weblinks, 30
website resources
  e-Banking, 226
  function key shortcuts, 3
  HM Revenue and Customs (HMRC),
    192, 193
  for Sage Instant Accounts, 30
  Sage Services, 30, 32, 33
  for this book, 3
  Weblinks, 30
Welcome screen, 22–23
Windows control panel, 256
Windows operating systems supported, 8
wizards
  accessing, 33
  Accountant Link wizard, 224–225, 261
  Accounts Installshield wizard, 10–11
  Active Set-Up wizard, 14–20
  creating records using, 57
  Global Changes wizard, 29, 260–261
  Month End Procedure wizard, 184–185,
    186–187
  New Bank Account wizard, 259
  New Customer wizard, 57, 257
  New Product wizard, 71, 259
  New Supplier wizard, 57, 258
  Nominal Record wizard, 258–259
  Opening and Closing Stock wizard,
    158–160, 259–260
  Opening Balances wizard, 78–86
Word, exporting data to, 223
Work Area, 26
write offs
  to customers, recording, 105–106
  from suppliers, recording, 124–125
write-off depreciation, 181
writing down your assets. *See* depreciation

• *Y* •

Year End screen, 189–190
year-end processes
  audit trail, clearing, 188
  performing, 189–190
  preparation for, 189
  program date for, changing, 29
  stock transactions, clearing, 187

About the Author

Jane Kelly trained as a Chartered Management Accountant while working in industry. Her roles ranged from Company Accountant in a small advertising business to Financial Controller for a national house builder. For the last few years Jane has specialised in using Sage accounting software and has taught a wide variety of small businesses and employees the benefits of using Sage. More recently Jane has been involved in writing *For Dummies* books, including *Bookkeeping For Dummies*, 3rd Edition and *Sage One For Dummies*.

Author's Acknowledgements

I hope that this book will help many of the small business owners who struggle to keep up to date with their finances.

This book aims to assist those who need a simple accounting system which will provide them with enough information to help make sensible business decisions. Throughout the book, I try and provide practical examples when using the software, to help make the monthly accounting process as straight forward as possible.

I'd like to thank the staff at Wiley, who have been very kind and supportive during the process of writing and reviewing this book, particularly Jo Jones and the rest of the development team, who have worked hard to produce the *For Dummies* book that you see before you.

Finally, I cannot possibly end without thanking my husband Malcolm and my daughter Megan, who have put up with my long absences from family life whilst I've been buried under paperwork in my office.

I hope you enjoy reading the book and find it useful.

Publisher's Acknowledgements

We're proud of this book; please send us your comments at `http://dummies.custhelp.com`. For other comments, please contact our Customer Care Department within the U.S. at 877-762-2974, outside the U.S. at (001) 317-572-3993, or fax 317-572-4002.

Some of the people who helped bring this book to market include the following:

Acquisitions, Editorial, and Vertical Websites

Project Editor: Jo Jones

Commissioning Editor: Claire Ruston

Assistant Editor: Ben Kemble

Copy Editor: Kim Vernon

Production Manager: Daniel Mersey

Publisher: Miles Kendall

Cover Photo: ©iStockphoto.com/s_white

Take Dummies with you everywhere you go!

Whether you're excited about e-books, want more from the web, must have your mobile apps, or swept up in social media, Dummies makes everything easier .

FOR DUMMIES

A Wiley Brand

BUSINESS

978-1-118-73077-5

978-1-118-44349-1

978-1-119-97527-4

MUSIC

978-1-119-94276-4

978-0-470-97799-6

978-0-470-49644-2

DIGITAL PHOTOGRAPHY

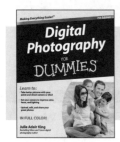

978-1-118-09203-3

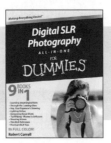

978-0-470-76878-5

978-1-118-00472-2

Algebra I For Dummies
978-0-470-55964-2

Anatomy & Physiology For Dummies, 2nd Edition
978-0-470-92326-9

Asperger's Syndrome For Dummies
978-0-470-66087-4

Basic Maths For Dummies
978-1-119-97452-9

Body Language For Dummies, 2nd Edition
978-1-119-95351-7

Bookkeeping For Dummies, 3rd Edition
978-1-118-34689-1

British Sign Language For Dummies
978-0-470-69477-0

Cricket for Dummies, 2nd Edition
978-1-118-48032-8

Currency Trading For Dummies, 2nd Edition
978-1-118-01851-4

Cycling For Dummies
978-1-118-36435-2

Diabetes For Dummies, 3rd Edition
978-0-470-97711-8

eBay For Dummies, 3rd Edition
978-1-119-94122-4

Electronics For Dummies All-in-One For Dummies
978-1-118-58973-1

English Grammar For Dummies
978-0-470-05752-0

French For Dummies, 2nd Edition
978-1-118-00464-7

Guitar For Dummies, 3rd Edition
978-1-118-11554-1

IBS For Dummies
978-0-470-51737-6

Keeping Chickens For Dummies
978-1-119-99417-6

Knitting For Dummies, 3rd Edition
978-1-118-66151-2